Afro-Future Females

Afro-Future Females

Black Writers
Chart Science Fiction's Newest
New-Wave Trajectory

Edited by

MARLEEN S. BARR

 THE OHIO STATE UNIVERSITY PRESS / Columbus

Library of Congress Cataloging-in-Publication Data
Afro-future females : black writers chart science fiction's newest new-wave trajectory /
edited by Marleen S. Barr.
   p. cm.
Includes bibliographical references.
ISBN-13: 978–0–8142–1078–9 (cloth : alk. paper)
1. Science fiction, American. 2. Science fiction, American—History and criticism. 3.
American fiction—African American authors—History and criticism. 4. American fic-
tion—Women authors—History and criticism. 5. Women and literature—United States—
History—20th century. 6. Women and literature—United States—History—21st century.
I. Barr, Marleen S.
PS648.S3A69 2008
813.'0876209928708996073—dc22
               2007050083

This book is available in the following editions:
Cloth (ISBN 978–0–8142–1078–9)
CD-ROM (ISBN 978–0–8142–9156–6)

Cover design by Janna Thompson Chordas.
Text design by Jennifer Shoffey Forsythe.
Type set in Adobe Minion.

9 8 7 6 5 4 3 2 1

Contents

PREFACE

"All At One Point"
Conveys the Point, Period

Or, Black Science Fiction Is Bursting Out All Over

> Race, far from being a special or marginal concern, was a central facet of the American story. On the evidence of Ellison's and Morrison's work, it is also a part of the story that defies the tenets of realism, or at least demands that they be combined with elements of allegory, folk tale, Gothic and romance.
>
> —A. O. Scott, "In Search of the Best"

Afro-Future Females: Black Writers Chart Science Fiction's Newest New-Wave Trajectory is my third effort in a series that began with *Future Females: A Critical Anthology* (1981, the first scholarly essay collection about women and science fiction). The series inception volume was followed by *Future Females, The Next Generation: New Voices and Velocities in Feminist Science Fiction Criticism* (2000, the first scholarly essay collection to emphasize the post–baby boom generation of feminist science fiction scholars). *Afro-Future Females* is the first combined science fiction critical anthology and short story collection to focus upon black women via written and visual texts. This anthology, published after the *New York Times Book Review* declared that Toni Morrison's *Beloved* "is the best work of American fiction published in the last 25 years" (Scott 17), emphasizes that the black writers who chart science fiction's newest new-wave trajectory share the enterprise of lauded black great American novelists. Toni Morrison—and the science fiction writers whose stories appear in this volume (Octavia E. Butler, Andrea Hairston, Nalo

Hopkinson, Nisi Shawl, and Sheree R. Thomas)—combine the tenets of realism with elements of allegory, folk tale, Gothic, and romance.

My preface tells a story about the inception of the black science fiction that is currently bursting out all over the science fiction universe.[1] I also emphasize why critics who pinpoint the best American fiction need to look to science fiction—to Harlan Ellison as well as to Ralph Ellison. Or: while a Philip Roth novel is a runner-up to *Beloved* on the *Times'* list and no fewer than four Roth novels are mentioned as recipients of multiple votes, Roth's contemporary, Samuel R. Delany, is an invisible man in relation to the *Times'* search for the best. The point (and I will have a lot to say about points): our late beloved Octavia E. Butler is no invisible woman eclipsed by Toni Morrison's stellar presence. Butler and Morrison, contributors to science fiction's black new wave, bring fantastic black diasporic narrative elements to bear upon denying the tenets of realism.[2] Both authors write in a manner that adheres to Frank Norris's definition of the great American novel: "Frank Norris wrote that 'the Great American novel is not extinct like the dodo, but mythical like the hippogriff'" (Scott 17). According to A. O. Scott, "the hippogriff, a monstrous hybrid of griffin and horse, is often taken as the very symbol of fantastical impossibility, a unicorn's unicorn" (Scott 17). The hippogriff represents the fact that black science fiction and the great American novel share the same trajectory in that they both center upon fantastical impossibility: *Beloved* is about a ghost, and Gloria Naylor's *Mama Day*, another example of how texts categorized as black realistic literature routinely incorporate the fantastic, includes mystical events and the supernatural. Black women science fiction writers focus upon ghosts, mystical events, and the supernatural too. Literary criticism that at once celebrates Morrison and her fellow black mainstream fiction writers while ignoring black science fiction should become as extinct as the dodo. Much of the best mainstream fiction incorporates the fantastic, a unicorn's unicorn. Afro-future female writers transcend ghettoizing generic classification; they join the best American writers in creating work that combines mainstream literature with science fiction and fantasy.

I. The Revenge of the Hippogriffs
Or, Black Science Fiction Writers Did Not Create Godzilla

A science fiction writer walks into a bookstore. "Do you have a black science fiction anthology?" she asks. The flummoxed clerk experiences a Eureka! moment. "No. No black science fiction anthology. But not to worry. We carry *The Best Japanese Science Fiction Stories.*"

I intend no *shtick*. Sheree R. Thomas is the science fiction writer who walked into the bookstore. Her idea to create the *Dark Matter* anthologies emanated from the anecdote I have related.[3] *Dark Matter*, the definitive science fiction anthologies of the new millennium, follow such representative anthologies for their time as Harlan Ellison's *Dangerous Visions*, Pamela Sargent's *Women of Wonder*, Bruce Sterling's *Mirrorshades*, and Larry McCaffery's *Storming the Reality Studio*. The bookstore clerk's response makes the need for black science fiction anthologies patently obvious.

It was not ludicrous for the clerk to respond to Thomas's request by equating black science fiction with Japanese science fiction: the two are not completely devoid of connection and can mutually illuminate each other. Karen Tei Yamashita, for example, writes fiction about Japanese Brazilians. Her *Circle K Cycles* concerns the second-class treatment Brazilian Japanese people receive when they immigrate to Japan. There is absolutely no biological difference between people born to Japanese parents in Brazil and people born to Japanese parents in Tokyo. It is nonsensical for Japanese to discriminate against those who are biologically identical to them. So, too, it is nonsensical for the literary establishment to discriminate against the black women's science fiction that is generically identical to Morrison's revered *Beloved*. With Yamashita's unusual multicultural perspective and the cross-cultural catalyst that generated *Dark Matter* in mind, I am quite comfortable using an Italian male writer's short story to serve as a central metaphor to pinpoint a black science fiction anthology.

II. Italo Calvino and the Point, Period

Period.

I do not evoke the finality of the grammatical period in terms of Frank Kermode's *The Sense of an Ending*. Instead, I refer to the inceptions Edward Said addresses in *Beginnings*. Look at a period: . A period printed on a page resembles a planet backgrounded by white space vastness. The black period situated amidst the page's white space can represent the science fiction generic white authorship space which has functioned as a void in relation to black science fiction. Thomas's encounter with the clerk exemplifies exactly why, until recently, black authors' presence on the science fiction radar screen (with the exception of Samuel R. Delany and Octavia E. Butler, of course) was aptly described by Isak Dinesen's title "The Blank Page." The period, the literal black densely filled-in circle, the figurative planet placed on the white outer space page, has lately reached a tipping point: the plethora of new black science fiction writers existing within the period are bursting out all over to become the newest new-wave trajectory of early-twenty-first-century science fiction.

Walter Mosley refers to the writer ensconced at the center of the black period/planet: "Mr. Delany is it. He is the *center*. He is one of our most amazing writers and thinkers. You're sitting in a room with one of the greatest men in American literature. *Period*" (Mosley, Conference, italics mine). Take heed, *New York Times Book Review*. Delany responds to Mosley in terms of my dark matter period/planet metaphor: "I was the only dark *spot* in the mix when I came into the largely Jewish liberal science fiction community. At one point you have to decide I'm going to do what I'm going to do. I can write it [science fiction] too" (Delany, Conference, italics mine). Delany is no longer America's lone black science fiction writer. Many more dark spots presently figure in the science fiction mix. Black science fiction writers are now converged all at "one point," the inception point of an exploding black science fiction presence that is newly positioned to become science fiction's most exciting new direction. The center cannot hold: the period/planet will expand and fill the surrounding white space/page.

Hélène Cixous characterized *écriture féminine* as the feminist literary texts that metaphorically replace black ink with white mothers' milk. Black science fiction writers create science fiction *écriture noire;* women and men use black ink to burst forth from the black/period planet and fill the space of the white page. Science fiction *écriture noire* is poised to eclipse the white page space that the science fiction publishing universe occupies. Delany says that you "learn about life from what is written on the page" (Delany, Conference). Using black ink, black science fiction writers create texts that reflect their lives, lives which center on the color black. Color black science fiction, science fiction *écriture noire,* fulfills Thomas's request: "I wanted to see my community reflected in a future I could live in" (Thomas, Conference).

Thomas calls for more room for black science fiction—rooms of black science fiction writers' own—more black science fiction black ink to fill white pages' white futures. Her point manifests itself in terms of Italo Calvino's "All At One Point." Calvino's story describes how the single point which contains everything and everyone creates the entire universe—the future—when it expands. So too for black science fiction. My point is that "All At One Point" can be read as a parable of black science fiction's explosive development. Thomas could comfortably inhabit the futures that emanate when the contained single point of the black science fiction period/planet explodes in the science fiction world.

Calvino imagines that the single point containing all the matter in the universe is populated: "[W]e were all there . . . where else could we have been? Nobody knew then that there could be space" (Calvino 43). In terms of black science fiction history, "then" is the time before the point first began to expand, the time before Delany entered the white science fiction coterie. Pre-Delany, few critics noticed black science fiction. The "we" who are all there in the point Calvino describes includes Mrs. Ph(i)NKo, the Italian mother whose articulated wish to cook noodles is the catalyst that starts the universe's expansion. Another woman is also present: "a cleaning woman— 'maintenance staff' she was called . . . she spent all her time gossiping and complaining" (Calvino 43–44). Mrs. Ph(i)NKo is the most important character in Calvino's story. It is the cleaning woman, however, who is the integral personality in relation to the story of black science fiction's inception— and, taking historical American race relations into account, a present-day American reader encountering a mid-twentieth-century story could justifiably construe the cleaning woman as being black. When the cleaning woman gossips, she might speak in the black female voice. When she complains, she might rail against the fact that comments about "immigrants" and the "unfounded prejudice" directed against them in "All At One Point" do not include the blacks who are most certainly also contained within the point. (Blacks, after all, first traveled intercontinentally as slaves, not as immigrants.) Calvino's narrator says that he is not convinced that the universe which emanated from a single point will ever be "condensed again" (Calvino 45). "Unfounded prejudice" would be a part of the alleged new all-at-one-point in that one of its former inhabitants says, "[T]he thing we have to make sure of is, this time, certain people remain out" (Calvino 45).

The condensed and about-to-burst science fiction point, a corrective to this prejudice, consists of particular people, black science fiction writers, who are the genre's new "in" group. Calvino's character who expresses unfounded prejudice against immigrants is "turning purple" when he contemplates being reunited with Mrs. Ph(i)NKo (Calvino 45). The color purple and Mrs. Ph(i)NKo are not the point vis-à-vis the recondensed science fiction universe. The point is that the cleaning woman's gossiping and complaining, the language of someone who might be a black woman, is the discourse that acts as a catalyst to science fiction's new expansion. "It was the cleaning woman who always started the slander" (Calvino 46). Perhaps she speaks out against unfounded prejudice, the point that Mrs. Ph(i)NKo who "welcomed us and loved and inhabited all equally" begins the universe when she says, "I'd like to make some noodles for you boys!" (Calvino 46).

I read "you boys" as white boys. When the cleaning woman speaks as I imagine she would and the science fiction universe expands again, she might make it clear that "every nebula, every sun, every planet" (Calvino

47) is, in addition to being white boys' real estate, an appropriate space for all black people in particular and all people in general. She might make it clear that the point—the black period/planet emanation point—expands to accommodate the black science fiction literature that ensconces black culture on every nebula, every sun, every planet. At the end of "All At One Point," Mrs. Ph(i)NKo is lost, "scattered through the continents of the planets" (Calvino 47). She is lost among the continents of the planets imagined by science fiction writers whose roots emanate from white Europe. Calvino's protagonists are "mourning her loss" (Calvino 47). The purpose of *Afro-Future Females* is to celebrate the fact that the black mother who is responsible for science fiction's new expansion has been found. Delany is no longer alone. "I'd like to make some plantains for you sistahs and boyz," I imagine her saying as science fiction's newest new-wave trajectory is born.

"Think about what exists. Black people can't have fiction without science fiction. Science fiction takes us away from the world which is so oppressive," says Mosley (Conference).

That is the point.

Period.

III. Science Fiction Will Overcome

The central point of *Afro-Future Females* is that black women impact upon science fiction as authors, protagonists, actresses, and editors. I wish to create a dialogue with existing theories of Afro-Futurism in order to generate fresh ideas about how to apply race to science fiction studies in terms of gender. *Afro-Future Females* at once applies Afro-Futurism to written and visual texts and offers something very different from existing scholarship. The volume's contributors expand Mark Dery's masculinist foundation for our understanding of Afro-Futurism by explaining how to formulate a woman-centered Afro-Futurism. Their essays and stories present a valuable argument concerned with repositioning previously excluded fiction to redefine science fiction as a broader fantastic endeavor. These texts can be used as a platform for scholars to mount a vigorous argument in favor of redefining science fiction to encompass varieties of fantastic writing and, therefore, to include a range of black women's writing that would otherwise be excluded.[4] The anthology's umbrella approach is not new in that it has for a long time been reflected by "speculative fiction" and by Eric S. Rabkin's notion of a "super genre."[5] While presenting a complex method to redefine "science fiction" is certainly beyond the purview of this preface, I note that my term "feminist fabulation"[6] encompasses black women's science fiction. The big-tent rubric figures in this collection's central argument which goes beyond the point that marginalized texts and authors have been excluded from the itself-marginalized science fiction genre. Instead, I emphasize that it is necessary to revise the very nature of a genre that has been constructed in such a way as to exclude its new black participants. It is necessary to rethink "science fiction" in light of Afro-Futurist fiction.

For example, the stories by Octavia E. Butler, Andrea Hairston, Nisi Shawl, Sheree R. Thomas, and Nalo Hopkinson which I have included collectively indicate the ways in which science fiction should be reconceptualized. Traditional constructions of science fiction have divided the genre into a fantastic continuum that often excludes fantasy, women, and people of color. The claim that black people do not write science fiction is dependent upon defining science fiction as texts that black people do not write. Expanding "science fiction" to include written and visual Afro-Futuristic imaginative visions changes the dynamic in which science fiction is always defined as inferior to mainstream realistic literature.[7]

For this change to occur—in order to end the marginalization of science fiction which relentlessly relegates the genre to subliterary status—it is necessary to define the broad fantastic tendency in Afro-Futurist texts as science fiction. In their contributions to this volume, Madhu Dubey and DeWitt Douglas Kilgore describe a new enlarged fantastic tendency. Kilgore points to the intermingling of fantasy, time, and history:

> I see their work [stories written by Nnedi Okorafor-Mbachu, Nisi Shawl, and Jarla Tangh] as part of a feminist tradition in African-American literature that imaginatively engages mythic and historical pasts in order to describe livable futures. These pasts have been visible but marginal in relation to Anglo-American science fiction and fantasy. I argue that Okorafor, Shawl, and Tangh bring these pasts into contact with the conventions and expectations fantastic literature fosters. Having no desire to erase the reading pleasures associated with speculative fiction, these authors use story telling conventions inherited from the Anglo-American literary tradition in unintended ways. The writers venture beyond merely moving black female characters and their histories into previously white and male precincts to create "diverse" versions of familiar tales. Instead, they directly engage genre conventions to change what and how we read. Thus, fantastic literature's resources are used to tell stories that have been impossible to imagine.

Black science fiction writers alter genre conventions to change how we read and define science fiction itself.

Dubey explains why previously impossible-to-imagine female Afro-Futurist stories emerge when black-centered fantasy interrogates "normal" science fiction premises. She discusses "magical modes of knowing and being that supplement and often override the principles of reason." Dubey continues: "The critique of scientific rationality forms such a strong impelling force in the fledgling field of black-authored science fiction as to almost warrant the term 'black anti–science fiction.' In science fiction novels by black men and women writers . . . scientific practice is relentlessly indicted for its predatory exploitation of black bodies and scientific theory for validating claims of black racial inferiority. Afro-diasporic systems of knowledge and belief, such as vodun, obeah, or Santeria, are consistently shown to confound and triumph over scientific reason." Dubey describes juxtaposing fantasies involving Afro-diasporic knowledge and belief systems with anti–science fiction. Anti–science fiction is science fiction imbued with black diasporic versions of fantasy, that is, fantasy-centered science fiction which includes such despised unrealistic tropes as dreams and magic. Anti–science fiction is black science fiction/fantasy—writing that falls under the auspices of feminist fabulation. *Beloved* is written in this vein. Recognizing that black science fiction writers combine science fiction with fantasy once and for all ends the tiresome debates about the differences between the definitions of science fiction and fantasy that once pervaded science fiction critical discourse. Black science fiction/fantasy is a new new-wave trajectory effective force. This force is with the science fiction critical empire when it strikes back against being relentlessly branded with the "C" word—and what I mean by the "C" word will become immediately clear. It is thankfully socially impossible currently to use racial epithets publicly and formally in American society. I wish the same for the "C" word as it is routinely used in the following pervasive elitist sentiment: "science fiction is crap."[8]

I read Dubey (in her contribution to this volume) as providing instructions about how to do things with words to end discrimination against science fiction. She clearly states that black women's science fiction and black women's mainstream literature are one and the same: the "resonance between [Nalo] Hopkinson and Morrison suggests that what is recently being marketed as the newly emergent phenomenon of black women's science fiction shares common generic traits with 'mundane' or 'mainstream' black women's novels such as Morrison's own *Song of Solomon, Beloved,* or *Tar Baby,* Toni Cade Bambara's *The Salt Eaters,* Ntozake Shange's *Sassafras, Cypress, and Indigo,* and Gloria Naylor's *Mama Day,* to name just a few." Dubey continues: "In its casual incorporation of magical and supernatural phenomena and its flouting of the norms of realism and rational explication, mundane as well as speculative fiction by black women writers can be said to exemplify the 'counterculture of modernity' that Paul Gilroy considers to be distinctive of Afro-diasporic culture." If black women's mainstream literature and black women's science fiction belong to the same genre just as surely as the Martians and the Earthlings depicted in Kurt Vonnegut's *The Sirens of Titan* belong to the same species, then—as *Star Trek*'s Vulcan Mr. Spock would say—discriminating against science fiction is illogical.

In terms of the female Afro-Futurism Dubey describes, applying the "C" word to science fiction generates the following logical imagined elitist critical conclusion: some literature created by Toni Morrison is crap. Why can the critics who routinely discriminate against science fiction texts apply the word "crap" to examples of Morrison's work? The answer: Morrison includes science fiction tropes in some of her writing. (If all science fiction is allegedly crap, then the science fictional aspects of Morrison's work must also logically be categorized as crap too.) To exemplify the notion that Morrison's work contains science fiction tropes, my introduction to *Future Females, The Next Generation* (Barr 2000, 1–2) explains that the feminist utopia Morrison depicts in *Paradise* is akin to the feminist utopias female science fiction writers envision. Equating "crap" with the science fictional elements present in the work of one of America's greatest living writers is as professionally impossible as publicly uttering racist language. Once and for all and finally, it is necessary to understand that the following knee-jerk literary critical assertion is absolutely illogical: if it is good, it can't be science fiction; and if it is science fiction, it can't be good. (This thinking led to the erroneous and irrational conclusion that Vonnegut's *Slaughterhouse Five,* a great American novel whose extraterrestrial protagonists hail from the planet Tralfamadore, is something other than science fiction. To the misguided critics who deny that *Slaughterhouse Five* is science fiction I say this: if it looks like an extraterrestrial and it quacks—or communicates in some other nonhuman manner—like an extraterrestrial, than it *is* science fiction. I note too that Philip Roth's lauded *The Plot against America* is a science fiction alternative history story.)

Dubey further explains that "Afro-diasporic and feminist writers of speculative and science fiction deploy magic in strikingly convergent ways, to reevaluate a whole set of gendered and racialized dichotomies that have helped to prop up the subject of modern science." In other words, Toni Morrison, Gloria Naylor, Nalo Hopkinson, and Tananarive Due, for example, produce female-centered Afro-Futurist texts; female-centered Afro-Futurist texts are part of science fiction's newest new wave, the Afro-diasporic, fantasy-infused, magic-centered science fiction I have described. Science fiction is rescued from discrimination when science fiction parameters are expanded to nullify the claim that black people do not write science fiction. Ditto for the false assertion that great American writers such as Morrison and Roth create purely realistic work that is devoid of science fiction tropes.

In addition to my aforementioned point about the similarity between the feminist utopia that Morrison depicts in *Paradise* and the feminist utopias that appear in science fiction, I have said that Virginia Woolf's *Orlando* is a science fiction time travel novel and that Ursula K. Le Guin should be recognized as the Virginia Woolf of our time.[9] I now situate Octavia E. Butler at the productive intersection of the intermingling between science fiction and Afro-diasporic fantasy I describe above. She participated at once in female Afro-Futurism fantasy and in conventional American genre science fiction traditions. Butler's *Kindred* is the time travel great American novel descendant of Mark Twain's *A Connecticut Yankee in King Arthur's Court* and *Orlando*. No crap-producing, marginalized, science fiction genre writer, Octavia E. Butler is absolutely the equal of Toni Morrison.

That is the point.

Period.

⟩ IV. Fantastic Voyage
What Lies Within

Afro-Future Females is divided into four sections: introductions, essays, stories, and commentaries. This is what lies within the sections:

Introductions

Hortense J. Spillers' "Imaginative Encounters" ponders the real and the imaginative, the juxtaposition of the familiar and the strange, in terms of black women writers' science fiction. In order to foster the needed interchange between black studies scholars and science fiction studies scholars, it is exceedingly important for one of the most noteworthy theorists of black feminism to address herself to black science fiction.

Mark Dery's "Black to the Future: Afro-Futurism 1.0" launched the discourse of Afro-Futurism. The piece appears here accompanied by a new explanatory note.

Marleen S. Barr, in "'On the Other Side of the Glass': The Television Roots of Black Science Fiction," argues that from the 1960s to the 1990s, television served as a remedial education program that mitigated against racism in the form of a temporal progression. I announce that black television stars are the mothers and fathers of black science fiction. My purpose is to explain how television laid the groundwork for the twenty-first-century outpouring of black science fiction.

Essays

Madhu Dubey, in "Becoming Animal in Black Women's Science Fiction," examines the device of women becoming animals in Octavia E. Butler's *Wild Seed* and Nalo Hopkinson's *Midnight Robber.* Dubey stresses that Butler and Hopkinson depict women changing into animals to critique scientific rationality, to "defamiliarize the modern Western discourse of the human."

Ellen Peel, in "God Is Change: Persuasion and Pragmatic Utopianism in Octavia Butler's *Earthseed* Novels," draws upon her *Politics, Persuasion, and Pragmatism: A Rhetoric of Feminist Utopian Fiction* to approach the *Earthseed* novels by questioning the nature of persuasion. Peel states that "since the Earthseed series tells the story of a movement both utopian and religious, these novels are also about persuasion."

Alcena Madeline Davis Rogan, in "Tananarive Due and Nalo Hopkinson Revisit the Reproduction of Mothering: Legacies of the Past and Strategies for the Future," argues that it is necessary to focus upon the American black woman's fraught relationship to her self and to the symbolic perpetuation of her self—her daughters. Rogan explores the theme of the racialized "reproduction of mothering" in Tananarive Due's "Like Daughter" and in Nalo Hopkinson's *Brown Girl in the Ring.* She brings the work of various theorists (such as bell hooks, Audre Lorde, Hortense J. Spillers, Gayatri Spivak, and Angela Davis) to bear upon this theme.

Jennifer E. Henton, in "Close Encounters between Traditional and Nontraditional Science Fiction: Octavia E. Butler's *Kindred* and Gayl Jones's *Corregidora* Sing the Time Travel Blues," undertakes a twofold objective: she describes a new conception of science fiction which allows the genre to include Other voices, and she exemplifies this inclusiveness by reading *Kindred* in terms of *Corregidora* being newly defined as science fiction. Henton establishes that both Butler and Jones are science fiction ladies who sing the time travel blues when she makes it "possible for a black woman's traditionally science fictional text to closely encounter a black woman's text which has never before boldly gone within genre science fiction."

De Witt Douglas Kilgore, in "Beyond the History We Know: Nnedi Okorafor-Mbachu, Nisi Shawl, and Jarla Tangh Rethink Science Fiction Tradition," focuses upon the experimental tradition of emerging writers, a strategy that "helps [to] reveal the rich play of influences, conversations and movements that are remaking contemporary science fiction and fantasy." Kilgore points out that these emerging writers bring African-American mythic and historic pasts to bear upon fantastic literature conventions. The three writers Kilgore discusses respond to his ideas in the following pieces: Shawl's "Bubbling Champagne Power Trip," Okorafor-Mbachu's "'Of Course People Can Fly,'" and Tangh's "Carla Johnson/Jarla Tangh: A Close Encounter with My Pseudonym."

Stories

Afro-Future Females includes five short stories that exemplify exactly how black women are boldly going into science fiction: Octavia E. Butler's "The Book of Martha," Andrea Hairston's "Double Consciousness," Nisi Shawl's "Dynamo Hum," Sheree R. Thomas's "The Ferryman," and Nalo Hopkinson's "Herbal."

Commentaries

Of course, no one would question why an anthology devoted to black women and science fiction includes science fiction written by black women. But not so for the commentaries Steven Barnes, Samuel R. Delany, and Kevin Willmott contribute: Barnes's "Can a Brother Get Some Love? Sociobiology in Images of African-American Sensuality in Contemporary Cinema: Or, Why We'd Better the Hell Claim Vin Diesel as Our Own"; an interview with Delany conducted by Carl Freedman, "A Conversation with Samuel R. Delany about Sex, Race, Writing—and Science Fiction"; and "Black 'Science Faction': An Interview with Kevin Willmott, Director and Writer of *CSA, The Confederate States of America*," an interview that I undertook. What are such nice male science fiction practitioners doing in an anthology like this—an anthology that focuses upon women? They discuss real women, imagined women, and sex and gender issues. To honor Butler, I frame the commentary section with pieces representative of the established writers and emerging talents who continue her legacy: Due's "On Octavia E. Butler," and the younger Okorafor-Mbachu's "Octavia's Healing Power: A Tribute to the Late Great Octavia E. Butler."

Finally, I include a personal afterword, "The Big Bang: Or, the Inception of Scholarship about Black Women Science Fiction Writers." Ruth Salvaggio, who participated in the events my afterword describes, offers her response, "Connecting Metamorphoses: Italo Calvino's Mrs. Ph(i)NKo and I, Dr. Ph(d)SalvagGIo."

Since the issue of who is authorized to speak about particular writers, and which writers should be included in the conversation, is vexed and troubling, I want briefly and directly to address it. Scholarly considerations of black science fiction must include Delany. (Delany, the author of *Triton*, is, after all, a feminist science fiction writer.) Hence, men contribute to this anthology about black women's science fiction. I took care to include scholars and writers who are well-known, as well as those who are at the inception of their careers. *Afro-Future Females: Black Writers Chart Science Fiction's Newest New-Wave Trajectory* celebrates the flowering, the burgeoning, the expansion of the newly born black female science fiction universe.

That is the point.

Period.

V. Postscript: Future Afro-Future Female (and Male) Award Winners
Or, the Imagined Triumph of the Hippogriffs

A. O. Scott says that "the thing about mythical beasts is they don't go extinct; they evolve. The best American fiction of the past 25 years is concerned . . . with sorting out the past, which may be its way of clearing ground for the literature of the future. So let me end with a message to all you aspiring hippogriff breeders out there: 2030 is just around the corner. Get to work" (Scott 19).

So let me end with a hopeful message about science fiction's future in relation to mainstream literature.

Scott's year 2030 is presently a science fiction projection. The presence of the science fictional 2030 in Scott's text means that science fiction, the "literature of the future," appears in the *New York Times'* search for the best American fiction after all! Today's hippogriff breeders—the recently established black science fiction writers and the emerging talents who follow them—sort out their historical past in order to generate the literature of the future. Once upon a future time, in Scott's 2030, for example, I hope that today's new science fiction writers will win prizes for writing the best American fiction. I also hope that Samuel R. Delany wins a major literary award well before 2030.

VI. Post-Postscript: Back to the Future

Butler was once described as "one of the finest voices in fiction—*period*" [italics mine] by *The Washington Post* (Lamb 8).

The point: black science fiction is the most exciting literature of the twenty-first-century present.

Period.

Notes

1. I wish to call attention to my use of the word "story" in this sentence. Please know that I am concerned about the fact that literary criticism distances itself from readers to the extent that some university presses are refusing to publish it. To assuage this situation, building upon my work as a pioneering feminist science fiction critic and an emerging fiction writer, I am now turning my hand toward pioneering a new critical writing style. Hence, in the manner of Maureen Dowd's *New York Times* editorial page columns, I am very purposefully writing this preface in an unorthodox mode. Many people did not welcome feminist science fiction criticism, and I am fully aware that not everyone will welcome the critical writing style I advocate. I hope that those who do not concur with me will at least be open to the creation of a space for new forms of critical expression. For another example of how "story" figures in my critical writing, see Marleen S. Barr, "Textism—An Emancipation Proclamation," *PMLA*, May 2004, 429–41.

2. Similar points were raised at Wiscon 30 (May 26–29, 2006), the feminist science fiction conference held in Madison, Wisconsin. The following is the program description for a panel called "Tearing Down the Walls and Windows" whose participants were Claire Light, Candra K. Gill, Ian K. Hagemann, Diantha Day Sprouse, and Sheree R. Thomas: "People sometimes ask 'Why don't people of color write speculative fiction?' 'We do,' says Nalo Hopkinson, 'but it's unlikely that you'll find it on the SF shelves in your bookstores.' Why don't genre readers recognize novels such as Gloria Naylor's *Mama Day* or Devorah Major's *An Open Weave* as belonging to our own? Why does even a writer as solidly genre-identified as Octavia Butler find most of her fans from elsewhere?"

3. Thomas related this anecdote to me. She also referred to it at the 2006 National Black Writers Conference.

4. Jennifer E. Henton's contribution to this volume exemplifies one method of how to frame this in-depth argument. Please know that in my capacity as editor, I helped to generate her essay's topic and structure. Hence, rather than including a complex critical argument that would repeat the intention of Henton's essay, I instead elect to have my preface focus upon a creative analogy involving Calvino's "All At One Point."

5. See Eric S. Rabkin, *The Fantastic in Literature*. Princeton, NJ: Princeton University Press, 1976.

6. See Marleen S. Barr, *Feminist Fabulation: Space/Postmodern Fiction*. Iowa City: University of Iowa Press, 1992.

7. I am grateful to this volume's anonymous outside readers who helped me to formulate the points I make at the start of this section.

8. The word "crap" resonates strongly within the science fiction community. When defending the genre against elitist critics, science fiction writer Theodore Sturgeon famously said "95 percent of science fiction is crap . . . but then, 95 percent of everything is crap." For a science fiction critic who satirically comments upon the pervasiveness of using "crap" to describe science fiction, see Eric S. Rabkin, "What Was Science Fiction?" *Envisioning the Future: Science Fiction and the Next Millennium*. Ed. Marleen S. Barr. Middletown, CT: Wesleyan University Press, 2003. 191–98.

9. See Marleen S. Barr, "*Searoad Chronicles of Klatsand* as a Pathway toward New Directions in Feminist Science Fiction: Or, Who's Afraid of Connecting Ursula Le Guin to Virginia Woolf?" *Foundation* (Spring 1994): 58–67.

Works Cited

Apostolou, John L. and Martin Harry Greenberg. *The Best Japanese Science Fiction Stories.* New York: Norton, 1989.

Bambara, Toni Cade. *The Salt Eaters.* New York: Random House, 1980.

Barr, Marleen S. *Future Females, The Next Generation: New Voices and Velocities in Feminist Science Fiction Criticism.* Lanham, MD: Rowman & Littlefield, 2000.

———. *Future Females: A Critical Anthology.* Bowling Green, OH: The Popular Press, 1981.

Butler, Octavia E. *Kindred.* Garden City, NY: Doubleday, 1988.

———. *Wild Seed.* Garden City, NY: Doubleday, 1980.

Calvino, Italo. 1965. "All At One Point." In *Cosmicomics,* trans. William Weaver. New York: Harcourt Brace & World, 1968. 43–47.

Delany, Samuel R. Speculative Fiction Panel. April 1, 2006. The National Black Writers Conference. Medgar Evers College, The City University of New York, March 30–April 2, 2006.

———. *Triton.* New York: Bantam, 1976.

Dinesen, Isak. "The Blank Page." In *Last Tales.* New York: Random House, 1957.

Ellison, Harlan. *Dangerous Visions.* Garden City, NY: Doubleday, 1967.

Hopkinson, Nalo. *Midnight Robber.* New York: Warner, 2000.

Jones, Gayl. *Corregidora.* New York: Random House, 1975.

Kermode, Frank. *The Sense of an Ending: Studies in the Theory of Fiction.* New York: Oxford University Press, 1967.

Lamb, Yvonne Shinhoster. "Science Fiction Writer Octavia Butler, 58." *Washington Post.* February 28, 2006. B8.

McCaffery, Larry. *Storming the Reality Studio: A Casebook of Cyberpunk and Postmodern Science Fiction.* Durham, NC: Duke University Press, 1991.

Morrison, Toni. *Paradise.* New York: Knopf, 1998.

———. *Beloved.* New York: Knopf, 1987.

———. *Tar Baby.* New York: Knopf, 1981.

———. *Song of Solomon.* New York: Knopf, 1977.

Mosley, Walter. Speculative Fiction Panel. April 1, 2006. The National Black Writers Conference. Medgar Evers College, The City University of New York, March 30–April 2, 2006.

Naylor, Gloria. *Mama Day,* New York: Vintage, 1993

Roth, Philip. *The Plot against America.* Boston: Houghton Mifflin, 2004.

Said, Edward. *Beginnings: Intention and Method.* New York: Basic Books, 1975.

Sargent, Pamela. *Women of Wonder: Science Fiction Stories by Women about Women.* New York: Vintage, 1974.

Scott, A. O. "In Search of the Best." *New York Times Book Review.* May 21, 2006. 17–19.

Shange, Ntozake. *Sassafras, Cypress, and Indigo,* New York: St. Martin's Press, 1982.

Sterling, Bruce. *Mirrorshades: The Cyberpunk Anthology.* New York: Arbor House, 1986.

Thomas, Sheree R. Speculative Fiction Panel. April 1, 2006. The National Black Writers Conference. Medgar Evers College, The City University of New York, March 30– April 2, 2006.

———. *Dark Matter: Reading the Bones.* New York: Warner, 2004.

———. *Dark Matter: A Century of Speculative Fiction from the African Diaspora.* New York: Warner, 2000.

Vonnegut, Kurt. *Slaughterhouse Five.* New York: Delacorte, 1969.

———. *The Sirens of Titan.* New York: Dell, 1959.

Woolf, Virgina. *Orlando.* London: Hogarth Press, 1928.

Yamashita, Karen Tei. *Circle K Cycles.* Minneapolis: Coffee House Press, 2001.

INTRODUCTIONS

"Dark Matter" Matters

HORTENSE J. SPILLERS

Imaginative Encounters

On 20 July 1969, *Apollo 11* successfully landed Neil Armstrong on the surface of the moon; to that moment, "the site of humankind's only manned exploration of another celestial body" (Parrett 1), this achievement arguably rendered wishing on the moon moribund. Now that going to the moon no longer counted as a patent impossibility, the figurative dimension suddenly shifted into the literal, and the act of imagination that had fired the engines of poets and songwriters and graced the most youthful eroticisms with the stuff of myth and dreaming now belonged to the precincts of the engineer and the computer specialist. But there is every reason to believe that the moon landing, as well as space exploration more generally, owes its fruition as much to poetry and the range of the imaginative arts as to the initiatives of science and technology; in short, the imitation of art by the real world is not usually the way we think it goes, but it must be so, according to the dynamic dance of mimesis that Oscar Wilde celebrates in the "Decay of Lying" (970–93). We might describe it this way: the writings of the imaginative artist, among which the "extraterrestrial" prominently figures—one scholar calls them the "translunar narrative"—deposit traces that the thickest empiricisms may well translate into products after their own encodations. To this ancient tradition of symbol-making, running back over the centuries, black women writers continue to make significant contributions.

The realm of the extraterrestrial, or the entire gamut of fictions that pose alternative models of reality, including the fictions of science, magic, and the fantastical, might be thought to have something of a pro-hibitive relationship to certain historical formations. Put another way, cer-tain historical formations that arise in the world of *realpolitik* bear a critical relationship, one might well believe, to literary realism; if the latter defines narrative strategy and modes of characterization according to mimeti-cally vivid and verifiable principles, engendered by the real world of power relations, then realism would seem to match up well with its origins in the problematic of the everyday. By this logic, African-American literary development would locate its center of gravity in realism. But if there is more than one way "to make it real," then the work of fantasy and make-believe has a genuine role to play in processes of social construction and identity formation.

Among black women writers in the genre of science fiction, Octavia E. Butler has created entire alternative worlds that uncannily reflect reality and deflect and undermine it at the same time by generating subjects who improve on the available human models; in that regard, science fiction puts into play something that we know, that is rather familiar, while it so rearranges the signposts that the outcome is strange and defamiliar-ized. The melding of the familiar and the strange is not only the essence of the marvelous, but the very ground of the uncanny, which returns us to what we know in a way that we had not known and experienced before. Butler's fictional projects in the reterritorializations and displacements of realism's objects trace back to the 1970s and her "Patternist" series that immerses the reader in the cosmos of the immortal and hermaphroditic Doro, encompassing *Patternmaster* (1976), *Mind of My Mind* (1977), *Sur-vivor* (1978), *Wild Seed* (1980), and *Clay's Ark* (1984) (Gates and McKay 2515–29). Butler's "Xenogenesis" series that tells the story of a new Lilith (Iyapo) takes us across the '80s decade of the writer's career and includes *Dawn, Adulthood Rites,* and *Imago;* perhaps the writer's best-known novel, *Kindred* (1988), belongs to the same period, as it reverses the logic of futurism and time travel by taking us backward in time, or, more precisely, back to the future. From the '90s, Butler's Lauren Olamina transports us deep inside the twenty-first century by way of *The Parable of the Sower* and *The Parable of the Talents.* On the basis of this substantial, single-authored canon, Octavia E. Butler most certainly inhabits a central chapter of a revised African-American literary history, alongside a sustained reassess-ment of the powers of the uncanny.

When Dana, the protagonist of *Kindred,* finds herself on a path of reentry onto slavery's old ground, she and the reader make the one return journey that they have both determined is the most dreadful event that the mind could conjure up and that the body, in utter recoil to terror, shudders in the very act of imagining. Not only does one try to think that such an occurrence is impossible, and to rest assured in that impossibility—after all, there is that fragile membrane-moment that we like to call the Constitution—but one also wants to believe that the thought itself is, paradoxically, *unthinkable*. That Butler indeed *thought* it, plucking this contemporary character out of a world that parallels our own and from the nesting place of an interracial marriage, inscribes the most daring of fictional moves with a result that is profoundly disturbing: if fictional time lays claim to plasticity, then it can retrogress as well as progress. In this case, Dana's return demarcates a proleptic leap, insofar as she must go back in order to give birth to her ancestors and, thus, to someone called Dana, which violent act of parturition will tear her arm off when she eventually makes it back to the novel's diegetic time frame. We have no fiction quite like it in joining so terrible a historical contingency to the canons of the magical; *Kindred* is also rare in its refusal of a unidirectional concept of time and the inevitability of progress. We do not want to know that the cost of our being here has been inestimable and that the way to our current peace swims in blood and the truncated bodies of the violent dead. Forced from our slumber of feigned innocence, we awaken here to full consciousness and its blasts of discomfort. In this instance, we have seen the future that is represented from one of its angles—the terrible past—and it is a cautionary tale that we dare not disbelieve. This volume of criticism on science fiction with its brilliant new stars opens a path here to considerations of other worlds that illuminate the one we now so uncertainly inhabit.

Works Cited

Gates, Henry Louis, Jr., and Nellie Y. McKay, eds. "Octavia E. Butler." In *The Norton Anthology of African-American Literature*. New York: W. W. Norton, 2004.

Parrett, Aaron. *The Translunar Narrative in the Western Tradition*. Aldershot Hampshire, England: Ashgate, 2004.

Wilde, Oscar. "The Decay of Lying." In *Complete Works of Oscar Wilde*, introd. Vyvyan Holland. London: Collins, 1976.

Black to the Future

Afro-Futurism 1.0

"Black to the Future" was originally written for *Flame Wars: The Discourse of Cyberculture* (Duke University Press, 1994), an anthology I edited. Arguably the first serious scholarly inquiry into digital culture, *Flame Wars* grappled with feminist and Afrocentric issues at a time when the alt.geek underground was A Guy Thing—more precisely, A White Guy Thing. Its aspirational bibles were the upwardly mobile *Wired* and its cyberslacker cousin, *Mondo 2000:* its natural habit the rave, the videogame console, and the virtual realities dreamed up by the novelist William Gibson and coded into being by the hacker Jaron Lanier. In the largely uninhabited vastness of cyberspace, a few colonists were founding subcultural enclaves, but the Net was still a terra simulacrum to most, marooned unawares in the Desert of the Real.

The introduction to a suite of interviews (with the African-American SF novelist Samuel R. Delany, professor of Africana Studies Tricia Rose, and cultural critic Greg Tate), "Black to the Future" launched the discourse of Afro-Futurism. I minted the term to describe African-American culture's appropriation of technology and SF imagery—this at a moment when *Wired* was lambasted for featuring nothing but white guys on its covers. As the prominent cultural theorist Ron Eglash confirms, in "The Race for Cyberspace: Information Technology in the Black Diaspora" (http://www.rpi.edu/~eglash/eglash.dir/ethnic.dir/r4cyb. dir/r4cybh.htm), "Mark Dery (1994) coined the term . . . to describe the self-conscious appropriation of technological themes in black popular culture, particularly that of rap and other hip-hop representations."

At last count, a Google search for "Afro-Futurism" racked up 1,500 hits. A burgeoning field of study, it has inspired a website (http://www. Afro-Futurism.net/); a members-only Yahoo discussion group (http://groups.yahoo.com/group/Afro-Futurism); a Hypertext project (http://www.vanderbilt.edu/AnS/english/English295/carroll/gateway.html); and critical anthologies such as *Race in Cyberspace, Technicolor: Race, Technology, and Everyday Life* and a special issue of the journal *Social Text,* titled, unsurprisingly, *Afro-Futurism.*

A decade on, Gibsonian visions of disenfranchised "Lo-Teks" and "orbital rastas" ripping off the Empire's brutally cool hardware and refunctioning it into weapons of mass resistance make a tinny irony when clanged against the everyday ugliness of the twenty-first century. Yesterday's cyberpunk bricoleurs are today's "entrepreneurial" jihadi, to use Chairman of the House Committee on Homeland Security Christopher Cox's term of art. Selecting their victims from multiple options in a target-rich environment, they improvise their ordnance from the innocuous stuff of consumer culture, turning cars into bombs, jetliners into missiles, and junk mail into booby traps rigged with anthrax or exploding match-heads. Fast, cheap, and out of control, the Improvised Explosive Devices (IEDs) wreaking havoc in Iraq as this is written are a sign of our times. Third-world insurgents sow the wind with first-world scrap, killing and maiming U.S. troops and private contractors with the trickledown products of American industry. "Highly sophisticated IEDs have been constructed from arming devices scavenged from conventional munitions and easily purchased electronic components, as well as consumer devices such as mobile phones," notes the online encyclopedia Wikipedia. "The degree of sophistication depends on the ingenuity of the designer and the tools and materials available." These are ad-hoc horrors, jury-rigged nightmares that make a mockery of cyberpunk fantasies, with their earnest, late-night dorm-room talk of appropriated technologies and "sites of resistance"—Islands in the Net, to use the SF novelist Bruce Sterling's patented phrase. Is there a place, in these days of Terrorist Futures and Total Information Awareness, for a naïve faith in guerrilla semiotics—the "deconstructionist ability to crack complex cultural codes"? In a time of human bombs and ad campaigns for the unspeakable (videotaped atrocities, with postproduction effects), such phrases sound like the litany of a forgotten religion, a millennial cult whose end days never came.

Afro-Futurism 1.0

[I]f all records told the same tale—then the lie passed into history and became truth. "Who controls the past," ran the Party slogan, "controls the future: who controls the present controls the past."
—George Orwell

There is nothing more galvanizing than the sense of a cultural past.
    —Alain Locke

Yo, bust this, Black
To the Future
Back to the past
History is a mystery 'cause it has
All the info
You need to know
Where you're from
Why'd you come and
That'll tell you where you're going
    —Def Jef

Hack this: Why do so few African-Americans write science fiction, a genre whose close encounters with the Other—the stranger in a strange land— would seem uniquely suited to the concerns of African-American novelists? Yet, to my knowledge, only Samuel R. Delany, Octavia E. Butler, Steven Barnes, and Charles Saunders have chosen to write within the genre conventions of SF. This is especially perplexing in light of the fact that African-Americans are, in a very real sense, the descendants of alien abductees. They inhabit a sci-fi nightmare in which unseen but no less impassable force fields of intolerance frustrate their movements; official histories undo what has been done to them; and technology, be it branding, forced sterilization, the Tuskegee experiment, or tasers, is too often brought to bear upon black bodies.

Moreover, the sublegitimate status of science fiction as a pulp genre in Western literature mirrors the subaltern position to which blacks have been relegated throughout American history—in which context William Gibson's observation that SF is widely known as "the golden ghetto," in recognition of the negative correlation between the genre's market share and its critical legitimation, takes on a curious significance. So, too, does Norman Spinrad's glib use of the phrase "token nigger" to describe "any science fiction writer of merit who is adopted . . . in the grand salons of literary power."

Speculative fiction that treats African-American themes and addresses African-American concerns in the context of twentieth-century technoculture—and, more generally, African-American signification that appropriates images of technology and a prosthetically enhanced future—might, for want of a better term, be called Afro-Futurism. The notion of Afro-Futurism gives rise to a troubling antinomy: Can a community whose past has been deliberately rubbed out, and whose energies have subsequently been consumed by the search for legible traces of its history, imagine possible futures? Furthermore, don't the technocrats, SF writers, futurologists, set designers, and streamliners—white to a man—who have engineered our collective fantasies already have a lock on that unreal estate? Samuel R. Delany has suggested that "the flashing lights, the dials, and the rest of the imagistic paraphernalia of science fiction" have historically functioned as "social signs—signs people learned to read very quickly. They signaled technology. And technology was like a placard on the door saying, 'Boys' Club! Girls, keep out. Black and Hispanics and the poor in general, go away!'" What Gibson has termed the "semiotic ghosts" of Fritz Lang's *Metropolis;* Frank R. Paul's illustrations for Hugo Gernsback's *Amazing Stories;* the chromium-skinned, teardrop-shaped household appliances dreamed up by Raymond Loewy and Henry Dreyfuss; Norman Bel Geddes's Futurama at the 1939 New York World's Fair; and Disney's Tomorrowland all still haunt the public mind, in one guise or another.

But African-American voices have other stories to tell about culture, technology, and things to come. If there is an Afro-Futurism, it must be sought in unlikely places, constellated from far-flung points. We catch a glimpse of it in the opening pages of Ralph Ellison's *Invisible Man,* where the proto-cyberpunk protagonist—a techno-bricoleur "in the great American tradition of tinkerers"—taps illegal juice from a line owned by the rapacious Monopolated Light & Power, gloating, "Oh, they suspect that their power is being drained off, but they don't know where." One day, perhaps, he'll indulge his fantasy of playing five recordings of Louis Armstrong's version of "What Did I Do to Be So Black and Blue" at once, in a sonic Romare Bearden collage (an unwittingly prescient vision, on Ellison's part, of that 1981 masterpiece of deconstructionist deejaying, "The Adventures of Grandmaster Flash on the Wheels of Steel"). Jean-Michel Basquiat paintings such as *Molasses,* which features a pie-eyed, snaggletoothed robot, adequately earn the term "Afro-Futurist," as do movies like John Sayles's *The Brother from Another Planet* and Lizzie Borden's *Born in Flames.* Jimi Hendrix's *Electric Ladyland* is Afro-Futurist; so, too, is the techno-tribal global village music of Miles Davis's *On the Corner* and Herbie Hancock's *Headhunters,* as well as the fusion-jazz cyberfunk of Hancock's *Future Shock* and Bernie Worrell's *Blacktronic Science,* whose liner notes herald "reports and manifestoes from the nether regions of the modern Afrikan American music/speculative fiction universe." Afro-Futurism manifests itself, too, in early '80s electro-boogie releases such as Planet Patrol's "Play at Your Own Risk," Warp 9's "Nunk," George Clinton's "Computer Games," and, of course, Afrika Bambaataa's classic "Planet Rock," records steeped in "imagery drawn from computer games, video, cartoons, sci-fi and hip-hop slanguage," notes David Toop, who calls them "a soundtrack for vidkids to live out fantasies born of a science-fiction revival courtesy of *Star Wars* and *Close Encounters of the Third Kind.*"

Techno, whose name was purportedly inspired by a reference to "techno rebels" in Alvin Toffler's *Third Wave*, is a quintessential example of Afro-Futurism. The genre was jump-started in the Orwellian year of 1984 in Detroit, appropriately enough, a city equally famous for Motown and the mechanical ballets of its spot-welding robots. The Ur-tune "Techno City" was hacked together by Juan Atkins, Kevin Saunderson, and Derrick May, a band of button-pushers who went by the name Cybotron. Matthew Collin notes that their worldview was "shaped by playing video games, by watching Ridley Scott's *Blade Runner*, and by the idea of a new computer world replacing industrial society as framed in both Kraftwerk's records and futurologist Alvin Toffler's book *The Third Wave*." According to Collin, the portentous chords and robotic clangor of their music reflected Motor City's moribund economy, its dark passage from the birthplace of the auto industry to its burial ground. Atkins, Saunderson, and May appropriated "industrial detritus" to create sparse, kinetic funk with drums like thunderbolts, yet mournful and deeply romantic, as if the machines were whispering a lament about what it was like to be young and black in postindustrial America. At the same time, they were young enough to be perversely fascinated by the very technologies that had downsized the American dream for factory workers in black Detroit. "Berry Gordy built the Motown sound on the same principles as the conveyor belt system at Ford's," explained Atkins. "Today they use robots and computers to make the cars. I'm probably more interested in Ford's robots than Berry Gordy's music." But Afro-Futurism bubbles up from the deepest, darkest well-springs in the intergalactic big-band jazz churned out by Sun Ra's Omni-verse Arkestra, in Parliament-Funkadelic's Dr. Seuss-ian astrofunk, and in dub reggae, especially the bush doctor's brew cooked up by Lee "Scratch" Perry, which at its eeriest sounds as if it were made out of dark matter and recorded in the crushing gravity field of a black hole ("Angel Gabriel and the Space Boots" is a typical title).

The Rastafarian cosmology, like the Nation of Islam's, with its genetically engineered white devils and its apocalyptic vision of Elijah Muhammad returning on a celestial mothership, is a syncretic crossweave of black nationalism, African and American religious beliefs, and plot devices worthy of a late-night rocket opera. Perry—arguably the preeminent prac-titioner of the audio juju known as dub—incarnates the Afro-Futurist sen-sibility. Erik Davis asserts that "what is most important about Perry and his astounding musical legacy is how they highlight an often ignored strain of New World African culture: a techno-visionary tradition that looks as much toward science-fiction futurism as toward magical African roots." Writes Davis, "This loosely Gnostic strain of Afro-diasporic science fiction emerges from the improvised confrontation between modern technology and the prophetic imagination, a confrontation rooted in the alienated conditions of black life in the New World." He quotes the African-American critic Greg Tate: "Black people," says Tate, "live the estrangement that science-fiction writers imagine."

Which explains the seemingly counterintuitive conjunction of black dance music and SF imagery in hip-hop. Tricia Rose argues that South Bronx hip-hoppers such as Afrika Bambaataa embraced the robotic synth-pop of Kraftwerk because what they saw reflected in the German band's android imagery was "an understanding of themselves as already having been robots." Says Rose, "Adopting 'the robot' reflected a response to an existing condition: namely, that they were labor for capitalism, that they had very little value as people in this society. By taking on the robotic stance, one is 'playing with the robot.' It's like wearing body armor that identifies you as an alien: if it's always on anyway, in some symbolic sense, perhaps you could master the wearing of this guise in order to use it against your interpolation."

Afro-Futurism percolates, as well, through black-written, black-drawn comics such as Milestone Media's *Hardware* ("A cog in the corporate machine is about to strip some gears. . . ."), about a black scientist who dons forearm-mounted cannons and a "smart" battle suit to wage guerrilla war on his Orwellian, multinational employer. Milestone's press releases for its four titles—*Hardware, Blood Syndicate, Static,* and *Icon*—make the Manhattan-based company's political impulses explicit: a fictional metropolis, Dakota, provides a backdrop for "authentic, multicultural" superheroes "linked in their struggle to defeat the S.Y.S.T.E.M." The city is a battlefield in "the clash of two worlds: a low-income urban caldron and the highest level of privileged society."

Icon, an exemplar of Afro-Futurism that sweeps antebellum memories, hip-hop culture, and cyberpunk into its compass, warrants detailed exegesis. The story begins in 1839, when an escape pod jettisoned from an exploding alien starliner lands, fortuitously, in the middle of a cotton field on Earth. A slave woman named Miriam stumbles on "a perfect little black baby"—in fact, an extraterrestrial whose morphogenetic technology has altered it to resemble the first lifeform it encounters—in the smoldering wreckage of the pod and raises it as her own. The orphan, christened Augustus, is male, and echoes of the Old Testament account of Moses in the bullrushes, the fay changelings of European folklore, and the infant Superman's fiery fall from the heavens reverberate in the narrative's opening passages.

Like his Roman namesake, Augustus is a "man of the future"; the man who fell to Earth is seemingly deathless, outliving several generations of his adopted family and eventually posing as his own great-grandson—

Augustus Freeman IV—in present-day Dakota. A rock-ribbed conservative who preaches the gospel of Horatio Alger and inveighs against the welfare state, Freeman is a highly successful attorney, the only African-American living in the city's exclusive Prospect Hills neighborhood. His unshakable belief in bootstrapping is challenged, however, when he takes a homegirl from the projects, Rachel "Rocket" Ervin, under his wing. A juvenile delinquent and Toni Morrison (!) fan, the streetwise teenager opens Augustus's eyes to "a world of misery and failed expectations that he didn't believe still existed in this country." She calls on him to use his otherworldly powers to help the downtrodden. When he does, in the guise of a mountain of bulging abs and pecs called Icon, she joins him as his sidekick. "As the series progresses," we are told, "Rocket will become the world's first superheroine who is also a teenage, unwed mother."

The New York graffiti artist and B-boy theoretician Rammellzee constitutes yet another incarnation of Afro-Futurism. Greg Tate holds that Rammellzee's "formulations on the juncture between black and Western sign systems make the extrapolations of [Houston] Baker and [Henry Louis] Gates seem elementary by comparison." As evidence, he submits the artist's "Ikonoklast Panzerism," a heavily armored descendant of late '70s "wild style" graffiti (those bulbous letters that look as if they were twisted out of balloons). A 1979 drawing depicts a Panzerized letter "S": it is a jumble of sharp angles that suggests the *Nude Descending a Staircase* bestriding a jet ski. "The Romans stole the alphabet system from the Greeks through war," explains Rammellzee. "Then, in medieval times, monks ornamented letters to hide their meaning from the people. Now, the letter is armored against further manipulation."

In like fashion, the artist encases himself during gallery performances in Gasholeer, a 148-pound, gadgetry-encrusted exoskeleton inspired by an android he painted on a subway train in 1981. Four years in the making, Rammellzee's exuberantly low-tech costume bristles with rocket launchers, nozzles that gush gouts of flame, and an all-important sound system.

> From both wrists, I can shoot seven flames, nine flames from each sneaker's heel, and colored flames from the throat. Two girl doll heads hanging from my waist and in front of my balls spit fire and vomit smoke. . . . The sound system consists of a Computator, which is a system of screws with wires. These screws can be depressed when the keyboard gun is locked into it. The sound travels through the keyboard and screws, then through the Computator, then the belt, and on up to the four mid-range speakers (with tweeters). This is all balanced by a forward wheel from a jet fighter plane. I also use an echo chamber, Vocoder, and system of strobe lights. A coolant device keeps my head and chest at normal temperature. A 100-

watt amp and batteries give me power.

The B-boy bricolage bodied forth in Rammellzee's "bulletproof arsenal," with its dangling, fetishlike doll heads and its Computator cobbled together from screws and wires, speaks to dreams of coherence in a fractured world, and to the alchemy of poverty that transmutes sneakers into high style, turntables into musical instruments, and spray-painted tableaux on subway cars into hit-and-run art.

Rammellzee's Afro-Futurist appropriation of the castoff oddments of technoculture is semiotic guerrilla warfare, just as his "slanguage"—a heavily encrypted hip-hop argot—is the linguistic equivalent of graffiti "tags" all over the mother tongue. In an essay on English as the imperial language of the Internet, the cultural critic McKenzie Wark argues for the willful, viral corruption of the *lingua franca* of global corporate monoculture as a political act. "I'm reminded of Caliban and Prospero," he writes. "Prospero, the Western man of the book, teaches Caliban, the colonial other, how to speak his language. And Caliban says, 'You give me words, that I might curse you with them.' Which is what happens to imperial languages. The imperial others learn it all too well. Make it something else. Make it proliferate, differentiate. Like Rammellzee, and his project for a Black English that nobody else could understand. Hiding in the master tongue. Waiting. Biting the master tongue." Wark's analysis resonates with Tricia Rose's notion of hip-hop countersignage as "master[ing] the wearing of this guise in order to use it against your interpolation."

African-American culture is Afro-Futurist at its heart, literalizing Gibson's cyberpunk axiom, "The street finds its own uses for things." With trickster élan, it retrofits, refunctions, and willfully misuses the techno-commodities and science fictions generated by a dominant culture that has always been not only white but a wielder, as well, of instrumental technologies. As Henry Louis Gates, Jr. reminds us:

> Black people have always been masters of the figurative: saying one thing to mean something quite other has been basic to black survival in oppressive Western cultures. . . . "Reading," in this sense, was not play; it was an essential aspect of the "literacy" training of a child. This sort of metaphorical literacy, the learning to decipher complex codes, is just about the blackest aspect of the black tradition.

Here at the end of the twentieth century, there's another name for the survival skill Gates argues is quintessentially black. What he describes as a deconstructionist ability to crack complex cultural codes goes by a better-known name, these days. They call it hacking.

MARLEEN S. BARR

"On the Other Side of the Glass"

The Television Roots of Black Science Fiction

Why, with the noted exception of Octavia E. Butler and Samuel R. Delany, have black authors only lately begun to impact upon science fiction? "Black to the Future," Walter Mosley's media-related answer, predicts a postmillennial black science fiction explosion and notes the pervasive presence of media images that link whiteness with power: "Media images of policeman, artists, and fireman from before the mid-sixties were almost always white. Now imagine blackness. There you will find powerlessness, ignorance. . . . Or you will simply not find anything at all—absence. . . . Only within the last thirty years have positive images of blackness begun appearing in even the slightest way in the media" (Mosley 203). Science fiction, as we all know, reflects reality. How, before the mid-1960s, could blacks see themselves as starship captains if reality denied them the opportunity to pilot airplanes? Why would blacks recast themselves as extraterrestrial aliens if they were alienated from everyday American life? Certainly blacks were disinclined to write about aliens because they had to struggle with being perceived as aliens. Why would blacks imagine, say, black Alpha Centauri denizens when alien encounters were defined as blacks showing up in white suburbia? I combine the ideas of Mosley, Neal Gabler, and Neil Postman to argue that from the '60s to the '90s, television served as a remedial education program which taught viewers how to see blacks as normal people. I wish to announce that black television stars are the mothers and fathers of black science fiction. My purpose is to explain that television laid the groundwork for the twenty-first-century outpouring of black science fiction Mosley describes.

⟩ I. Defining Black Normalcy
Or, Bill Cosby Has Not Lost His Mind

I rely upon the complex claim that television normalized black reality to pave the way for the black fantastic. There are, of course, myriad definitions of black authenticity and subjectivity. Within the milieu of television, *Amos 'n Andy* was faulted for omitting successful blacks while *The Cosby Show* was faulted for omitting impoverished blacks. Bill Cosby himself has famously chastised the black underclass for irresponsible parenting—and Michael Eric Dyson has countered him in *Is Bill Cosby Right?: Or Has the Black Middle Class Lost Its Mind?* As John McWhorter argues, the "normal" black reality debate involves the "old way focused on assimilation" and the "new way [which] elevated separatism" (McWhorter A23). I link televised images of blacks to the assimilation Cosby advocates.

Cosby's vision of black normalcy is quite congruent with the one John H. Johnson published in *Ebony Magazine*. Johnson created *Ebony* (1945) to show that "Negroes got married, had beauty contests, gave parties, ran successful businesses, and did all the other normal things of life" (McWhorter A23). My use of the term "black normalcy" coincides with the views of black normalcy that Johnson, McWhorter, and Cosby advocate. According to McWhorter, "the fact remains that since the 60's, blacks have found that some assimilation and striving in the mainstream is usually a surer path to success than embracing angry separatism. *Ebony* and *Jet* have covered this triumph lovingly . . . given the eternal static in the air claiming that the scowling poses of the likes of *Vibe* magazine are the essence of the 'real' for black people" (A23). The approach found in *Ebony* and *Jet* "is a victory" because "it shows that blacks hitting the heights in the mainstream arena are no longer extraordinary" (A23). Television established that the fact of blacks accomplishing "all the other normal things of life" is the essence of the real for black people. And McWhorter calls today's pervasive presence of blacks on television "something to celebrate" (A23). Because television now pervasively portrays black normalcy, blacks are finally free to imagine themselves confronting the science-fictional alien Other, to see themselves as protagonists within the pages of a work such as Joanna Russ's *Extra (Ordinary) People*. The postmillennial black science fiction explosion is occurring after television took forty years to establish that black normalcy, as Johnson and Cosby define it, is very real—not at all extraordinary.

Hence, I claim that in order to account for the recent outpouring of black science fiction, it is necessary to attribute this proliferation to the televised progression that made it possible.

Black science fiction characters emanate from very real stars, the black television personalities who inhabit the space that Gabler, in *Life: The Movie: How Entertainment Conquered Reality,* calls "on the other side of the glass" (185). According to Gabler, there are two Americas consisting of the privileged people who live behind the television glass and the lesser citizens who don't, those on the wrong side of the television broadcast signal tracks/divide who cannot go through the looking glass/television screen. Spending forty years viewing the positive images of the black protagonists who live behind the glass had myriad positive results. For example: the impenetrable looking glass television screen—the mirror mirror pervading interior domestic spaces—progressed from framing *Amos 'n Andy* to emphasizing this new fact of American life: the respectively black and white *The Facts of Life* protagonists Dorothy "Tootie" Ramsey and Blair Warner both attend the same elite private girls boarding school. The pictures behind the glass morph. Viewers watching the black *Star Trek: Deep Space Nine* Captain Benjamin Sisko boldly ensconced within outer space where no black starship captain had gone before could see his real counterparts: the faces of black space shuttle pilots behind the glass of real space helmet visors. Fiction is usually pictured on the other side of the television screen glass. The demise of minstrel-show blackface and the new rise of successful blacks on television led to the reality of the black face behind the space helmet glass—and the black writer on the science fiction novel cover. As Postman said in a video documentary that featured him, "the growth of more tolerance in America is because of television. There was a time when people could not see someone different from them. This can't happen today. Television is responsible" (Urbano). Television is responsible for the postmillennial black science fiction surge.

I illuminate this statement by giving black television actresses equal representation with the black male television stars we all know. I argue that after forty years during which black characters on television became ever more normal, these characters gave rise to new characters—and real people (such as Colin Powell and Condoleezza Rice)—who jump to the other side of the glass to represent—and act as—social power brokers. Media ecologists see communications systems as environments. I argue that crosspollination has occurred between television and reality which establishes a new late-twentieth-century normalcy for blacks and makes the burgeoning of black science fiction possible.

II. Outlining Black Science Fiction's Television Heritage
Or, I Spy Dominique Deveraux Knocking Amos, Andy, and Beulah's White Socks Off

Amos 'n Andy has a female-centered counterpart born from racist caricature: *Beulah,* which focuses upon an overweight black maid. Before black science fiction could come into its own, Will Smith[1] had to supplant the shuffling, buffoonish Amos and Andy, and attractive clothes horse Hilary Banks (Smith's cousin on *The Fresh Prince of Bel Air)* had to supplant Beulah. This transition began with what I call the short black boy syndrome. Gary Coleman and Emmanuel Lewis were the abnormally short boys who respectively starred in *Diff'rent Strokes* and *Webster,* the stories of poor black children adopted by rich white families. These boys, who were short to the point of resembling midgets, at once became the economic betters of the *Amos 'n Andy* protagonists and did not threaten white manhood. Short black girls never had sitcoms of their own.

George Jefferson (played by Sherman Hemsley), television comedy's first successful black male entrepreneur, was also short. Despite his business acumen, Jefferson also did not threaten white manhood. *The Jeffersons* made it patently clear that Jefferson differed in both appearance and demeanor from his economically successful WASP neighbor, Tom Willis. Jefferson's wife, Louise, a person of intelligence and integrity, looked very much like Beulah. Despite the negative stereotypes that characterized George and Louise, *The Jeffersons* was groundbreaking because it emphasized that the black community is characterized by economic stratification. The black Jeffersons had a black maid, Florence Johnston (who preceded Geoffrey, the Banks family's black butler). The physical difference between the corpulent Louise and her thin, elegant, sophisticated black neighbor Helen Willis was patently obvious to viewers. Helen is a normal upper-class person, and, as such, she is a precursor to Will Smith's aunt on *Fresh Prince,* Vivian Banks. The Jeffersons are indeed "movin' on up," as the show's theme song announces, when their son Lionel marries the Willis's beautiful and normal-in-every-way mixed-race daughter Jenny. *The Cosby Show*'s Cliff and Clair Huxtable are a more mature version of Jenny and Lionel Jefferson.

Benson improves upon *The Jeffersons* in that Benson is exceedingly well-spoken and of normal height. But Benson is always subordinate to the governor throughout the various manifestations of his employer/employee relationship with him. Benson, the governor's culturally sophisticated, foreign-accented right-hand man, has more in common with the Banks family's British, socially sophisticated butler, Geoffrey, than with the rather boorish, typically American Philip Banks. Americans do not emulate uppity foreign cultural codes. Benson is no Will Smith. It was, of course, Bill Cosby starring in *I Spy* who first played a black man acting as a white man's social and action adventure hero equivalent. *I Spy* made it possible for Will Smith to star in the film version of *I, Robot*. Bill Cosby is the father of black science fiction.

Before blacks could imagine themselves confronting intergalactic heights, it was necessary to establish that it is normal for them to integrate, say, Brooklyn Heights. The Huxtables, who made Brooklyn Heights their home, normalized the image of a black professional family. No television teenage girl was ever cooler than Denise Huxtable. Even now, more than twenty years after *The Cosby Show* first aired, the Huxtable family does not appear to be dated. In fact, Clair Huxtable, who manages perfectly to balance being a high-powered lawyer with raising five children, is a fantasy vision in relation to women's still very real difficulty resolving their domestic and professional responsibilities. Cosby, in addition to being the father of black science fiction, emphasized black fatherhood. Cliff Huxtable's relationship with his married daughters, Sondra and Denise, is more complex than that of Sholom Aleichem's Tevye with his five daughters. In *Fiddler on the Roof,* Tevye's daughters get married and leave his house; Sondra and Denise get married and bring husbands *and* children into the Huxtable home. So much for stereotypes about dysfunctional black nuclear families. Cliff's ever-increasingly complex domestic situation does not position him as a precariously balanced black fiddler on a Brooklyn Heights roof.[2] Instead, in terms of their comfort with black culture, the Huxtables are groovin' to opening shot theme song jazz while literally standing on the Apollo Theater's roof.

Little Rudy Huxtable could grow up to be "Jewish-American Princess" incarnate Hilary Banks. Before *The Cosby Show* ended, in the manner of Philip Banks, Cliff Huxtable welcomed a poor cousin into his affluent home. Unlike *Webster* and *Diff'rent Strokes, Cosby* and *Fresh Prince* portray blacks making economic strides via deriving assistance from their own families, not from white strangers. *Fresh Prince* more overtly emphasizes the black economic success *The Cosby Show* portrayed. In economic terms, Dr. Huxtable is to Philip Banks as Dr. Kildare is to Mr. Drysdale (Jed Clampett's rich banker neighbor on *The Beverly Hillbillies*). Unlike Jed, who in his pre-oil strike days is a white version of caricatured *Amos 'n Andy* protagonists, Philip Banks truly belongs in Bel Air. Unlike Beulah, Hilary Banks is a black pretty woman.

And Professor Vivian Banks is a pretty—and intelligent, professionally competent—black woman.[3] Vivian is a "sistah" of Clair Huxtable. Professor Banks owes her existence to a protagonist who came before her: Diahann Carroll playing nurse and single mother Julia Baker on *Julia*. Diahann Carroll, not Phylicia Rashad, is the mother of black science fiction. Clair, despite her professional expertise which is mostly enacted offstage, is an appendage to Cliff, but Julia stands alone. Diahann Carroll's role in *Julia* is the equivalent of Cosby's in *I Spy*. Carroll is the first black woman on television to play an intelligent professional who functions as an independent agent. Julia's son, Corey, is as cute as Rudy Huxtable. Most importantly, Diahann Carroll, who later appeared on *Dynasty,* is as compellingly beautiful as Joan Collins and Linda Evans.

The most important moment for black female science fiction on twentieth-century television does not involve the infamous *Star Trek* interracial kiss scene involving Lieutenant Uhura and Captain Kirk ("Plato's Stepchildren" 1968). The most important moment for black female science fiction on twentieth-century television involves the words Carroll uttered on *Dynasty* when she played Dominique Deveraux. Wearing a stunningly elegant white outfit replete with a white hat (the director obviously wanted to emphasize that Deveraux is a good guy), Dominique stands alone in Blake Carrington's office, faces the camera, and directly addresses the audience. "When they [the Carrington family] find out that I am a Carrington they will drop their socks off," she says. Dominique, Blake's half-sister, is in fact biologically a Carrington. Race does not prevent her from being a part of the superrich and exceedingly attractive Carrington dynasty.

The images of Dominique and her suave husband (played by Billy Dee Williams) negates "step and fetch it" black stereotypes. Dominique fits right in as a native of the Carrington's home planet (which is, after all, a different world from the one most Americans inhabit). Dominique is as important to black science fiction as Lieutenant Uhura: she shows that black women's reality in terms of beauty and economic power is equal to that of white women. Dominique can hold her own with Alexis vis-à-vis power and beauty. Even blonde bombshell Krystle does not outshine her. Black science fiction springs from the once almost-nonexistent black-empowered reality that *I Spy* and *Dynasty* portrayed. These shows function as behind-the-glass crystal balls, windows on the future, twenty-first-century worlds in which empowered black reality is exceedingly normal. Ashley Banks, normal American teenager incarnate, absolutely fits into contemporary Bel Air. Her father, Will Smith's Uncle Phil, is no Uncle Tom. True, Philip Banks is noticeably fat as surely as George Jefferson is noticeably short. His corpulence, however, is normal in that it makes him look like America. Ensconced within her elite neighborhood economic comfort zone, no *Twilight Zone* fiction, Ashley can grow up to become a science fiction writer. No alien herself, she can comfortably invent alien encounter fictions.

Today, the real Will Smith lives in one of the most expensive neighborhoods in Los Angeles. He and his wife, Jada Pinkett-Smith, exemplify the glamour and wealth that Dominique Deveraux and her husband exude. The Smiths can be themselves, not the Carringtons. The Smiths are not aliens; they just play alien encounterers in the movies. The progression I chart, which moves from the negative stereotypes of blacks depicted in *Amos 'n Andy* and *Beulah* to the reality of black affluence shown on *Cosby* and *Fresh Prince,* has influenced black reality and, in turn, black science fiction. After forty years of television development, normal black protagonists have jumped to the other side of the television glass into reality *and* science fiction. Jada Pinkett-Smith, Halle Berry, and Vivica A. Fox have appeared in science fiction movies. But there is no female counterpart to Will Smith as blockbuster science fiction movie hero. Smith—star of *Independence Day; I, Robot;* and *Men In Black*—is the hottest science fiction movie star of our day. *Fresh Prince* functioned as Smith's on-the-other-side-of-the-glass portal: he jumped through to become the fresh black face of the male science fiction movie hero.

His jump is rooted in television. The upper-middle-class black protagonists on *The Jeffersons* begat the rich professional protagonists on *Cosby* who begat the hyperrich characters on *Fresh Prince.* Propelled forward by his role on *Fresh Prince* and the black-action-hero role Cosby pioneered on *I Spy,* Smith became the premiere action adventure science fiction film actor of the new millennium. This is not the case for black female actors and protagonists. Black women did not jump from behind the television glass into roles as stellar movie science fiction adventure heroes. Instead, individual black women attained real-world power which science fiction did not foresee. There is no science fiction example of a black woman becoming a secretary of state or a media tycoon. Yet, in the manner of Will Smith, Condoleezza Rice and Oprah Winfrey owe their success—success which even defies science fiction parameters—at least partly to television's images of black normalcy.[4]

Nurse Julia begat the business-savvy Dominique Deveraux who begat lawyer Clair Huxtable. Clair Huxtable begat Professor Vivian Banks and her daughter, talk show host Hilary Banks. Professor Vivian Banks is a contemporary of Professor Condoleezza Rice; Hilary Banks is a young Oprah Winfrey. We are comfortable with real black woman holding positions of power which even science fiction did not portray; we watched these roles evolving on television for forty years. Black normalcy is busting out all over from a forty-year-old television incubation period. Due to television, Butler and Delany no longer stand as the lone exemplars of blacks who write science fiction. The positive and normal images of blacks that jumped from behind the glass into prominent, real-world roles places them on the brink of creating science fiction's newest new wave: the burgeoning of black science fiction that Walter Mosley describes (and that is exemplified by the black science fiction writers I include here in *Afro-Future Females*).

III. Transcending Stereotypical Racial Categorization

Diahann Carroll, the mother of black science fiction, engendered black female progeny who inhabit science fiction worlds. Whoopi Goldberg famously played Guinan, the all-knowing *Star Trek* black female alien. The omnipotent black female called The Oracle in *The Matrix* certainly springs from Guinan. Another seemingly garden-variety woman who makes everything happen appears in John Singleton's film *Four Brothers*—and she is white. I connect Singleton's Evelyn Mercer to Guinan and The Oracle to argue that she signals a new understanding of black science fiction—and of racial categorization itself.

Mercer adopts four sons; three are black and one is white. The four biologically unrelated men become a band of brothers when they eschew racial categories and band together to avenge their adoptive mother's death. A movie plot involving four exceedingly tough men who are obsessed with their mother's memory is as incongruous as one with all-powerful science fiction aliens (such as Guinan and The Oracle) being depicted as black women. *Four Brothers,* using a white woman as a catalyst, calls for an end to categorization in regard to race. Despite the male protagonists' differing parentage, they do function as brothers; racial difference plays no part in their relationship. Singleton presents this eradication of racial difference in terms of science fiction. In the confrontational denouement which takes place on the frozen Lake Michigan, when one of the most notorious hoodlums in Detroit is forced to dig his own grave on the ice, one observer says, "this is science fiction and he [the hoodlum] is an Eskimo." No matter how incongruous the prospect of a black Eskimo may be, the hoodlum digging a hole on the ice *is* acting like an Eskimo. And this ice scene *is* comparable to science fiction in that it functions as an analogue to how readers respond to Genly Ai and Estraven's encounter on the ice in Ursula K. Le Guin's *The Left Hand of Darkness.* When Genly Ai and Estraven interact on the ice, readers do believe that they have transcended gender. When the interracial brothers interact on the ice, viewers do believe that they have transcended biology, that they are in fact brothers. Evelyn Mercer *is* their mother. Her race and her biological disconnection to her sons are of no importance.

Diahann Carroll is the mother of black science fiction which, regardless of Mercer's race, situates Guinan, The Oracle, and Mercer functioning similarly as omnipotent female protagonists. *Four Brothers* shows that Guinan, The Oracle, and Mercer—like the mythological Fates—are sisters.

This sisterhood constitutes a new way to interpret the relationship between characters. Such newness should also apply to actors as well. Diahann Carroll and Bill Cosby, as I have stressed, are the television star messengers in regard to the development and understanding of the new burgeoning medium which is black science fiction. Black science fiction stands ready to surge forth from the positive black image incubation period which took place behind the television glass and dive into the wreck of racism. We all want to be members of the Huxtable family. We all want to live like and look like Dominique Deveraux and her husband. Guinan, The Oracle, and Evelyn Mercer are the real and fictitious mothers of us all.

IV. Katrina Storms the Racial Reality Studio[5]

I have described how television depictions of blacks generated images that led to the acceptance of black normalcy and, in turn, now function as a foundation for the proliferation of black science fiction. Now, during the early twenty-first century, television broadcasts pictures of unprecedented American natural catastrophes, and all viewers can see that while many American blacks do in fact live analogously to the Huxtable family, the newly accepted normal images of professional blacks do not apply to the majority of blacks. Hurricane Katrina's destruction underscores this point. Katrina inverted Gabler's "on the other side of the glass" divide between the blacks who are on the same economic level as the Huxtables and the underprivileged black masses. The multitudes of New Orleans blacks who were impoverished to the extent that they lacked bus fare to escape from their city were newly positioned behind the glass; the whole world watched the roots of American racism. Floodwaters placed an entire urban poor black population behind the television glass and washed away the social constructions that had rendered this population invisible.

This point was lost on no one—except President Bush. The pervasive television coverage of Katrina made the obvious absolutely clear: "The whites got out. Most of them, anyway. If television and newspaper images can be deemed a statistical sample, it was mostly black people who were left behind. Poor black people, growing more hungry, sick, and frightened by the hour. . . . What a shocked world saw exposed in New Orleans . . . wasn't just a broken levee. It was a cleavage of race and class, at once familiar and startling new, laid bare in a setting where they suddenly amounted to matters of life and death" (DeParle 1). The shocked world saw something new located on the other side of the glass: a reality show of unprecedented historical proportions that revealed the life-threatening manifestations of the Grand Canyonesque cleavage between race and class in America. The relationship between this horrific newness and black science fiction was not articulated. Images of black men carrying looted televisions are indelible; the looted televisions, in reality patently useless because there was no electricity available in New Orleans, symbolize the complete lack of analysis devoted to interpreting the catastrophe in terms of science fiction.

Nor did commentators equate Bush's September 15, 2005 speech—delivered in New Orleans' Jackson Square in front of the St. Louis Cathedral—with science fiction. Lighting made Bush's shirt and the cathedral appear to be the same grayish-blue color. Bush seemed to merge with the cathedral to become a brave new creature: a cyborgian juxtaposition of human and building to communicate that the president has literally become one with the city. The word "future" resonated throughout Bush's speech. He imagines a new New Orleans, the future of a predominantly black city, as surely as Delany imagines Bellona, the ruined city in *Dhalgren*. Bush, in the manner of a science fiction writer, describes a future urban vision, a vision that will impact predominantly upon black residents. His speech, which evokes Franklin Roosevelt's New Deal and Lyndon Johnson's Great Society, also alludes to the black science fiction writers who build new black worlds. Casting Bush as analogous to a black science fiction writer is no less absurd than his handlers' efforts to position him as Roosevelt's and Johnson's elocutionary force clone.

Maureen Dowd understands Bush's Jackson Square speech in terms of Walt Disney: Bush "looked as if he'd been dropped off by his folks in front of an eerie, blue-hued castle at Disney World. . . . His gladiatorial walk across the darkened greensward, past a St. Louis Cathedral bathed in moon glow from White House klieg lights, just seemed to intensify the sense of an isolated, out of touch president clinging to hollow symbols. . . . The president is still looking for a gauzy beam of unreality in New Orleans" (A15). Frank Rich concurs with Dowd's linkage between the televised image the speech conveyed and Disney. He describes "Karl Rove's Imagineers" directing Bush's "laughably stagy stride across the lawn to his lectern in Jackson Square. (Message: I am a leader, not that vacationing slacker who first surveyed the hurricane damage from my presidential jet)" (12). When Rove's Imagineers bathed the flooded New Orleans in "moon glow" klieg lights, they inadvertently evoked imagery straight out of a grade B science fiction movie. Bush seems to have been staged by Chief Engineer Scotty in the *Star Trek* transporter room rather than by Rove's Imagineers: he seems to have beamed down on a "gauzy beam of unreality" emanating from his presidential jet recast as spaceship. The gray-blue-shirt–clad President Bush striding across the grass in front of the gray-blue-lit St. Louis Cathedral edifice flanked by the statue of Andrew Jackson astride his horse presents a picture that evokes the clichéd little green male alien who lands on the White House lawn and demands, "Take me to your leader." Message: George W. Bush, the leader, is no Andrew Jackson—and no Captain James T. Kirk. Science fiction has taught every culturally literate American that the president is supposed to be the leader to whom the White House lawn ensconced alien is taken, not the alien slacker who beams down to the St. Louis Cathedral lawn belatedly to claim responsibility for governmental ineptitude that resulted in an unprecedented ruined American city disaster —a disaster which renders apocalyptic science fiction real.

The *New York Times* reported that Katrina disaster "scenes that could have been lifted from *The Grapes of Wrath* or maybe the Book of *Exodus,* continued to be played out" (Barry 9). True enough. But the horrific scenes could have been more pertinently lifted from Delany's *Dhalgren* and Butler's *The Parable of the Sower.* New Orleans is now most certainly analogous to Delany's Bellona, the destroyed city that exposes the veneer of civilization, the perpetual disaster zone emanating from failed race relations. Further, all the young black women evacuees newly speaking from behind the television screen represent many versions of Butler's Lauren Olamina, a refugee who flees from a ruined urban environment laid waste by global warming and racial strife. George W. Bush might meet his Waterloo because the whole world watched him fail to show any symptom of the disease which afflicts Lauren: "hyperempathy syndrome," the ability to directly feel the suffering of others.[6] Instead of trying to save face by surrounding himself with the conservative black leaders who do not wish to be associated with him, Bush would have done well to consult with Butler and Delany. Butler and Delany created the science fiction scenarios that predict the fate of New Orleans. It has become a cliché to say that, in relation to such newness as cloning and ever-increasing technological advances, we live in a science fiction world. We need to recognize that post-9/11 Americans now inhabit a black science fiction postapocalyptic, post-Katrina world.[7]

Katrina names this non–brave new world born from cowardice in the face of the need to spend federal government money to improve levees, as well as the need to deconstruct the social barriers that separate impoverished blacks from economically secure whites. Katrina names the failure adequately to spotlight this schism in the strobe lights illuminating the stage sets ensconced behind the glass (television viewers never saw Amos, Andy, and Beulah literally drown in a sea of poverty). Countering the sexism which until recently called for hurricanes to be designated solely by female names, Katrina rewrites the cliché about frailty in relation to women. Frailty thy name is now the racist American social class stratification system, Katrina announces. Frailty thy name is George W. Bush in particular and the American federal government's ability to protect its citizens in general, Katrina goes on to say. The worldwide attention given to the televised eye of the storm will make it more difficult to continue to turn a blind eye to the conditions that caused impoverished and vulnerable American citizens to become forever unidentifiable and nameless corpses. It is unlawful to picture the coffins containing dead Americans who fought in Iraq; the federal government's attempts to block televising pictures of the New Orleanians who became corpses failed. Rebuilding New Orleans and our divisive social systems involves building black science fiction and building upon the no-longer science-fictional scenarios that Butler and Delany imagined. New Orleans just might emerge as the prototype equalitarian American city of the future, a brave new American world we can now only imagine. Due to the television roots of black science fiction I have described, people are now comfortable seeing fictitious lawyer Clair Huxtable appear as the very real, absolutely not science-fictional Michelle Obama.

Notes

1. The character Will Smith plays on *Fresh Prince* is named Will Smith.

2. My reading of the Huxtable family in terms of Jewish culture is not idiosyncratic. Jazz, for example, as Harvey Fierstein pointed out when he narrated "From Shtetl to Swing," emanates from both black and Jewish culture. Echoing the obliteration of rigid racial and ethnic stereotypes I advocate, the PBS Great Performances Web site states, "'From Shtetl to Swing' tells the story of the cross-pollination of Jewish and African-American musical influences, two traditions born out of exile and longing, yet charged with an energy and freedom that gave voice to a new multicultural America" (http://wwwpbs.org/wnet/gperf/shows/shtetl/). So too for black sitcoms. *The Fresh Prince*, for instance, was created by Andy and Susan Borowitz. The Borowitzes were probably quite conscious of Hilary Banks's resemblance to a Jewish-American princess which I note. I heard Andy Borowitz say that Hilary Banks is based upon Quincy Jones's princess-like daughter.

3. Vivian Banks was said to be a professor only during the first three seasons of *Fresh Prince* when she way played by Janet Hubert-Whitten. No mention was made about Vivian being a professor when she was played by Daphne Maxwell Read during seasons 4 through 6.

4. For a discussion of how to understand Condoleezza Rice in terms of science fiction, see Marleen S. Barr, "A Last Situation: Secretary of State Condoleeza Rice and Cultural Critic Leslie Fiedler," *Political Science Fiction*, ed. Donald M. Hassler and Clyde Wilcox (Columbia: University of South Carolina Press, 2008).

5. I refer to Larry McCaffrey's title *Storming the Reality Studio*.

6. Unlike Bush, Bill Clinton, as we are all aware, has marvelous hyperempathy skills. The *New York Times* describes how Clinton applied these skills to Katrina victims: "He kissed babies, hugged their parents, felt their pain and smiled for cell phone photos. Bill Clinton was back in his element . . . on a tour of Louisiana, and at times even seemed to forget his status as a former president" (Strom A24).

7. It is not farfetched to use a hurricane as a setting for a science fiction story. The premise for a television show called *Invasion* is that a hurricane serves as a smokescreen to mask a conspiracy about an extraterrestrial alien takeover. The premiere of *Invasion* (September 21, 2005) coincided with the devastating impact of Katrina.

⟩ Works Cited

Amos 'n Andy, 1951–53. Produced by Freeman Gosden and Charles Correll.

Barr, Marleen S. "A Last Situation: Secretary of State Condoleeza Rice and Cultural Critic Leslie Fiedler." In *Political Science Fiction*, ed. Donald M. Hassler and Clyde Wilcox. Columbia: University of South Carolina Press, 2008.

Barry, Dan. "Texas Way Station Offers A First Serving of Hope." *New York Times*. September 5, 2005, 9.

Benson, 1979–86. Produced by Paul Junger Witt, Tony Thomas, Susan Harris, and Don Richetta.

Beulah, 1950–53. Produced by Roland Reed.

The Beverly Hillbillies, 1962–71. Produced by Paul Henning, Al Simon, and Joseph De Pew.

Butler, Octavia E. *The Parable of the Sower*. New York: Warner, 1995.

The Cosby Show, 1984–92. Produced by Marcy Carsey, Tom Werner, Caryn Sneider, and Bill Cosby.

Delany, Samuel R. *Dhalgren*. New York: Bantam, 1974.

DeParle, Jason. "What Happens to a Race Deferred." *New York Times*. September 4, 2005, Section 4:1.

Diff'rent Strokes, 1978–86. Produced by Maxwell Anderson, Benn Starr, and Martin Cohan.

Dowd, Maureen. "Disney on Parade." *New York Times*. September 17, 2005, A15.

Dynasty, 1981–89. Produced by Richard and Esther Shapiro, Aaron Spelling, E. Duke Vincent, Philip Parslow, Elaine Rich, and Ed Ledding.

Dyson, Michael Eric. *Is Bill Cosby Right?: Or Has the Black Middle Class Lost Its Mind?* New York: Basic Books, 2005.

The Facts of Life, 1979–88. Produced by John Maxwell Anderson, Jack Elinson, Paul Haggis, and Irma Kalish.

Fiddler on the Roof, 1964–70. Directed by Jerome Robbins. Produced by Harold Prince. Music by Jerry Block. Lyrics by Sheldon Harnick.

Four Brothers, 2005. Directed by John Singleton. Written by David Elliot and Paul Lovett.

The Fresh Prince of Bel Air, 1990–96. Produced by Quincy Jones, Gary H. Miller, Kevin Wendle, and Winifred Hervey.

From Shtetl to Swing. Written and directed by Fabienne Rousso-Lenoir. Narrated by Harvey Fierstein. PBS Great Performances, October 5, 2005.

Gabler, Neal. *Life: The Movie: How Entertainment Conquered Reality*. New York: Vintage, 2000.

Independence Day, 1996. Directed by Roland Emmerich. Written by Dean Devlin and Roland Emmerich.

Invasion, 2005–6. Produced by Shaun Cassidy and Thomas Schlamme.

I, Robot, 2004. Directed by Alex Proyas. Written by Jeff Winter (screenplay) and Isaac Asimov (book).

I Spy, 1965–68. Produced by Sheldon Leonard, David Friedkin, and Mort Fine.

The Jeffersons, 1975–85. Produced by Ron Leavitt, Jay Moriarty, Michael G. Moye, and George Sunga.

Julia, 1968–71. Produced by Hal Kanter and Harold Stone.

Le Guin, Ursula K. 1964. *The Left Hand of Darkness*. New York: Harper & Row, 1980.

The Matrix, 1999. Directed and written by Andy and Larry Wachowski.

McCaffery, Larry. *Storming the Reality Studio: A Casebook of Cyberpunk and Postmodern Science Fiction*. Durham, NC: Duke University Press, 1991.

McWhorter, John. "Black and White and Read All Over." *New York Times*. August 11, 2005, A23.

Men In Black, 1997. Directed by Barry Sonnenfeld. Written by Lowell Cunningham and Ed Solomon.

Mosley, Walter. "Black to the Future." In *Envisioning the Future: Science Fiction and the Next Millennium*, ed. Marleen S. Barr. Middletown, CT: Wesleyan University Press, 2003. 202–4.

Rich, Frank. "Message: I Care About the Black Folks." *New York Times*. September 18, 2005, Section 4:12.

Russ, Joanna. *Extra(Ordinary) People*. New York: St Martin's, 1984.

Star Trek, 1966–69. Produced by Gene Roddenberry, John Lucas, Gene L. Coon, and Fred Freiberger.

Star Trek: Deep Space Nine, 1993–99. Produced by Ira Steven Behr, Hans Beimler, and Rick Berman.

Strom, Stephanie. "Clinton Lends His Expertise and an Ear In Louisiana." *New York Times*. October 5, 2005, A24.

Urbano, Toni. 2003. "A Conversation with Neil Postman." New York University TV Productions.

Webster, 1983–89. Produced by Madeline and Steven Sunshine.

ESSAYS

The Blackness of
Outer Space Fiction Blast(off)
from the Past

MADHU DUBEY

Becoming Animal in
Black Women's Science Fiction

Until recently, the very presence of women writers within the genre of science fiction was seen as something of a contradiction in terms, given that the field of modern Western science has historically been constituted as a masculine preserve from which women have been both actually and symbolically excluded.[1] If we agree with Sharona Ben-Tov that science fiction was "the product of the death of nature and the emergence of modern science" (16), women's access to the genre was necessarily constricted by their imputed identification with a nature construed in modern science as a passive object of knowledge. Ben-Tov's quote echoes the title of Carolyn Merchant's influential study, *The Death of Nature,* which lays bare the gendered dichotomy at the heart of the modern scientific project. The Scientific Revolution, Merchant argues, achieved a decisive shift away from organicist ideas of a living nature infused with spiritual presence to mechanist notions of nature as inert matter to be controlled by the agency of reason, science, and technology. As a consequence of this shift, women and certain other social groups that were deemed to lack the faculty of reason came to be not only subordinated by the processes of industrial moderniza-tion unleashed by the Scientific Revolution, but also discursively con-structed as the "others" of modern rationality, as objects rather than subjects of scientific inquiry.[2]

Whether science fiction as a genre perpetuates or interrogates the gendered dichotomy that is constitutive of modern science remains a matter of debate. Some feminist critics believe that the binary opposi-tion between a feminized nature and a masculinist science is foundational to the genre, in fact representing, in Jane Donawerth's opinion, one of the "defining constraints" of science fiction for women writers (xvii). Scott Sanders agrees that the vast bulk of science fiction equates women with nature, body, and feeling, and men with science, intellect, and reason; in "the epistemology characteristic of the genre," the subject of knowledge is typically assumed to be masculine and the object of knowledge feminized (42–43). Not surprisingly, then, science fiction itself has been traditionally perceived as a masculine genre dealing with "hard" science and valorized over the "soft" feminine genre of fantasy, driven by the suprarational and putatively antiscientific principles of magic.[3] When a critical mass of women writers began to write and publish science fiction during the 1970s, the gendered split that was formative of the genre was called into question in a number of different, sometimes conflicting, ways.[4]

Some women writers claimed the domain of "hard" science by featuring women characters in the role of scientists—a strategy that does not necessarily call into question the gendered constitution of the subject of scientific knowledge. Others pursued the opposite route, making a calculated choice to surrender the category of science altogether as one that is too deeply implicated in a masculinist logic to be worth seizing for feminist purposes. Such writers—whom we might associate with radical feminism—instead affirmed supposedly unscientific faculties, such as empathy or intuition, as the distinctive property of women. The critical potential of this particular strategy also remains open to question, with some feminists, such as Robin Roberts, arguing that inverse valorization forms a necessary first step for those seeking to overturn binary oppositions that have historically devalued women (92), and others, such as Evelyn Fox Keller, cautioning against essentialist mythologizing that only reifies the position of women as the "others" of science. Keller suggests that a more effective approach might be to question the very social construction of science as a masculinist category antithetical to women (143). Some women writers of science fiction have followed exactly this approach, by extending definitions of science so as to include bodies of knowledge, such as herbal medicine, midwifery, or magic, which have been dismissed as unscientific because of their association with women. As Roberts observes, many women writers deconstruct the binary opposition between "hard" and "soft" science by radically undermining the distinction between science and magic, often valorizing magic as a form of legitimate, albeit unrecognized, science (5, 7). This effort to reclaim science for women entails the elaboration of an alternative model of the scientific enterprise, one that acknowledges the subjectivity and embodiment of the scientist; emphasizes human connection with nature; and supplements rationality with intuition, emotion, and imagination.[5]

In a particularly pointed critique of modern science from the stand-point of radical feminism, science fiction writer Sally Miller Gearhart castigates its arrogant moral separation of human beings from the rest of nature—a hierarchical separation dictated by an overestimation of reason (178). From within the scientific belief-system, all non- and suprarational modes of knowing are presumed to "cast the knower back into the primitive methods of lower animals" (174).[6] Some women writers of science fiction are in fact appropriating and converting the symbolic identification of women with lower animals into a potent literary device for critiquing the gender ideology of modern science. As Lisa Tuttle notes, the device of animal metamorphosis—of women literally or figuratively becoming animals—recurs with heightened frequency in women's science fiction published since the 1980s.[7] Women becoming animals are not unfamiliar in mainstream science fiction, but this trope serves vastly different purposes in science fiction written by men and women. Male writers have largely employed the trope to convey the genre's endemic hostility toward a nature conceived as menacing to human rationality. Like the bug-eyed monsters that pervade the landscapes of science fiction, images of women becoming animals evoke a monstrous nature that threatens the autonomy and stability of masculine identity and that must therefore be subdued by the power of reason. Women's science fiction often draws on the mythological tradition of animal metamorphosis to question this model of identity whereby individuation is always achieved by means of differentiation and alienation from nature. Women writers tend to blur the boundaries between human and animal in order to explore and affirm women's difference from masculinist notions of science and culture defined in opposition to nonhuman nature. If science fiction written by men has typically represented women as the others of reason, women writers revalorize this otherness as the basis of a more responsible and reciprocal relation to nature. Accordingly, animal metamorphoses in women's science fiction often celebrate the irrationality and physicality traditionally associated with women and nature.

In her essay on animal tropes in women's science fiction, Tuttle elaborates some further purposes served by this device: to revel in the wild side of nature, to narrate the eruption and reintegration of repressed sexual desire, to express overpowering emotions, and to call into question dualistic definitions of nature and culture (98). In a similar vein, Donawerth argues that animal tropes allow women writers to explore the pleasures of carnality and sexuality. But Donawerth also remarks on less celebratory uses of animal tropes to explore the messiness of biological reproduction, in particular its blurring of the self-other boundaries that are so fiercely defended in mainstream science fiction (68–71). Pregnant females form such an enduring object of obsession in science fiction written by men precisely because they embody the transgression of self-other boundaries, threatening the integrity and self-mastery of the Cartesian subject assumed in so much science fiction. Tropes of women becoming animal aid feminist critiques of the enterprise of modern science, freeing women writers to imagine different—more relational and embodied—models of knowledge and identity.

In this essay, I will examine the device of women becoming animals in two novels by the best-known black women writers of science fiction: Octavia E. Butler's *Wild Seed* and Nalo Hopkinson's *Midnight Robber*. Becoming animal in these novels is associated with magical modes of knowing and being that supplement and often override the principles of reason. The critique of scientific rationality forms such a strong, impelling force in the fledgling field of black-authored science fiction as to almost warrant the term "black anti–science fiction." In science fiction novels by black men and women writers, including Tananarive Due, Steven Barnes, and Levar Burton, scientific practice is relentlessly indicted for its predatory exploitation of black bodies and scientific theory for validating claims of black racial inferiority.[8] Afro-diasporic systems of knowledge and belief, such as vodun, obeah, or Santeria, are consistently shown to confound and triumph over scientific reason.[9] It is surely telling that two anthologies of nonmundane fiction by Afro-diasporic writers steer clear of the generic label "science fiction": *Dark Matter: A Century of Speculative Fiction from the African Diaspora*, edited by Sheree R. Thomas, and *Whispers from the Cotton Tree Root: Caribbean Fabulist Fiction*, edited by Nalo Hopkinson. Hopkinson's account of her experience as editor of this anthology vividly captures the disaffiliation of black writers from the tradition of science fiction. For this collection, Hopkinson called for science fiction from Caribbean writers, but most of the stories she received "were dreams (a no-no in the science fiction world)" (xii). She decided to use the label "fabulist" instead of "science fiction," explaining their generic and epistemological discontinuities as follows:

> Northern science fiction and fantasy come out of a rational and skeptical approach to the world: That which cannot be explained must be proven to exist, either through scientific method or independent corroboration. But the Caribbean, much like the rest of the world, tends to have a different worldview: The irrational, the inexplicable, and the mysterious exist side by side with the daily events of life. (xii–xiii)

Hopkinson's description of the "different worldview" of Caribbean writers strongly echoes Toni Morrison's account of a specifically black "cosmology" marked by a seamless blending of the supernatural and the mundane. In her essay "Rootedness: The Ancestor as Foundation," Morrison claims that one of the features that makes black fiction uniquely black is its recovery of "discredited knowledge," based in intuition and other suprarational faculties, that has been marginalized by the Enlightenment legacy (342). This resonance between Hopkinson and Morrison suggests that what is recently being marketed as the newly emergent phenomenon of black women's science fiction shares common generic traits with "mundane" or "mainstream" black women's novels, such as Morrison's own *Song of Solomon, Beloved,* or *Tar Baby;* Toni Cade Bambara's *The Salt Eaters;* Ntozake Shange's *Sassafras, Cypress, and Indigo;* and Gloria Naylor's *Mama Day,* to name just a few. In its casual incorporation of magical and supernatural phenomena and its flouting of the norms of realism and rational explication, speculative fiction by black women writers can be said to exemplify the "counterculture of modernity" that Paul Gilroy considers to be distinctive of Afro-diasporic culture (36).

Historically defined as the others of modern Western rationality, Afro-diasporic and feminist writers of speculative and science fiction deploy magic in strikingly convergent ways to revaluate a whole set of gendered and racialized dichotomies that have helped to prop up the subject of modern science. Afro-diasporic as well as Euro-American women's science fiction exploits the trope of becoming animal not only to explore the implications of (black people and women) being identified with animal nature, but also to call into question dualistic and overlapping oppositions between nature and culture, magic and science, animal and human, body and mind, female and male, European and African, and so forth. In common with other women writers of science fiction, Octavia E. Butler and Nalo Hopkinson use the trope of woman becoming animal in order to defamiliarize the modern Western discourse of the human. But *Wild Seed* and *Midnight Robber* also depart in crucial ways, pulling back from a total identification of black woman with animal, for reasons that I will elaborate over the course of this essay.

The occult ways of knowing that are privileged in both Afro-diasporic and feminist critiques of modern science are central to Octavia E. Butler's *Wild Seed.* The protagonist of the novel, Anyanwu, is captured and transported from Africa to the New World by Doro, an immortal male who practices a unique form of reproductive slavery. Described as a "breeder of witches" (29), Doro collects and mates those who are seen as strange because they possess special physical and mental powers, such as psionics or telekinesis. Anyanwu considers herself to be primarily a healer, but the extraordinary gift that makes her so valuable to Doro's reproductive colony is her ability to assume animal forms. This ability, along with her unconventional methods of healing, causes Anyanwu to be categorized as a "witch" in both her native African village and the New World. In common with other women writers of speculative fiction, Butler uses the terms "magic" and "witchcraft" to legitimate distinctively female bodies of knowledge that are discredited by the standards of modern Western science.[10] In addition to her expertise in herbal medicine, Anyanwu cures disease in herself and others through medicines produced within her own body. For example, when Doro's hand becomes infected, Anyanwu bites it in order to take the infection into herself, and then spits on the wound, healing it with her saliva. She explains this treatment to Doro in the following terms: "There were things in your hand that should not have been there . . . Living things too small to see. I have no name for them, but I can feel them and know them when I take them into my own body. As soon as I know them, I can kill them within myself" (29). Described as "magic" (36), this form of alternative medicine is valorized in the novel as better than medical practices that carry the stamp of scientific approval.

Butler's presentation of Anyanwu's magic and witchery is consistent with the tradition within women's speculative fiction that seeks to undermine hard-and-fast distinctions between (female) magic and (male) science and to elaborate an alternative feminist epistemology grounded in empathy and embodiment.[11] If the practitioner of modern science proceeds by way of a rationality that stands apart from and works upon the object of knowledge, Anyanwu knows disease by feeling it within her body, by means of ingestion and direct experience rather than abstraction and distanciation. When Anyanwu cures herself of disease through the same method she uses to treat Doro's infected hand, her body operates simultaneously as object (that which is diseased) and subject/scientist (that which produces medicines to cure the disease).

This unique form of embodied knowledge is more fully illustrated in a scene in which Anyanwu explains to Doro how she acquires knowledge of other species, a dolphin in this particular instance. Her knowledge of the fish depends on a process of literal ingestion and symbolic incorporation. Anyanwu eats the flesh of the fish so that her body can read the creature's "physical structure" as well as "its story" (79). As with her alternative healing, Anyanwu's method of knowing is presented as superior to accepted scientific methods because of its immediacy: "She told him of the messages she had read within the flesh of the fish. 'Messages as clear and fine as those in your books,' she told him. Privately she thought her flesh-messages even more specific than the books he had introduced her to, read to her from. . . . 'It seems that you could misunderstand your books,' she said. 'Other men made them. Other men can lie or make mistakes. But the flesh can only tell me what it is'" (80). Perfectly in keeping with the epistemology developed in much women's speculative fiction, Anyanwu's knowledge of the fish heals the dichotomy between mind and body, taking the body as an active agent rather than an inert and alienated object of knowledge. The knowledge gained from the body is shown to be virtually infallible because it is free of any mediation or interpretation, consisting as it does of direct flesh-to-flesh transmission of vital information.

Anyanwu obviously must kill other animals in order to eat them and to read their "flesh-messages," but this violence implicit in her way of knowing other species goes unacknowledged in the novel. What is emphasized instead about Anyanwu's way of knowing animals is its logic of empathetic identification rather than violent domination. Anyanwu's most exceptional power, as mentioned earlier, is her ability to take animal forms, and it is in the service of this power rather than the power to tame and control non-human nature that Anyanwu eats animal flesh. Eating animals so as to read their flesh-messages enables her to become animal more effectively, and the experience of becoming animal spurs her to combat human exploitation of other species.

Although, as I have been arguing so far, Octavia E. Butler's novel elaborates the embodied and relational model of knowing nature that is privileged in much women's speculative fiction and feminist theory, its treatment of animal metamorphosis takes a rather unexpected direction as animal nature is presented as precisely *not* a domain of irrationality, sexuality, wild nature, or messy reproduction. To be sure, there are moments in the novel when Anyanwu assumes an animal shape—usually that of a leopard—in order to unleash violent anger and other fierce emotions deemed improper for women. She also occasionally takes animal form in order to experience the sheer wonderment of becoming another species. But for the most part, Anyanwu changes herself into an animal to escape the sexual perversions and reproductive slavery inflicted on her by Doro. If the animal realm usually offers women writers the license to explore sexuality and motherhood outside the constraints of patriarchal culture, in *Wild Seed* this realm offers Anyanwu the freedom not to be a sexual, reproductive creature.

The novel's recurrent allusions to antebellum U.S. slavery suggest one explanation for Butler's unusual deployment of the device of animal metamorphosis. In *Wild Seed,* becoming animal does not exemplify a joyful transgression of sexual norms, because black women in particular and people of African descent in general have quite literally been defined and used as animals. In some significant respects, the animal tropes in Butler's novel extend the strategic manipulation of animal-human distinctions that has formed such a vital part of antislavery literature from Frederick Douglass's *Narrative* to Toni Morrison's *Beloved*. In the slave narratives of Douglass and Harriet Jacobs, animal imagery is first used to castigate the ways in which slavery strips the slaves of their humanity, and then is reversed to disclose the barbarity of the slave owners. *Beloved* renews this critique through the image of Schoolteacher's notebook, with its columns listing the "animal" and "human" characteristics of slaves (193). In Butler's novel as well, animal/human distinctions are explicitly exploited to rationalize U.S. racial slavery. White people implicated in the institution of slavery are repeatedly shown to categorize Africans as "animals" lacking culture and religion (43, 102, 158).

Although Butler wrote in the historical shadow of racialized U.S. slavery, this historical context did not exhaust her use of the device of animal metamorphosis. Not only is this device utterly unthinkable within the genre of the slave narrative, but its implications in *Wild Seed* exceed an exclusively racial explanation. The novel is full of references to racialized antebellum U.S. slavery, but this is pointedly not the form of slavery to which Anyanwu is subjected. Her slave master is a male of African descent, and his methods and practices of enslavement are clearly distinguished from those of the more familiar "peculiar institution." This narrative choice indicates not that race is irrelevant to the novel's use of animal tropes, but that it does not work as the sole lever of interpretation. The burden of bestiality is most heavily borne by slave women in the novel, who embody all shades of the racial spectrum. Most of the animal references in the novel appear in relation to the reproductive dimensions of slavery. What reduces women slaves to the level of cows, goats, or mares is that they are bred and mated like cattle, and their offspring expropriated as the property of their masters (123, 124, 167, 210, 213, 215, 220). The term "animal" in *Wild Seed* is most frequently used to describe a female creature that is deprived of sexual and reproductive agency.

It is in order to elude Doro's more outrageous sexual pairings or reproductive schemes that Anyanwu usually decides to cross over into animal territory. In other words, the impetus for her transformation of herself into an animal is usually the human treatment of other human beings as animals. This seemingly paradoxical statement begins to make sense as we track more closely Butler's finely discriminating elaboration of animal/human distinctions. At the more immediately accessible level, the novel is strewn with conventional usages of the word "animal" to describe that which is the savage other of "human." This discourse of binary opposition, relegating slaves to the status of subhuman beasts, bolsters both of the forms of slavery (Doro's reproductive slavery and racialized antebellum U.S. slavery) presented in the novel. In an inversive strategy reminiscent of the nineteenth-century fugitive slave narratives, Anyanwu often turns these binary oppositions against her master, labeling Doro an "animal" in order to expose the ways in which slavery dehumanizes both its perpetrators and its victims (131, 184, 196). At this level, the term "animal" appears as a human construct, the product of a discursive operation that rationalizes the exploitation of women's bodies.

But when Anyanwu becomes a dolphin or a bird, readers are transported out of this discursive universe into the nonhuman world of actual animals. At this level, "a true animal" is defined as "a creature beyond his [Doro's] reach" (89). Significantly, it is only when Anyanwu makes herself over into an animal that she is able to escape Doro's mental tracking of her. From this dimension, she can relativize the human and conduct a thorough revaluation of the animal/human opposition underpinning racial and reproductive slavery. Passage after passage describing her experience among the dolphins emphasizes the sexual violence and reproductive exploitation that is uniquely human, adding up to a powerful indictment of the human male. For example, Anyanwu is relieved to find herself in the dolphin world, where there are "no slavers with brands and chains" (84). She feels fortunate as a female dolphin because "only in her true woman-shape could she remember being seriously hurt by males—men" (83). Anyanwu's observation of the sexual and mating rituals of the dolphins reveals them to be gentle, "honorable," and "innocent" creatures (196). The barbaric sexual behavior of human males is thereby shown to be a product of patriarchal and racist culture rather than intrinsic to nature.

Feminist critics have acclaimed *Wild Seed* for its "feminization of power": through her animal metamorphoses, Anyanwu is said to dissolve binary oppositions, to render permeable the boundaries between male and female, white and black, human and animal, culture and nature (Wolmark 43–44; Doerksen 32). Without denying the critical force of Butler's interrogation of these dualisms, it is equally important to ask why the novel ultimately preserves certain clear divisions between the animal and the human. Anyanwu's animal changes, as well as the novel's narrative account of these changes, are subject to significant limitations. The one scene in which Anyanwu is on the verge of drifting into sexual intercourse with a dolphin is abruptly foreclosed not just by Doro's interference but also by her own belief that "intercourse with an animal was abomination" (84).[12] In this and other scenes, some human kernel of Anyanwu is left untouched by her animal transformations. We are told that she "was still partly human in most of her changes long after she had ceased to look human" (189). The precise reference here is to the hybrid physiology—part human and part animal—of Anyanwu's internal organs once she has undergone transformation, but these changes never actually affect the substance of her identity. Anyanwu always retains a human mind as well as a strongly integral sense of her identity: "she was who she was" (220). References to her "true shape" and her "true form" as a black female abound in the novel (250,

219). Through all her metamorphoses, Anyanwu never loses the ability to "still know [her] self" (219).

The constancy of Anyanwu's human consciousness is reinforced by the fact that her experience while she is an animal is always narrated from a human point of view. The most extended account of her experience as a dolphin (82–83) gives us a description of a dolphin body mediated by a human mind. In this respect, the dolphins (even when Anyanwu assumes dolphin form) remain the objects rather than subjects of knowledge and narration. In *Wild Seed,* the world of animal nature is wholly contained by the human, not only in the sense that it can be narratively rendered only in human terms, but also in the sense that it is serviceable for human purposes. The animal world is instrumental to Anyanwu's struggle against Doro as well as to her quest for knowledge of nonhuman nature. In other words, the interaction between Anyanwu and the dolphins is not reciprocal but unidirectional, in favor of the human. We cannot ever know if Anyanwu does make a splash in the dolphin world, because the novel cannot render dolphin consciousness or dolphin point of view.

Although science fiction perhaps more than any other genre traffics in otherness, its conventions strongly discourage direct representations of that which is alien to humanity. The alien is typically encountered, comprehended, and subsumed by a human perspective; rarely (if ever) is the alien the subject of narration. This is in part a consequence of the peculiar realism of the genre, which can allow human characters to become dolphins within certain parameters of plausibility (in *Wild Seed,* Anyanwu is explained to have inherited this special capability), but which precludes the emergence of a dolphin perspective unfiltered by the human. Ben-Tov provocatively argues that science fiction is structurally incapable of representing the otherness of nature. As a product of the Scientific Revolution, the genre constructs an "alienated nature"—a nature that has been so completely mastered as an object of scientific knowledge that it has been drained of mystery and vitality (10). Ben-Tov claims that because science fiction precludes unrationalized phenomena, its epistemology is necessarily antimagical, in that magic subscribes to an animist conception of nature numinous with presence. According to Ben-Tov, "alienated nature" persists even in feminist science fiction as long as it follows the genre's cardinal rule of submitting all phenomena to the standard of rational, realist explanation (137). "[M]agic can't win" in science fiction in the sense that the genre can never bring us face to face with the true otherness of a nature that exceeds the explanatory grasp of human rationality (80).

Wild Seed features a protagonist who is characterized as a witch possessing magical powers, as part of its critique of the epistemology of modern science and its exploration of an alternative feminist mode of knowing nature. Yet, as I have been arguing, the novel ultimately presents nature as fully knowable by human beings (as is clear from Anyanwu's infallible knowledge of dolphin flesh and dolphin story) and entirely subordinate to human ends. Nothing about the natural, animal world eludes Anyanwu's or the reader's comprehension, and Ben-Tov would argue that the reason is the novel's adherence to psychological realism. Although *Wild Seed* features magic as a significant component of its plot and theme, it does not project a magical worldview or epistemology in Ben-Tov's sense insofar as it remains largely faithful to the realist expectations of the science fiction genre.

Does the otherness of nonhuman nature become more fully representable in fiction that flagrantly flouts these realist protocols, deploying magic at a generic as well as a thematic level? Hopkinson's *Midnight Robber* offers an interesting point of comparison with *Wild Seed*, a text that also centrally focuses on animal/human distinctions and interactions, but by way of yoking together the genres of science fiction and animal fable. Hopkinson's novel reads as a legend or folk tale about a young girl named Tan-Tan, whose story begins on the planet of Toussaint, colonized by Caribbean migrants. When Tan-Tan is on the verge of puberty, her father kills his wife's lover and is exiled to New Half-Way Tree, the planet into which Toussaint dumps its criminals and transgressors. New Half-Way Tree is described as the "mirror planet," the "dub" or "dark" side of civilization, separated from Toussaint by a "dimension veil" (2). Excessively attached to her father, Tan-Tan follows him to this planet inhabited not only by exiled humans but also by douens, a sentient animal species that seems to be a cross between bird and reptile. When Tan-Tan's father rapes and impregnates her, she kills him and escapes into the animal world, and much of the rest of the novel intricately recounts her struggle to understand and adapt to douen ways of life.

Although *Midnight Robber* does not feature the literal metamorphosis of woman into animal, it treats the animal/human theme in ways strikingly similar to those in *Wild Seed*. The female protagonists of both novels flee into the animal world out of a sense of alienation from patriarchal human society. For Tan-Tan, as for Anyanwu, this alienation springs from her experience of sexual abuse and reproductive exploitation at the hands of human males. But instead of going animal in order to identify with a wild, carnal, feminized nature that is suppressed in patriarchal culture, Anyanwu and Tan-Tan alike enter into an animal nature that allows them to exist as desexualized beings. Tan-Tan is hypersexualized by nearly every man she encounters, a process that culminates in incestuous rape. During her sojourn among the douens, Tan-Tan heals herself from sexual violence not only by becoming an entirely asexual creature but also by discovering that such violence is not organic to nature. Like the dolphins in Butler's novel, the douens are kind and honorable creatures, throwing into bold relief the savagery of human sexual and reproductive behavior. Tan-Tan describes her father's rape and impregnation of her through images of planting (260), or human cultivation of nature. Animal nature, in contrast, reveals to her an alternative norm of sexual and reproductive relations that serves to defamiliarize human gender relations. Tan-Tan learns that both male and female douens are born with wings, but males lose theirs as they mature, whereas females begin to fly once they enter puberty—a model of delightful and liberating female maturation very different from Tan-Tan's entry into puberty, marked by rape.

Because Tan-Tan is impregnated by her father at the age of sixteen, she cannot view pregnancy and childbirth as anything but monstrous aberrations. As with the dolphin realm in *Wild Seed*, the animal nature of the douens is precisely that which is not monstrous in its approach to sexuality and reproduction. In a telling scene, a female douen, Abitefa, responds with total incomprehension when Tan-Tan agonizes over her unwanted pregnancy, because such horrors are unimaginable in the douen world. Tan-Tan's stint with the douens introduces her to a radically different—and more equitable—way of organizing reproductive relations whereby biology does not determine social destiny. Although only female douens have the biological capacity to reproduce, parenting is not socially constituted as an exclusively female responsibility. The male douen Chichibud is shown to be as gentle and protective in his nurturing relation with Tan-Tan as are the females Abitefa and Benta. Instead of the human practice of worshipping a disempowered and sublimated Mother Nature, each douen nation lives in a Papa Bois, or a "Daddy Tree" (179). Detailed descriptions of their living arrangements reveal a symbiotic relation to a nature that they invest with both male and female properties. Her experience of the Daddy Tree, or of a paternally nourishing nature, enables Tan-Tan to denaturalize "the nightmare daddy world" (213) in which human males rape their daughters. Although, unlike Anyanwu, Tan-Tan never physically becomes an animal, her growing psychological identification with the douens gradually allows her to de-pathologize her own body, sexuality, and pregnancy. Through a process of critical distancing from human patriarchy, Tan Tan is finally able to attribute "monstrosity" where it really belongs—to the sexually abusive human male rather than to the female body or to nonhuman, animal nature (323).

In common with *Wild Seed*, Hopkinson's novel gives us a two-layered depiction of animal nature, first presenting the human definition of animals as monstrous others, and then going on to topple this hierarchy, showing that in fact it is humans who are monsters. At the first level, we see that human civilization is made possible by the physical displacement and subordination of native animal life. On the seemingly utopian planet of Toussaint, the douens are remembered as "indigenous fauna, now extinct" as a result of human colonization (33). Douens still exist on the dystopian planet of New Half-Way Tree, but in a rigidly hierarchical order wherein they are compelled to work as "servants" for their human "masters" and "bosses." The material exploitation of douens is reinforced by discursive conventions that maintain sharp distinctions between the two species: as a douen points out, "Oonuh tallpeople [the douen term for human beings] quick to name what is people and what is beast" (92).

As we saw earlier, in *Wild Seed* Butler deploys animal tropes to denaturalize hierarchical and dualistic conceptions of racial as well as gender differences. Butler does this by way of explicit reference to American slavery, which institutionalized the status of black people as subhuman beasts. Hopkinson only obliquely alludes to American slavery (by naming her fictional planet Toussaint), elaborating instead the imperialist inflections of the human/animal opposition. In Hopkinson's novel, differences between human beings and animals become paradigmatic of a cluster of polarities— between culture and nature, civilization and savagery, science and magic— that have historically served to consolidate the West's assumed superiority over those constituted as its others. Like slaves and colonized natives, the douens are situated within a developmental narrative that sanctions their material oppression by defining them as the very antithesis of modernity. The humans on New Half-Way Tree justify their repressive control over the douens by describing them as "simple" primitives (139) in need of paternal supervision: "You have to watch them all the time. . . . Them like children" (128). Recalling the conventional tropes used in colonial accounts of native land, the area inhabited by the douens is depicted as the realm of wild, uncultivated nature, as a "bush with no food and shelter" (91).

But as Tan-Tan later discovers, the douen have developed highly sophisticated systems for feeding and housing themselves—systems so complex that Tan-Tan and the novel's readers have to strain to grasp their intricacies. In its revaluation of the human/animal dichotomy imposed by a colonizing culture, *Midnight Robber* depicts the douens as noble savages rather than degenerate primitives. Extended descriptions of feeding and living arrangements highlight the organicism of douen life. Their culture is harmoniously integrated into nature: they bathe in bromeliad tubs, and they live in flexible yet sturdy structures nested into the branches of trees. Elaborate accounts of their feeding habits evoke the familiar anthropological opposition between raw and cooked, primitive and modern cultures. Tan-Tan's greatest difficulty in accommodating herself to douen life is her revulsion at eating living creatures such as worms: "she preferred her food good and dead" (220). Her civilized human tastes are relativized by the douens' disgusted perception of cooking as "remov[ing] all the life" from food (221). The rawness of douen culture reinforces Tan-Tan's and the reader's initial impression of the douens as noble savages who live in organic symbiosis with nature.

Tan-Tan's recourse to the noble savage archetype serves the positive functions of redeeming the douens from the human classification of them as degraded beasts and of indicting instead the monstrous savagery of civilized human society. Like the dolphins in *Wild Seed*, the douens are compassionate and generous creatures who, in marked contrast to the human beings presented in the novel, are endowed with a strong sense of respect and responsibility toward other living beings. This is brought out most clearly in the difference between human and douen standards of justice: whereas human beings abide by a merciless tit-for-tat creed that dictates that "murder must always get repaid with murder" (151), the douens believe that you must save two lives for each one that you destroy: "It ain't have no magic in do-for-do, / If you take one, you must give back two" (290).

The use of the word "magic" is crucial here, for it is through its subtle treatment of magic at a generic as well as thematic level that *Midnight Robber* most effectively overturns hierarchical oppositions between the modern West and its others. In *Wild Seed*, magic indexes a premodern sphere that is primarily associated with women, although certain passages in the novel also describe this sphere in racial terms. Along with women, people of African descent and Native Americans—the enslaved and the colonized—are most closely aligned with magic, which Butler's novel presents as a residual belief-system fast being eroded by the spread of modern Western rationality:

> The Indians were rich in untapped wild seed that they tended to tolerate or even revere rather than destroy. Eventually, they would learn to be civilized and to understand as the whites understood that the hearing of voices, the seeing of visions, the moving of inanimate objects when no hand touched them, all the strange feelings, sensitivities, and abilities were evil or dangerous, or at the very least, imaginary. (149)

In *Midnight Robber* as well, "magic" is the signifier for a residual worldview menaced by the encroachment of modernity, but here the natives have learned to manipulate the rhetoric of primitivism in order to preserve their own ways.

The douens exploit the familiar dichotomy between magic and technology so as to abet human misperceptions of them as a backward, uncultivated species. For example, Chichibud disingenuously explains to Tan-Tan that douen woodcraft is more closely affiliated with magic and art than with technology: "it was because the douens had worked obeah magic upon the wood. 'Douen man grow them, douen women paint them,' he would say with pride. 'The woman—them does work obeah into them as they painting them. Is for so the patterns come in like they alive. . . . Men make things and women magic them. Is so the world does go, ain't, doux-doux?' Then he'd laugh *shu-shu*" (153). As is clear from his laughter, Chichibud cannily encourages the customary linkage of magic with women and natives in order to protect douen culture; as long as the colonizers perceive douens as innocent of technology, douen culture can thrive behind the screen of primitivism. Chichibud's sly usage of the term "magic" also affiliates douen-created objects with totemic art rather than technological artifact, mocking the fetishism that marks modern Western appreciation of the culture of the colonized. Tan-Tan eventually realizes, however, that the distinctiveness of douen woodwork "wasn't magic, it was craft and cunning" (153). As the novel progresses, various apparently primitive facets of douen culture are rendered through technological metaphors, and technological skills are described in magical terms, thoroughly scrambling the dichotomy between primitivism and modernity, magic and technology. For example, douen language, which human beings hear as a cacophonous racket of "nonsense phrasings" (173), is ultimately presented as a sort of technology, with its advanced skills of "sonar and echolocation" (234). Conversely, douen foundry workers are described as being engaged in "working obeah magic with hammer and fire" (228).

This fusion of magic and technology offers an alternative to the over-rationalized worldview of modern science, contributing to the novel's critique of the abuses and excesses of advanced technology—a critique found in much feminist as well as other science fiction. In *Midnight Robber,* the douens view human technological artifacts as "killing things" (283), and they are proved right when their community is violently disrupted by the intrusion of human beings with cars and guns. In clear opposition, douen technology is presented as a vital force that synthesizes pleasure and use, art and industry. The "magic" of douen technology is that it makes objects come "alive" (152), in contrast to the death-dealing technology of a human culture that instrumentalizes and converts objects into inert matter.

What makes *Midnight Robber* such an unusual novel is not this thematic deployment of magic to critique an aridly rationalist worldview, but its use of magic to revitalize the genre of science fiction. To better appreciate this dimension of Hopkinson's novel, let us recall Ben-Tov's argument that magic—with its animist and organicist notion of nature—cannot win in science fiction because of the genre's realist imperative to rationalize everything. *Midnight Robber* draws on the magical worldview of folk animal tales as a means of animating and reenchanting the alienated nature that customarily appears in science-fictional texts. In the Introduction to her edited anthology of "Caribbean Fabulist Fiction," quoted earlier, Hopkinson explicitly characterizes folk fabulism as antithetical to the tradition of science fiction in key respects. Hopkinson's assertion—that in her anthology she "was essentially trying to marry two traditions of writing that have different priorities and protocols" (xiii)—is equally applicable to her own novel. In *Midnight Robber,* the animal species of the douen are like "an anansi story folk tale come to life" (229). Three main features of this folk tradition are salient to Hopkinson's subversion of the generic protocols of science fiction. First, the fabulism of animal tales confounds the realist reading codes of science fiction. Not only are the douens, jumbies, and rolling calves of the novel creatures of myth and legend, but Tan-Tan's own story as well is narrated in these registers, making it difficult for readers to disentangle fact from fiction. Second, magical realism at the generic level enables the restoration of an animist rather than scientific notion of nature, a fertile and numinous nature that often defies human comprehension. Significantly, however, Hopkinson does not merely reverse the conventional hierarchical ordering of these terms, but instead seeks to undo the dichotomy altogether, presenting the magical art of folk storytelling as "word science" rather than antiscience (320). Finally, the tradition of folk fabulism posits a very different relation between human beings and animal nature than does mainstream science fiction. While the bug-eyed monsters of science fiction primarily function as objects of antagonistic differentiation and conquest for human beings, animal fables elicit empathetic identification of the human with the animal. In keeping with this tradition, Tan-Tan arrives at a mature sense of her identity as a human being only after integrating certain aspects of douen culture into herself, the most notable example being her adoption of the douen creed of "two for one." Unlike Anyanwu's animal changes, which leave intact the core of her human identity, Tan-Tan's interaction with the douens substantively transforms her understanding of what it means to be human.

Although *Midnight Robber* draws on elements of animal fable to subvert the reading codes of science fiction, the novel is a generic hybrid rather than a pure instance of animal fable. Instead of being wholly embedded within the animal world, as would be the case in an animal tale, the narrative perspective in *Midnight Robber* is that of a human visitor to a strange land, a convention common to utopian/dystopian, travel, and science fiction. In these kinds of narratives, the aliens (whether animal or extraterrestrial) are generally mediated to the reader by the visiting human's narration, and made instrumental to the visitor's moral, cultural, or psychological education. Hopkinson's novel bends these conventions to a certain extent. Although douen life is filtered primarily through Tan-Tan's point of view, this perception accommodates the douens' estranging perception of human beings. What's more, the novel's narrative voice is dominated by but not confined to Tan-Tan's perspective. Inflected by communal myths, legends, and rumors, the narrative voice evokes the same folk fabulist imagination that spawns creatures like douens and jumbies, thereby bridging the customary gap between human and animal, narrator and alien.

Midnight Robber also dramatizes a more two-sided relation between human and animal than does *Wild Seed* in that we are shown the repercussions of human interference with douen life. By the end of Tan-Tan's visit, two douens have been killed, and they have been forced to dismantle and relocate their settlement. Qualifying the idealist dream of empathetic communion and reciprocal recognition between different species, said to distinguish feminist from mainstream science fiction, Hopkinson's novel ends with a disenchanted separation of the species: "Maybe your people and mine not meant to walk together," says a douen to Tan-Tan (283). *Midnight Robber* starkly clarifies the power imbalances that skew interactions between different species or races, the structural inequalities that cannot be wished away through empathy or love. As a result of Tan-Tan's visit, the more vulnerable species learns the important lesson that even the most well-disposed human visitor brings nothing other than disruption to douen ways of life. The most asymmetrical aspect of the human-douen encounter is that it contributes primarily to the story of Tan-Tan's development, rendering the animal species once again serviceable to the human.

Midnight Robber closes with Tan-Tan's departure from the douen world and her decision to stake a claim to human rather than animal identity and sociality. To be sure, her human identity has been transformed in significant ways by her social intercourse with the douens. What Tan-Tan learns from the douens, and Anyanwu from the dolphins, is that bestiality does not inhere in the black woman's body and that the animal nature with which black women have been historically identified is not in itself degenerate. A human character in *Midnight Robber* blames Tan-Tan's rape on her own supposedly degraded nature, her "leggobeast ways" (323). Butler and Hopkinson are writing against the long history of this sort of dehumanizing hypersexualization of black women's bodies. This history helps explain the distinctive ways in which Butler and Hopkinson deploy the trope of becoming animal: notably, their choice of animals that are innocent and noble rather than wild and carnal; their skepticism toward the feminist ideal of reciprocal interspecies identification; their retention of certain boundaries between the animal and the human; and their ultimate reappropriation of the category of the human.

Ben-Tov has argued that the most frightening moments in science fiction occur when the boundaries of the Cartesian subject are crossed, when nature threatens to come back to life and overwhelm the autonomy and rationality of the humanist subject of modern science (40). Postmodern feminists such as Donna Haraway revel in such boundary crossings as part of their assault on modern humanism. But although Haraway might seem to agree with feminist writers and critics of science fiction who seek "connection across the discredited breach of nature and culture" (152), her own essay about science fiction, "A Cyborg Manifesto: Science, Technology, and Socialist-Feminism in the Late Twentieth Century," is actually committed to a very different idea of nature. As I noted earlier, Ben-Tov bases her argument about science fiction's built-in hostility to nature on Merchant's *The Death of Nature,* which decisively aligns the feminist project with a premodern, animist, magical conception of nature. Haraway, to the contrary, explicitly refers to Merchant's book in order to caution feminists against the appeal to "an imagined organic body" as the foundation of "progressive" politics (154). In Haraway's own utopian fiction of the cyborg, woman/animal fusions must work to dispel the ideal of the whole, self-possessed body implicit in modern humanist variants of progressive politics.

Haraway mentions Butler's *Wild Seed* as a preeminent example of her cyborg myth (179), but the representations of human beings and animals, culture and nature in Butler's and Hopkinson's novels do not really qualify them as cyborg, or posthumanist, fictions in Haraway's sense. In neither novel is boundary confusion in itself presented as a progressive or feminist or even necessarily a cyborg phenomenon. The starting point of both novels is violation, not joyful transgression, of bodily boundaries—Anyanwu's capture into reproductive slavery and Tan-Tan's impregnation by rape. This violence is what reduces both women to the degraded level of animals, or creatures who are dispossessed of their bodies. When Anyanwu and Tan-Tan willingly repudiate human society and disappear into the animal world, this world is mediated to readers by way of a longstanding humanist tradition of representing nature as a source of primal innocence—the very view of nature that Haraway wishes to displace. The animal/woman mergers in *Wild Seed* and *Midnight Robber* open up their characters' imaginations not to the otherness of nature but to a view of *human* nature other than that which obtains in social reality. The most valuable lesson learned from Anyanwu's and Tan-Tan's animal changes is that sexual violence is not grounded in nature. The noble and innocent dolphins and douens, clearly products of an anthropomorphic imagination, testify to the seductions of organicist metaphors of nature for feminist and humanist writers alike. And as both novels would suggest, neither organicist nor cyborg metaphors are radical or political in themselves. Just as bodily boundaries can be transgressed with brutality and terror, so organic ideals of bodily integrity can inspire progressive politics. For both Butler and Hopkinson, the detour into the animal world serves to relativize and reimagine the nature of humanity, but not to surrender their own claim to the category of the human. When Anyanwu and Tan-Tan insist on the fundamental difference between themselves and animals, they appropriate toward feminist ends the humanism that has been so central to the genre of science fiction. Anyanwu's indignant retort to Doro, "I am not an animal!" (118) and Tan-Tan's furious quarrel with the label of "leggobeast" bespeak a continuing, albeit critical, investment in humanism.

Notes

1. For feminist critiques of science, see Harding; and Keller and Longino, eds. On the difficult relation of women writers to science, see Benjamin, Donawerth, and Roberts.

2. Merchant writes that one consequence of the Scientific Revolution was that "Nature, women, blacks, and wage laborers were set on a path toward a new status as 'natural' and human resources for the modern world system. Perhaps the ultimate irony in these transformations was the new name given them: rationality" (288).

3. On dualistic definitions of hard science versus soft science, science fiction versus fantasy, see Weedman (5–6). Some critics use the term "speculative fiction" as a way out of this gendered dichotomy. See, for example, Barr, for whom "speculative fiction" is a capacious category including "feminist utopias, science fiction, fantasy, and sword and sorcery" (xxi).

4. For a useful mapping of the various approaches taken by women writers struggling to appropriate both science and the genre of science fiction for their own purposes, see Donawerth.

5. On this model of what might be called an ecofeminist science, see Donawerth (7–28) and King (118–29).

6. Gearhart is drawing on Merchant's influential critique of the nature/culture dualism at the heart of modern humanism, which relegated women and animals to the realm of "lower nature" (143).

7. Some of the women science fiction writers whom Tuttle discusses in this context are Carol Emshwiller, Rhoda Lerman, Eleanor Arnason, Pat Murphy, Sara Maitland, Tanith Lee, and Suzy McKee Charnas.

8. On the complicity of modern Western science with racism, see Harding, ed., *The "Racial" Economy of Science.*

9. Three novels in which such Afro-diasporic belief systems win out over or supplement modern science and technology are Steven Barnes's *Blood Brothers,* LeVar Burton's *Aftermath,* and Tananarive Due's *The Between.*

10. See Merchant on the differences between the relation to nature posited in witchcraft and modern science (137–40).

11. Donawerth describes this kind of feminist epistemology as an effort to overcome the subject-object dualism of scientific ways of knowing (7, 28).

12. We are told later in the novel that Anyanwu did once mate with and bear dolphins, but the brief reference in not elaborated (219).

Works Cited

Barnes, Steven. *Blood Brothers.* New York: Tor Books, 1996.

Barr, Marleen S. *Alien to Femininity: Speculative Fiction and Feminist Theory.* Westport, CT: Greenwood Press, 1987.

Benjamin, Marina. "A Question of Identity." In *A Question of Identity: Women, Science, and Literature,* ed. Marina Benjamin. New Brunswick: Rutgers University Press, 1993. 1–21.

Ben-Tov, Sharona. *The Artificial Paradise: Science Fiction and American Reality.* Ann Arbor: University of Michigan Press, 1995.

Burton, LeVar. *Aftermath.* New York: Warner, 1997.

Butler, Octavia E. *Wild Seed.* New York: Warner, 1980.

Doerksen, Teri Ann. "Octavia E. Butler: Parables of Race." In *Into Darkness Peering: Race and Color in the Fantastic,* ed. Elisabeth Leonard. Westport, CT: Greenwood Press, 1997. 21–34.

Donawerth, Jane. *Frankenstein's Daughters: Women Writing Science Fiction.* Syracuse: Syracuse University Press, 1997.

Due, Tananarive. *The Between.* New York: HarperCollins, 1996.

Gearhart, Sally Miller. "An End to Technology: A Modest Proposal." In *Machina Ex Dea: Feminist Perspectives on Technology,* ed. Joan Rothschild. New York: Pergamon Press, 1983. 171–82.

Gilroy, Paul. *The Black Atlantic: Modernity and Double Consciousness.* Cambridge, MA: Harvard University Press, 1993.

Haraway, Donna. "A Cyborg Manifesto: Science, Technology, and Socialist-Feminism in the Late Twentieth Century." In *Simians, Cyborgs, and Women: The Reinvention of Nature.* New York: Routledge, 1991. 149–81

Harding, Sandra. *The Science Question in Feminism.* Ithaca: Cornell University Press, 1986.

———, ed. *The "Racial" Economy of Science.* Bloomington: Indiana University Press, 1993.

Hopkinson, Nalo. *Midnight Robber.* New York: Warner, 2000.

———. Introduction. *Whispers from the Cotton Tree Root: Caribbean Fabulist Fiction.* Ed. Nalo Hopkinson. Montpelier, VT: Invisible Cities Press, 2000. xi–xiii.

Keller, Evelyn Fox. "Women, Science, and Popular Mythology." In Rothschild, ed. 130–46.

────── and Helen E. Longino, eds. *Feminism and Science.* New York: Oxford University Press, 1996.

King, Ynestra. "Toward an Ecological Feminism and a Feminist Ecology." In Rothschild, ed. 118–29.

Merchant, Carolyn. *The Death of Nature: Women, Ecology, and the Scientific Revolution.* New York: Harper and Row, 1980.

Morrison, Toni. *Beloved.* New York: Penguin, 1987.

────── . "Rootedness: The Ancestor as Foundation." In *Black Women Writers (1950–1980),* ed. Mari Evans. New York: Doubleday, 1984. 339–45.

Roberts, Robin. *A New Species: Gender and Science in Science Fiction.* Urbana: University of Illinois Press, 1993.

Rothschild, Joan, ed. *Machina Ex Dea: Feminist Perspectives on Technology.* New York: Pergamon Press, 1983.

Sanders, Scott. "Woman as Nature in Science Fiction." In *Future Females: A Critical Anthology,* ed. Marleen S. Barr. Bowling Green, OH: Bowling Green State University Popular Press, 1981. 42–59.

Thomas, Sheree R., ed. *Dark Matter: A Century of Speculative Fiction from the African Diaspora.* New York: Warner, 2000.

Tuttle, Lisa. "Pets and Monsters: Metamorphoses in Recent Science Fiction." In *Where No Man Has Gone Before: Women and Science Fiction,* ed. Lucie Armitt. New York: Routledge, 1991. 97–108.

Weedman, Jane. Preface. In *Women World Walkers: New Dimensions of Science Fiction and Fantasy,* ed. Jane Weedman. Lubbock: Texas Tech University Press, 1985. 5–8.

Wolmark, Jenny. *Aliens and Others: Science Fiction, Feminism, and Postmodernism.* Iowa City: University of Iowa Press, 1994.

"God Is Change"

Persuasion and Pragmatic Utopianism in Octavia E. Butler's Earthseed *Novels*

> All that you touch
> You Change.
> All that you Change
> Changes you.
> The only lasting truth
> Is Change.
> God
> Is Change.
> —*Earthseed: The Books of the Living,* in *The Parable of the Sower* (3)

It is the near future. Abused, the natural environment has deteriorated to the point where global warming has caused dangerous climate change. The United States has disintegrated into a sea of anarchy dotted with islands of well-defended privilege. Except in armed enclaves, rape, robbery, and murder are commonplace; torture and cannibalism are not unknown. Police and fire departments charge for their services, which turn out to be ineffectual anyway. As government fades, predatory private corporations grow more powerful, creating company towns and indentured servitude.

Octavia E. Butler sets *Parable of the Sower* (1993) in this disturbingly plausible place. It is a bad one, in fact an appalling one, and getting worse, as becomes evident in the other novel in the *Earthseed* series, *Parable of the Talents* (1998; hereafter abbreviated *PT*), a winner of the 1999 Nebula Award.[1] In *Talents,* outright slavery is on the rise, made possible by "slave collars," remote-controlled electronic devices capable of administering a shock that can lead to convulsions, amnesia, and sometimes death. Meanwhile the ineffectual president depicted in

Sower has been replaced by a fascistic one. These novels, like the place they describe, are clearly dystopias, and yet some critics have perceptively observed that the texts can be more accurately called "critical dystopias," in part because they offer a thread of hope not just to readers but also to characters.[2] Rarely does literature present the founding of a religion, much less by a black woman, much less by a young person, and yet that is what happens here. The two books tell the story of Lauren Oya Olamina, a black teenager who, despite enormous obstacles, follows her "positive obsession" (*PT* 157), manages to found a utopian religion and, by the end of her long life, sees much of what she has sown bear fruit, including the beginning of the space travel that she sees as humanity's next step.[3] The series thus consists of a utopia within a dystopia.

Scholars have ably examined aspects of the series, such as its utopian and dystopian elements and its treatment of race and class,[4] but something else deserves deeper study in order to reveal the novels' sophistication and complexity: particularly since the *Earthseed* series tells the story of a movement both utopian and religious, these novels are also about persuasion.[5] "God Is Change," and persuasion is a form of change that imbues these texts. In such a desperate setting, persuasion matters because the texts are exploring "the role belief systems play in enhancing or impeding survival" (Keating 73), in particular through what I will be calling *pragmatic utopianism*. While the thought of persuasion in literature often raises the specter of crude propaganda, the sort of persuasion employed here works subtly, which in large part accounts for Lauren's success in converting other characters to her religion and accounts for the novels' skill in encouraging readers at least to entertain the idea of that religion.

The *Earthseed* series makes compelling reading for a variety of reasons: we wonder, with horrified fascination, if the future that Butler depicts will indeed be our own; we speculate on whether Lauren—female, feminist, and black in a sexist, racist society—will manage to prevail, or even survive; we are torn when she has to make excruciating choices, such as deciding to haggle when buying her own brother from a slave dealer; and we suffer when her "hyperempathy syndrome" causes her to feel the agonies of wounded people or—in some ways worse—the pleasure of a man who is raping her (*PT* 212). The books, however, are not in the least melodramatic; like Lauren herself, they are matter-of-fact. Nor is the utopia simplistic or saccharine—the heroine pays a price for almost every decision she makes. As Nicholas Birns says, "At best, [Butler's stories] portray a wise choice among almost equally uncompelling alternatives" (5). The need for self-defense means that, in Raffaella Baccolini's words, "the ethic of resistance and compromise, derived from slave narratives, is the very condition for both the endangerment of utopia and its survival" (26).

The series also exerts its power in a more nuanced way, because the second novel in a sense critiques the first—for being not wrong but incomplete. In the first novel, Lauren attracts other characters toward Earthseed, and the text addresses similar persuasion to readers. Although the first book also meditates somewhat on persuasion itself, that theme becomes much more prominent and negative in the second one. The latter novel suggests that, even when what is being advocated is desirable, some persuasive methods are questionable and that devoting oneself to advocacy, regardless of methods, can be questionable as well. Thus *Talents* adds a dimension, asking us to rethink *Sower*.

To analyze Butler's books, I will be drawing on some of the concepts that I have laid out in *Politics, Persuasion, and Pragmatism: A Rhetoric of Feminist Utopian Fiction* (hereafter abbreviated *PPP*)—first the theories about persuasion and later those about pragmatic utopianism. I define "persuasion" as the attempt to change or reinforce someone's beliefs, if only slightly, about states of affairs or about values. Often both sorts of beliefs are involved: a persuader convinces someone that things are a certain way and then convinces that person how to evaluate the situation. Thus, roughly speaking, persuasion involves "is" and "ought," description and prescription. In this study of the *Earthseed* books, I will be asking about the nature of the persuasion: what is its *subject* (what is being advocated), to whom is the persuasion addressed, and what techniques are used?[6] Finally, I explore how persuasion itself is commented upon. In order to answer these questions, we must first review the plots of the novels.

Parable of the Sower begins in 2024, when fifteen-year-old Lauren is living with her black father, her Latina step-mother, and her younger stepbrothers (whom she calls brothers) in a tiny, middle-class neighborhood of Robledo, outside Los Angeles. Because civil society has spiraled down to the point where public order has disappeared, Robledo is protected only by an encircling wall and the vigilance of its inhabitants, who rarely dare to leave the neighborhood except in armed groups. Although not privileged, the Robledo citizens live better than the homeless and poor who suffer outside, preyed upon by criminals of all sorts. Thieves sometimes scale Robledo's wall, one of Lauren's brothers is tortured and murdered outside, and her father disappears; yet most of the neighbors feel they are getting by and simply yearn for the stability of the past.

Lauren, however, looks to the future. She wants to leave Robledo and go north, where better opportunities lie. The wall that protects also imprisons and, she fears, cannot protect for long, so she makes meticulous, secret preparations to leave. But before she can flee, the enclave is invaded and burned to the ground by people addicted to a drug that causes them to set fires. Separated from her family and believing them dead, eighteen-year-old Lauren starts walking north along a freeway with the two other neighbors she can find who have escaped. Their journey is a nightmare, particularly for Lauren, whose hyperempathy syndrome causes her to feel any pain or pleasure she believes someone nearby is feeling. Yet, she and her companions survive and enlarge their group, thanks to careful preparation, quick wits, and luck. Helping the weak when possible, they also kill in self-defense when necessary.

Along the way they meet a doctor named Bankole, walking with his few remaining possessions in a pushcart; although he is fifty-seven, he and Lauren fall in love. Bankole is headed for an isolated area north of San Francisco, where he owns land that his sister has been living on. When, after a two-month journey, the group reaches Bankole's land, they find his sister and her family slaughtered and the house burned down. Deciding that this is nevertheless safer than more-inhabited areas, the group of thirteen settles down and establishes a community that is diverse in race, ethnicity, class, and age. The book ends as they plant oaks in memory of their dead and decide to call the settlement Acorn.

What unifies this somewhat episodic plot is the growth of Earthseed, the religion that Lauren conceives of at the age of twelve, when she ceases to share the faith of her father, a Baptist minister. She realizes that, facing the devastating changes still to come in society, the majority of people enter denial and just hope life will improve, while most of the rest become ruthless predators. "God Is Change"—the central tenet of Earthseed—"means that Change is the one unavoidable, irresistible, ongoing reality of the universe. To [Earthseed members], that makes it the most powerful reality, and just another word for God" (*PT* 73). "God Is Change" is intended as a wake-up call to bring awareness that one cannot escape change; one can only be prepared or unprepared for it, as seen in the contrast between the biblical Noah and those around him (*PS* 59–60). Lauren explains, "Nothing is going to save us. If we don't save ourselves, we're dead" (51). Change is inevitable, and yet its precise nature is not: "in the end, God *does* prevail. But we have something to say about the whens and the whys of that end" (264–65).

Another key slogan is "Shape God," bringing to mind the saying "God helps those who help themselves." The tough-minded, adaptable Earthseed members—willing to sacrifice a great deal, but not everything, for individual and species survival—occasionally steal from other people or plunder a corpse after killing in self-defense, though they do not kill in order to rob. Those who survive will be those with traits that Earthseed values, such as "learning to shape God with forethought, care, and work [and] to educate and benefit their community, their families, and themselves" (*PS* 234). For long-term species survival, Earthseed envisions humans settling on other planets.

Talents begins five years after the founding of Acorn, which has started to thrive. Lauren, now married to Bankole, learns that her half-brother, Marcus, survived the annihilation of Robledo but has been enslaved and severely traumatized. She buys him out of slavery and brings him to Acorn, where, now calling himself Marcos Duran, he gradually recovers and starts preaching Christianity. He soon leaves, however, frustrated by the Earthseed members' preference for his sister's preaching.

Andrew Steele Jarret has been elected President of the United States. He is the founder of Christian America (CA), a fundamentalist organization that promises to build a strong, safe country by imposing the uniformity of what CA's followers regard as traditional Christian values, such as the subordination of women. When Acorn is about six years old, it is invaded by a heavily armed group of men (later discovered to be Jarret's Crusaders). They abduct all the children, including Larkin (Lauren and Bankole's two-month-old daughter), and they put the adults in slave collars, one of which kills Bankole. The captives later learn that their children have been given to "good Christian homes" to be raised according to CA values (*PT* 189). Some of the captors at "Camp Christian" sincerely believe they are reeducating the wayward, but most are simply sadists. Despite the plans of Earthseed members, escape seems impossible, until the guards' overcutting of trees ultimately causes a landslide, which destroys the collars' master unit; only then can the slaves kill their captors and get away.

The Earthseed members agree to split up and look for their children, but, despite diligent searching, Lauren cannot find Larkin. She does find Marcos, now rising as a CA preacher and unwilling to believe her accusations about misdeeds perpetrated by his church. He advises her to seek her daughter by, in effect, going undercover in CA, but Lauren cannot bring herself to do so. Ever-pragmatic, she realizes Earthseed must adapt: since physical communities can be so easily obliterated, she writes, "I need to create something wide-reaching and harder to kill. That's why I must teach teachers. I must create . . . a movement" (*PT* 267). By the time the main text of the novel ends, the new strategy is working: twenty-six-year-old Lauren and a companion are flying all over the country propagating Earthseed. For various reasons, CA gradually declines, becoming "a smaller, somewhat defensive organization with much to answer for and few answers" (313). The epilogue skips ahead to 2090: Lauren has lived to feel great satisfaction at seeing "the first shuttles leave for the first starship" (362).

Unlike *Sower, Talents* includes narrators in addition to Lauren, some of whom criticize her, which lends the latter novel a very different tone. One of the critical narrators is the grown-up Larkin. Mother and daughter are not reunited until Larkin is an adult; at that time she accuses Lauren of caring more about Earthseed than her own child. Larkin feels that her mother's obsession with Earthseed not only led to the abduction by causing the family to live at Acorn instead of some place safer but also prevented Lauren from looking hard enough for her child. Butler wisely refrains from answering such questions definitively.

The Subject and Addressees of Persuasion

Throughout the series, the most important subject of persuasion is Earthseed. Both novels are liberally interspersed with quotations from *Earthseed: The Books of the Living*, an account of "truths" that Lauren has been writing in verse since she first conceived of her utopian religion (*PT* 117). I refer to her belief as a religion because she does so also and because, like a conventional religion, it gives hope, inspires faith, and inspires individuals to convert. But in a sense this creed is more like Deism or even a philosophy than an ordinary religion. What Lauren calls "God"—not personified, not supernatural, not good or evil—often seems more like "reality," for Earthseed exhorts people to face facts, no matter how grim or frightening. It is "very demanding but offering so little comfort from such an utterly indifferent God" (49). Yet Lauren has her reasons for calling it a religion. When someone asks, "Since change is just an idea, why not call it that?" she replies, "People forget ideas. They're more likely to remember God—especially when they're scared or desperate" (*PS* 198).

Unlike many religions, Earthseed offers no immortality for individuals—after death they will live on only insofar as they have furthered the Destiny, which is "to take root among the stars," meaning that humans are eventually to settle other worlds. In an interview, Butler referred to the idea "that the one insurance humanity can take out is to scatter among the stars. This is one way, probably, that some of us will survive somewhere" (Mehaffy and Keating 62). The Destiny is a desirable goal not only in itself but also as a way to help humanity mature. As one character puts it: "The Destiny is important for the lessons it forces us to learn while we're here on Earth, for the people it encourages us to become. It's important for the unity and purpose that it gives us here on Earth. And in the future, it offers us a kind of species adulthood and species immortality when we scatter to the stars" (*PT* 143–44). If necessary, space settlement will be an escape from an environmentally destroyed world, but in any case it will provide the challenge that humanity needs to evolve away from cycles of self-destructive solipsism. Here again, it helps to consider Earthseed a religion, as Lauren explains: "The truth is, preparing for interstellar travel and then sending out ships filled with colonists is bound to be a job so long, thankless, expensive, and difficult that I suspect that only a religion could do it. . . . [I]t will take something as essentially human and as essentially irrational as religion to keep [people] focused and keep it going . . . ." (323).

It is the principles of Earthseed, as put into practice, that make it utopian and attract other people to join Lauren's group. Small, almost impoverished, and initially homeless as the group is, it nevertheless offers "immediate rewards," even to those skeptical about its religious underpinnings or long-term "Destiny": "Here was real community. Here was at least a semblance of security. Here was the comfort of ritual and routine and the emotional satisfaction of belonging to a 'team' that stood together to meet challenge when challenge came. And for families, here was a place to raise children, to teach them basic skills that they might not learn elsewhere and to keep them as safe as possible from the harsh, ugly lessons of the world outside" (*PT* 62–63).

The term "utopia," an ideal society or a text about such a society, often conjures up images of static perfectionism of the sort that Butler herself criticized (Miller 339). But utopia can take another, more dynamic form, which I call *pragmatic*. As Jim Miller observes: "Utopian thinking . . . seeks to inspire us to desire, à la [Ernst] Bloch, but not necessarily for a predetermined solution" (339). He says that, in Butler's critically dystopian works, she "preserves utopian yearning while [she] rejects easy answers" (357). Earthseed's utopianism is pragmatic—certainly in the ordinary sense (it is nothing if not practical) but also in the philosophical sense, for it is committed to "provisional models and ceaseless, striving questioning" (*PPP* 4; emphasis removed). Such a utopia belongs to the tradition of pragmatism established by philosophers such as John Dewey, Charles Sanders Peirce, and William James (see *PPP* 3–15). As I have said:

> Faced with an existing structure—even one of their own creation—pragmatists neither leave it intact nor destroy it in a spirit of knee-jerk subversion. Rather, they tear down part of it in order to remodel: they critique something, modify their model a bit, critique something else, amend another part of the model, and so on. Through *bricolage,* in short, pragmatists create models provisionally, in stages, and criticize them in order to improve them. (8)

Pragmatism is particularly well suited to feminism. Although some feminists employ a static mode of thought, feminism generally questions patriarchy (often questioning itself as well) and evolves along multiple paths.

Although Earthseed is not in every way pragmatic, pragmatism does pervade it.[7] "God Is Change," and adapting to such a god means becoming pragmatic, particularly if one is to "Shape God." Earthseed's pragmatism begins with its founder. For example, Tom Moylan notes that, given Lauren's hyperempathy syndrome, "she adapts what could be a genetic disability into a personal gift that endows her with the extra transformative strength that eventually informs her work as a visionary and social reformer" (*Scraps* 228). Always improvising, the protagonist is as eager to learn as to teach: "I'm just feeling my way, using whatever I can do, whatever I can learn to take one more step forward" (*PT* 318; 52).[8] And her followers adopt an analogous openness toward change. Their weekly Gatherings, for instance, "are discussions. They're problem-solving sessions, they're times of planning, healing, learning, creating, times of focusing, and reshaping" the members (65). Moreover, the Earthseed community "is racially and culturally mixed and thus demands constant efforts of mediation and translation. The . . . porous lines between insiders and outsiders . . . must be continually redrawn" (Dubey 113).[9]

Pragmatic changes occur throughout the series. We first encounter Lauren's questioning spirit when she criticizes the conventional notion of staying in Robledo. Later, the harrowing journey northward and the development of Acorn represent significant phases in an ongoing process of pragmatic utopianism. Most notably, when Acorn is destroyed, its founder does not try to rebuild it but instead adapts and starts spreading the word differently. The end of the series sees the beginning of travel to the stars, fulfillment of Earthseed's Destiny, which also involves flexibility, a reaction against humanity's tendency to "keep falling into the same ditches" (*PT* 321). In an interview Butler summed up the need for a change such as space travel: "I think the best way to do something else is to go someplace else where the demands on us will be different. Not because we are going to . . . change ourselves, but because we will . . . be forced to change" (Potts 336).

The pragmatism of Butler's texts also affects the reading experience. As I have argued elsewhere, a static utopian society "might bore its inhabitants, and a book about such a society might bore its readers"; the *Earthseed* books, in contrast, are the sort that move "to something more possible and more vital: an ongoing, intricate, vibrant process of rethinking what [the ideal] might entail" (*PPP* 4, xix). Patricia Melzer finds significant additional ramifications in Earthseed:

> At the center of Butler's utopian desire lies the concept of change that adds an element of *process* to the feminist discourse on difference. It not only places categories of difference into a historical context, but also connects them with time. This temporal aspect that complicates absolute concepts of identity/subjectivity based on race, class, and gender, I believe, is a valuable contribution to the feminist debate on how to negotiate difference politically and theoretically. (31)

Thus the series can motivate feminist readers to rethink their views on difference.

With the pragmatic utopia of Earthseed as its main subject, persuasion is directed toward two groups: on the textual level, characters address each other, and on the extratextual level, the texts address the readers.[10] On the former level, the chief persuader is Lauren, who at first simply tries to convince a few other people in Robledo that clinging to the shreds of their past life will ultimately fail, leaving them dangerously vulnerable. As her ideas develop, her overall subject of persuasion becomes convincing others to embrace Earthseed. That general subject entails specific ones that gradually evolve: she encourages people to join her on the trek north, to found and develop Acorn, and finally to spread Earthseed by other means. She is not the only persuasive character, however: for instance, her father and her brother, Marcos, are both powerfully convincing preachers.

On the extratextual level, literature tries to influence readers' beliefs but usually does not ask us to rush out and take some specific action or, as in nonfiction, to believe every detail; rather, its persuasion encourages us to entertain certain possibilities. As Butler said in an interview, part of her role as a science fiction novelist is "to say what I feel is true. Obviously, I mean verisimilitude as well as the literal truth" (Jackson 5). In her case, we have interview evidence indicating that the real author has some thoughtful didactic purposes. But the phenomenon I am describing would occur even without such evidence (Jackson; Mehaffy and Keating). Having discussed this process in detail elsewhere, I will summarize it here (see *PPP* 18–34). Examining a text in isolation—unaided by the *real author*'s interviews, biography, or nonfiction writing—reveals nothing certain about that real person but does create an impression of an author as implied by the text—someone with various kinds of knowledge, skills, interests, and values. We cannot know definitely what the real author intends. But we do have a good sense of what the *implied author* intends. Similarly, we gather what the implied author, if not the real one, is advocating.

The addressee of the implied author is the *implied reader*, a figure located in the text. Although this figure is less solid than the implied author, we nevertheless can infer some traits. If they overlap significantly with those of a real reader (what I call *matching*), then it is likely that the implied author's intentions, such as persuasion, will be fulfilled in the case of that person (see *PPP* 27–34). (When I simply use the term "readers" below, I mean both implied and real ones.) Sometimes, however, a mismatch occurs—say, the real reader likes less-vehement persuasion than the implied one, has different prior knowledge, or has quite divergent values; then the real reader is not persuaded. In short (in these novels as, I believe, in all other literature), persuasion is addressed by the implied author to the implied reader and, through them, can reach real readers.

In the *Earthseed* books, on this extratextual level, readers are being asked to believe in a state of affairs—the society represented—and to evaluate it negatively, as a dystopia. Similarly, readers are being urged to think of the pragmatic Earthseed alternative as plausible and to evaluate it positively, as utopian. Real readers are not being asked to believe that these precise societies will actually exist in our future, but simply to consider the notion that they could believably develop out of our own.

The Techniques of Persuasion

Having discussed the major subject and the addressees of the persuasion, we can now turn to the specifics of how it occurs. In particular, how is persuasion constructed to convince characters and readers to value such a strange, demanding, pragmatic utopia? On both the textual and the extra-textual levels the main persuasive technique is *belief-bridging*, a device I consider crucial in all persuasion (see *PPP* 35–42). Trying to convince a person with whom one has nothing in common is doomed to failure. So in belief-bridging, the persuader begins with a belief already held by the addressee and associates a new belief with the first one. Like the friend of a friend, the new belief becomes appealing through its association with the old one. The smaller the distance between the old belief and the new belief, the more likely it is for someone to ease into accepting the new one (e.g., *PS* 174). A simple example of belief-bridging appears in Lauren's journal, where she writes that, having drawn a sketch of a potential convert, she added an Earthseed verse "that was intended to reach her through environmental interests that I had heard her express" (*PT* 343).

On the extratextual level, an instance of belief-bridging can be found in the verisimilitude of the dystopia. Readers share with the implied author awareness of trends that existed in the United States in the 1990s, when the *Earthseed* books were published, and continue now; to name a few examples: the environment is being corroded, private corporations are taking over government functions, and the middle and lower classes are losing ground. From belief in such conditions the novels build a bridge to belief in the possibility of the society of Lauren's time. Next, from readers' belief that violence and anarchy in general are undesirable, the text builds a bridge, urging readers to view that violent and anarchic society as dystopian.

One common form of belief-bridging starts when two people agree on the existence of a problem; then the persuader builds a bridge from that shared belief to a new belief, according to the efficacy of a suggested solution. Within the text, given the common belief that society is dangerously chaotic, Lauren does not have much trouble attracting people and urging her practical solutions. Then, once people believe in the practical side of Earthseed, Lauren can often build another bridge, to belief in its spiritual side, including the "Destiny" among the stars. Of course, there could be a book about a persuasive but villainous leader, a text in which the implied author described the protagonist's power over other characters but did not approve of it. In the *Earthseed* series, however, the implied author does endorse Lauren and her ideas and tries extratextually to persuade the reader of their value.

Belief-bridging addressed both to characters and to readers is aided by Lauren's authority as one whose beliefs should be taken seriously. She possesses a number of characteristics, such as intelligence, that are valued inside and outside the text. Her virtues are conveyed not by proclamations but by actions: instead of exhorting people to care about the young, she risks her life to rescue several terrified children whose parents have been shot (*PT* 32–42). Her judgments tend to be validated by later events, most notably when early on she correctly predicts that Robledo cannot remain safe for long. And Lauren is willing to do what she asks others to do, whether tilling a garden or killing an attacker. These traits and a number of others make it easier for someone to value her and to move from there to sharing her values, most notably respect for Earthseed. Lauren, moreover, through her journals and Earthseed verses, is the sole narrator of *Sower* and the narrator of most of *Talents*. Narrators normally have special authority unless shown to be unreliable. Since readers already trust a reliable narrator to convey the narrative itself, an especially strong bridge can be built from that person's beliefs to other beliefs.

Another technique that enhances persuasion in Butler's novels is what I have called *matching* between the real listener or reader and the implied one. Successful persuasion is possible when they match in such traits as prior knowledge and the level of persuasive vehemence (akin to loudness) that they desire. So, on the textual level, Lauren at times manages to win over skeptical characters not by an overbearing monologue but by "soft, nonpreachy verses" (*PS* 191). (This quiet method is well suited to advocating pragmatism, which itself entails evolution rather than revolution.) Lauren employs a similarly low-key approach when engaging in almost Socratic dialogue, permitting other characters to voice skepticism and then assuaging their doubts (e.g., *PS* 198–200). Allowing doubts to be voiced may seem like a gamble. But it pays off because, rather than ignoring potential objections, she answers them, ultimately making her argument all the stronger. Such incidents can have a similar effect extratextually as well: the text matches the tastes of doubtful readers by welcoming their questions (as voiced by characters) and then defusing them.

The seemingly paradoxical technique of fueling persuasion by subverting it intensifies in *Talents*. Until now I have mainly described the two books as if one flowed seamlessly into the other, and in some ways that is so. As summarized so far, *Talents*, like *Sower*, is Lauren's story—a story not only about Lauren but also by her, as recounted in her journals. But the later novel also diverges widely in form from its predecessor: about a fifth of it is narrated by other characters—more importantly, by characters who often criticize Lauren and Earthseed sharply and plausibly. The second novel thus adds a new layer of complexity to the series. As Melzer says, "By multiplying the perspectives on events in *Talents*, Butler problematizes the concept of a utopian vision that a single individual formulates" (36).[11] Butler remarked, "In some ways, having several narrators in the second novel serves, subtly, to, I hope, undermine the single-minded guiding voice of *Sower*—[Lauren] Olamina doesn't have the *only* truth" (Mehaffy and Keating 75). This change does not imply that readers who looked up to Lauren and Earthseed were foolish. The situation is merely that other facets need to be considered.

The main new voice we hear belongs to the compiler of *Talents*, Asha Vere—the name borne by Lauren's daughter since being abducted. After Lauren dies at age eighty-one, Asha not only assembles excerpts from Lauren's journals but also makes her own mark. The daughter selects the excerpts, groups them into chapters, and—most significantly—includes her own commentary at the beginning of each chapter, occasionally adding short texts written earlier by her father or her "Uncle Marc." Thus, regardless of content, these other voices divert some narrative power from the founder of Earthseed.[12]

The content shows a more shocking shift away from Lauren and her values. Asha's comments in the Prologue begin:

THEY'LL MAKE A GOD of her.

I think that would please her. . . . In spite of all her protests and denials, she's always needed devoted, obedient followers—disciples—who would listen to her and believe everything she told them. And she needed large events to manipulate. All gods seem to need these things. . . .

I have wanted to love her and to believe that what happened between her and me wasn't her fault. . . . But instead, I've hated her, feared her, needed her. I've never trusted her, though, never understood how she could be the way she was—so focused, and yet so misguided, there for all the world, but never there for me. . . .

At least she began with some species of truth. And now she's touched me one last time with her memories, her life, and her damned Earthseed. (7–9)

Asha's words can certainly upset a reader persuaded by the previous novel to regard Earthseed and its founder with approval or even awe. Meanwhile, the daughter's views may be shared by other readers, those who think the only kind of obsession proper for a woman is the search for a lost child or those who, like Tom Moylan (*Scraps* 238) and Darko Suvin (196), consider the "Destiny" among the stars to be mere escapism.

In an interview conducted between the publication dates of the two novels, Butler expressed her own doubts about Lauren's quest for power:

> I had a lot of trouble writing [*Sower*] because I knew I would have to write about a character who was power-seeking. I didn't realize how much I had absorbed the notion that power-seekers were evil. . . . I had to come to the realization that . . . power, money, knowledge, religion, whatever is common among human beings, can be beneficial or harmful to the individual and is judged by how it is being used. And also, of course, by the entrenched interests doing the judging. (Johnson 14)

Although in *Sower* Butler came to terms with her protagonist's power-seeking, in *Talents* the real author seems to be attributing some of her old doubts to Asha.

As the novel continues, so does the daughter's political and personal bitterness, albeit diluted by occasional grudging admiration (e.g., *PT* 63; 142).[13] We learn from her writings that, after being abducted, she is raised in an unloving and abusive CA household. At age 19 she is contacted by her Uncle Marc, by then a prominent CA preacher, who says that her parents are dead. Believing she has a good adoptive home, he has been keeping tabs on her for years. Thrilled to find a family member, Asha goes to live with him. Even before she realizes Lauren is her mother, the Earthseed leader's picture makes the younger woman suspicious: "She looked, somehow, like someone I would be inclined to like and trust—which scared me. It made me immediately dislike and distrust her. She was a cult leader, after all" (341). Only at age thirty-four does Asha figure out their relationship. Their reunion is prickly: Asha is distant, and Lauren becomes furious after learning that Marcos concealed her daughter's whereabouts, fury that Asha resents on behalf of her beloved uncle. To her, Earthseed seems like Lauren's "other kid [,] . . . her favorite" (265). Mother and daughter meet only sporadically after their initial reunion.

Since Asha is the overall compiler of *Talents*, her narration carries special weight in counterbalancing her mother's journal. But the words of Marcos and Bankole compete with it as well. We read excerpts from Marcos's *Warrior*, in which, for example, he extols the founder of CA (278). Unlike Marcos, Bankole loves Lauren deeply, but he would prefer her to give up Acorn and Earthseed in favor of an old-fashioned way of life, which he perceives as safer. His *Memories of Other Worlds* reveals his skepticism about Earthseed. For him the "Destiny," for instance, consists of "[g]rand words" (48). Just as the larger society's dystopia is modified into a critical dystopia by the Earthseed utopia within it, so that utopia in turn is modified into what Moylan calls a critical utopia by these three doubting voices (Moylan, *Demand* 10–12).

How can persuasion in favor of Earthseed function in a context as unpromisingly critical as that of *Talents?* Perhaps surprisingly, the persuasion can be supported by the criticism, for the latter facilitates matching between implied and real readers. The texts must avoid sounding propagandistic. *Sower* does not pose much of a problem: since Earthseed is new and strange to readers, it needs to be advocated strongly. Its downtrodden members hardly risk seeming complacent, and its founder herself often expresses doubt about her abilities. Even Asha says she might have liked her mother when Lauren was "struggling, focused, but very young, very human" (*PT* 29). In *Talents,* however, except for the grueling concentration camp episode, Lauren and Earthseed generally do better than in *Sower.* Before Jarret's Crusaders invade, Acorn is growing and prospering, though, of course, not without hardships.[14] Again, after the prisoners flee the camp, Earthseed manages to survive and soon to grow anew, so that, by the end of the main text, it is starting to accumulate supporters all across the United States.

Such success can backfire, especially given the values of contemporary readers: if they have been rooting for Earthseed positioned as an underdog, they may cease to sympathize with it positioned as top dog, and therefore few pages are devoted to its later, more thriving phase. Lauren's dreams, so inspiring when fresh, may seem stultifying when brought into being. To keep readers from turning away, she needs her flaws. To use Sheldon Sacks's term, she is constructed as a "fallible paragon," someone who represents the implied author's values without being annoyingly, improbably perfect (110–11). In short, to avoid seeming dogmatic or simplistic, the implied author must to some extent undercut Earthseed and its founder, doing so increasingly as the series progresses. In a chiasmus pattern, as Earthseed rises, the persuasive volume must be turned down.[15]

Moreover, when the second novel adds a dimension missing in the first, the implied author is modifying her initial model, thus herself engaging in a process of pragmatism and urging readers to do the same. The *Earthseed* books are among those texts that draw implied readers

> into a process of [pragmatism] that proceeds *simultaneously* with their experience of the narrative, for they are to engage in the process about

which they are reading. Instead of merely presenting an ideal for readers to pursue in the future, these books present a model, then modify it, then replace it with another, which in turn is modified, and so on; in order to follow the narrative, readers need to employ the very agility and openness that the book is advocating. Because novels based on pragmatic [utopianism] urge readers to participate more actively than usual in the reading process, these narratives combat passivity and gain persuasive force. (*PPP* 14)

▶ The Commentary on Persuasion

So far my discussion of the Earthseed texts has dealt with the nature of their vigorous persuasion, an element present in various other novels, though not always so subtly. But what makes Butler's novels truly remarkable is their self-consciousness, their complex and somewhat ambiguous commentary on persuasion. All literature, in my view, is persuasive, and myriad subjects of persuasion are possible. But when the values and states of affairs about which literature is seeking to persuade readers are themselves specifically related to persuasion, the literature becomes self-referential—persuasion about persuasion. (The *Earthseed* series is also self-referential in regard to the weight it gives to reading and writing; Lauren frequently reflects on what compels her to write in her journal and on the need for literacy in her society.)

The series calls attention to persuasion from the very beginning by naming both books "parables," which are, after all, stories that teach.[16] All teaching is to some degree a form of persuasion—that a certain state of affairs exists, that certain values are desirable, or both—and Butler's titles allude specifically to the strongly persuasive teachings of Jesus, who was not only teaching but preaching, attempting to convert and inspire. (The mention of Jesus' stories is reinforced at various other points in the books, especially at the end, when each quotes the heart of the parable after which it is named [*PS* 295; *PT* 365].) The *Earthseed* novels, pervaded by the theme of education, place themselves in the genre of strongly persuasive teaching narratives both by alluding to Jesus' parables and by calling themselves parables.

Furthermore, it is significant which parables the novels allude to—the Parable of the Sower (Luke 8:5–8) and the Parable of the Talents (Matthew 25:14–30)—for both of these stories are themselves self-referential commentaries on persuasion. In the case of the Parable of the Sower, Jesus makes the self-referentiality explicit. After telling a tale about how seed may languish or thrive, depending on where it is sown, Jesus cries, "'He that hath ears to hear, let him hear'" (authorized King James version). When his disciples ask him to explain the parable, he gives a detailed answer, beginning, "'Unto you it is given to know the mysteries of the kingdom of God: but to others in parables; that seeing they might not see, and hearing they might not understand'" (Luke 8:9–10). He is explaining that the word of God may be lost or effective, depending on who hears it.[17] The Parable of the Talents concerns a master who, when leaving on a journey, gives talents, or money, to his servants. On his return, he rewards the servants who invested and multiplied their talents, whereas he punishes the servant who merely buried his talents in the ground. Although not only about persuasion, the parable can be interpreted in that way, with the money resembling the sown seed: some people profit from what they receive (words or something else), while others do not.[18] Thus both parables can themselves be read as self-referential, as parables about parables.

The *Earthseed* series mostly refers to persuasion positively. To begin with, the most frequent and skilled persuader is Lauren, and her subject—Earthseed—is usually presented as worthy. Furthermore, persuasion is shown as clearly preferable to the main alternative—force. In the future society, slave collars, concentration camps, and the threat of murder are all-too-common ways that some characters compel others to do their bidding. Such violent coercion would seem appalling in any novel. But its horrors are especially vivid here because of the hyperempathy of some characters, particularly Lauren, the main point-of-view character.

Nevertheless, the series does not idealize persuasion. It presents some characters' subjects as inadequate (Lauren's father, though aware of his neighborhood's fragility, argues that people should stay there and is proved wrong) or pernicious (President Jarret is a rabble-rouser [*PT* 25], and Marcos also promotes Christian America, which—even in the guise he permits himself to perceive—is rigid and bigoted). And even charismatic characters' persuasive methods can prove ineffectual. At times, however, these failures provide the moments when persuasion is understood best. For instance, when Lauren tries to convince Joanne Garfield, a close friend in Robledo, that they should get ready because the community will soon collapse and that Joanne should keep Lauren's preparations secret, Joanne, unwilling to believe the bleak warning, betrays the secret (*PS* 45–54). Lauren is reprimanded by her father, who explains, "'It's better to teach people than to scare them'" (58).

Marcos sometimes fails as well. Soon after Lauren rescues him from slavery, he tries to turn the residents of Acorn away from Earthseed and toward Christianity (*PT* 136–40). Because they do not value hierarchy and tradition as much as he does, there is not enough initial sharing of values for belief-bridging to function. (Interestingly, though, something else contributes to his failure; he is not yet ready to preach, and Lauren knows that when she grants his request to do so [140]. This is one of the first examples where we see her put Earthseed above family and mislead someone other than an enemy.) Lauren later runs into a similar obstacle to belief-bridging, when she tries to convince Marcos that the "re-education camps" run by Christian America, in which he is now a minister, imprisoned not just criminals but also the residents of Acorn (280–84; 290–91). She evokes such rivalry and distrust in him, and he feels such a strong need for the "order, stability, safety, control" offered by CA (103), that he is unwilling to believe any substantial criticism of it. His beliefs do not overlap enough with his sister's for belief-bridging to work: as the biblical Parable of the Sower says, he lacks ears to hear. Whether or not the characters themselves analyze such incidents, these events can teach readers about what persuasion needs in order to function.

Ironically, it is when Lauren's persuasion succeeds most that readers may feel the most uncomfortable. Especially in the second book, she reflects more and more on which techniques to use and on how effective they are. Also near the end of *Talents,* when Lauren begins traveling with Len (a woman who assists her), Len often comments on her companion's persuasive power, remarks that can engage readers in considering and potentially critiquing it. Although Len usually makes her observations admiringly, they can give readers pause.

For instance, Lauren writes:

> Best not to push people. Best, as Len says, to seduce them. . . . The Elfords may be bored and hungry for both novelty and purpose, but they're not fools. I had to be more open with them than I have been with people like Isis [a homeless woman].
>
> "What will you ask them to do?" Len said to me. . . . "You have them, you know, even if they don't realize it yet."
>
> I nodded. "I think they'll have some suggestions themselves. They'll feel better if they make the first suggestions. . . . Later, I want them to take Allie in."
>
> "The Elfords have all but seduced themselves for you," Len said. (*PT* 342; 344–45)

At another point a woman is strongly attracted to Lauren, who has dressed as a man, as she often does for safety while traveling. Having sketched the woman, Lauren writes: "drawing a person helps me *become* that person and, to be honest, it helps me manipulate that person. . . . I could have finished it much more quickly. But working on it, adding detail, gave me a chance to talk about Earthseed without seeming to proselytize.

I quoted verses as though quoting any poetry to her until one verse caught her interest" (*PT* 329). Lauren ultimately reveals her true gender, yet plans not only to help the woman but also to exploit her lingering and somewhat reciprocated attraction. Lauren writes:

> I'll have to visit her again soon . . . to hold on to her, and I intend to do that. . . . She needs purpose as much as I need to give it to her.
> "That was fascinating," Len said to me . . . , "I enjoyed watching you work."
> "Thank you for working with me."
> She smiled, then stopped smiling. "You seduce people. My God, you're always at it, aren't you?"
> "People fascinate me," I said. "I care about them. If I didn't, Earthseed wouldn't mean anything at all to me." (334)

As I have found, criticism of Lauren by Asha, Marcos, and Bankole makes her, or at least Earthseed, all the more appealing. But, interestingly, her own matter-of-fact comments and Len's insights cast more of a shadow. *Talents* hints that something may be wrong with the ways in which Lauren seeks to convince people, or perhaps with all persuasive methods. Furthermore, if Lauren's obsession with Earthseed induced her to search less than she might have for her daughter, then something may be wrong with devoting oneself to persuasion, regardless of how one does it. Thus, while a good deal of evidence suggests that the implied author is trying to persuade readers to look favorably on Earthseed, there is less evidence for how we are to evaluate persuasion itself. The implied author leaves the implied reader with some doubt about the ethics of persuasion. Since Earthseed itself is never seriously called into question, Butler's series functions almost as a controlled experiment, in effect asking, "Even if the subject of persuasion is fine, might something be wrong with persuasion itself?"

People have debated the meaning of Jesus' parables for millennia: it is agreed that the parables are meant to persuade, but in many cases the subject of persuasion remains hazy. In the same way, by bearing the title of "parable," Butler's texts identify themselves as teaching narratives but, particularly in *Talents,* may also be signaling the ambiguity of some of their subjects. Naomi Jacobs, writing about Butler's *Xenogenesis* series, says, "As is typical of Butler's work, this . . . will arrive at only a qualified resolution of the problems it raises" (102).

I have been arguing that persuasion is a major theme and technique in the *Earthseed* series. I have observed that the main subject of persuasion, Earthseed, is pragmatically utopian, encouraging its followers to question, rethink, and adapt, and that the methods of persuasion are themselves gradual and subtle, as befits pragmatism. Advocacy of Earthseed is addressed both to characters on the textual level and to readers on the extratextual level. Just as Earthseed members act pragmatically on the textual level, so the *Earthseed* series acts pragmatically on the extratextual level, as when *Talents* asks readers to rethink *Sower*. On both levels the key concepts of belief-bridging and matching have enabled us to understand how persuasion works, even when it seems paradoxical: for example, the more that Lauren succeeds, the more that additional voices are needed to represent her as fallible.

Most strikingly, the series is self-referential, consisting of parables about parables, persuasion about persuasion. Butler wanted to persuade her readers to think. When asked how a text like hers might affect readers, she replied, "To bend their minds a bit?"—a goal pragmatic both in its modesty and in its ambition (Mehaffy and Keating 63–64). In *Sower* and *Talents* the commentary on persuasion is itself pragmatic. Instead of being handed a single definition and evaluation of persuasion, we are urged to question, rethink, and adapt.

> To survive,
> Know the past.
> Let it touch you.
> Then let
> The past
> Go.
> (*Earthseed: The Books of the Living,* in *The Parable of the Talents* 337)

Notes

1. Butler intended to write at least four more novels in the series. She said she decided to stop after *Talents* because it "was too hard to write the first sequel; and now I'm focusing on and having fun with a completely different text and a new narrator" (Mehaffy and Keating 76).

2. The hope is generated through open endings, mixed genres, and other techniques. The term "critical dystopia" is applied to *Sower* by Miller (337), by Baccolini in "Gender and Genre" (13), by Moylan in *Scraps* (223), and to both *Sower* and *Talents* by Moylan in "The moment" (138). Baccolini and Moylan trace the complex genesis of the term in "Introduction. Dystopia and Histories" (3–8).

3. I summarize the plots of both books. For a longer summary, see Moylan (*Scraps* 223–45; 321–25). The names of the characters deserve a separate study: several central figures bear names that have special meanings and are changed, by choice or against the characters' will. Regarding the notion of "positive obsession," see Butler's essay of that

title, concerning her own writing.

4. Scholars who pay substantial attention to utopian and dystopian elements (often feminist ones) in Butler's writings include: Andreolle, Baccolini, Gant-Britton, Melzer, Miller, Moylan (*Scraps* 223–45; 321–25), Stillman, and Zaki. Analysis of race in the *Earthseed* books often refers to ramifications of both the racially mixed identity of Earthseed and the specifically African-American identity of the protagonist and the author, including elements such as the texts' allusions to slavery and the employment of the slave narrative genre. Among texts that discuss Butler in terms of race are those by Baccolini, Birns, Dubey, Gant-Britton, Melzer, Moylan (*Scraps* 223–45; 321–25), and Zaki, and the interviews by Mehaffy and Keating and by Rowell. Class is examined by Dubey, Miller, and Moylan (*Scraps* 223–45; 321–25). As Third-Wave feminist texts, the novels emphasize gender, race, and class but do not foreground any single one of them.

5. In the interview by Mehaffy and Keating, Butler reflected on the potential of her work to persuade readers in the direction of social change. Some critics have briefly mentioned persuasion in the *Earthseed* series (e.g., Melzer 37, Pfeiffer 150, and Sands). Although beyond the scope of this study, it would be worthwhile to explore how the persuasive aspects of the series fit into the tradition of African-American preaching.

6. I ask to whom the persuasion is addressed rather than who is persuaded, because persuasion is not always successful within the text. By reading only the text itself, one cannot tell whether persuasion has succeeded in convincing readers outside the text. For similar reasons I sometimes must refer to attempts to persuade rather than persuasion.

7. Melzer provides insightful comments about the relation of change and utopia in the series, though without mentioning philosophical pragmatism. Dubey points out that the book of Earthseed verses is "a process rather than a finished product" because Lauren writes it throughout her journey northward, though its content "remains fixed and unrevised by its readers' contestations" (118). Birns compares Earthseed to "various forms of process theology" (13).

8. Butler thought in the same pragmatic way about constantly honing her skills (Rowell 48).

9. Pragmatism can prove particularly helpful for certain groups. Focusing on women of color, Gant-Britton observes that "for many exploited people, change is often a matter of starting with almost nothing and making incremental advancements. . . . Butler's model privileges proactive rather than reactive thinking. This different attitude is potentially more empowering for . . . previously marginalized peoples" (282–83).

10. I use the term "extratextual" to indicate that, through real readers, more than the text is involved, though, of course, the text is involved too.

11. Moylan feels that this problematization should go further (*Scraps* 244).

12. Interestingly, in both novels the epigraph of each part and each year is a quote from *Earthseed: The Books of the Living*. Even if Asha is the one who has chosen the *Talents* epigraphs, she still is following the format Lauren employed in *Sower*. In Asha's sequel are Lauren and Earthseed being privileged—or co-opted?

13. Stillman provides an even-handed evaluation of Asha's criticisms.

14. Even in *Sower* the founding of Acorn at the end strikes Madhu Dubey as too

much, a betrayal of the novel's earlier innovative rejection of the "localist and organic notions of community" that many other African-American novelists rely upon (Dubey 105).

15. Just as we may admire a blossom without brown spots and yet criticize it for looking artificial, so readers may long for perfection but tend not to believe in it if a text presents it. Thus the faults of Lauren and her religion contribute to belief-bridging as well as to belief-matching: if we believe that people and religions tend to be flawed, then we will believe more easily in fallible ones than flawless ones.

16. Pfeiffer asserts that "the single most pervasive reference in [Butler's] writing has been the Judeo-Christian Bible" (140). Andreolle places *Sower* in the tradition of Christian fundamentalism.

17. It is unclear whether he means that, because direct communication is lost on some listeners, they need parables; that even parables are wasted on some individuals, so that such an audience will never understand; or that he uses parables to keep the mysteries from some people.

18. Lauren also refers to herself as recipient of a "talent," Earthseed, which circumstances have forced her to bury at Acorn (*PT* 25). Her followers resemble the seed sown (e.g., *PS* 135). Actually, richer possibilities exist for interpreting how the two parables relate to the two novels. For example, Lauren might be the seed or the ground as well as the sower, and so might be the master or a talent as well as the recipient of a talent.

Works Cited

Andreolle, Donna Spalding. "Utopias of Old, Solutions for the New Millennium: A Comparative Study of Christian Fundamentalism in M. K. Wren's *A Gift upon the Shore* and Octavia Buler's *Parable of the Sower.*" *Utopian Studies* 12 (2001): 114–23. *Humanities Full Text,* 15 March 2004, http://0-spweb.silverplatter.com.opac.sfsu.edu/c10914.

Baccolini, Raffaella. "Gender and Genre in the Feminist Critical Dystopias of Katharine Burdekin, Margaret Atwood, and Octavia E. Butler." In *Future Females, The Next Generation: New Voices and Velocities in Feminist Science Fiction Criticism,* ed. Marleen S. Barr. Lanham, MD: Rowman & Littlefield, 2000. 13–34.

—— and Tom Moylan, eds. *Dark Horizons: Science Fiction and the Dystopian Imagination.* New York: Routledge, 2003.

—— and Tom Moylan. "Introduction. Dystopia and Histories." In *Dark Horizons: Science Fiction and the Dystopian Imagination,* ed. Raffaella Baccolini and Tom Moylan. New York: Routledge, 2003. 1–12.

Birns, Nicholas. "Octavia Butler: Fashioning Alien Constructs." *The Hollins Critic* 38.3 (June 2001): 1–14.

Butler, Octavia E. *Parable of the Sower.* New York: Warner Books, 1993.

——. *Parable of the Talents: A Novel.* New York: Seven Stories, 1998.

——. "Positive Obsession." *Bloodchild and Other Stories.* New York: Four Walls Eight Windows, 1995. 123–36.

Dubey, Madhu. "Folk and Urban Communities in African-American Women's Fiction: Octavia Butler's *Parable of the Sower.*" *Studies in American Fiction* 27 (1999): 103–28.

Gant-Britton, Lisbeth. "Octavia Butler's *Parable of the Sower:* One Alternative to a Futureless Future." In *Women of Other Worlds: Excursions through Science Fiction and Feminism,* ed. Helen Merrick and Tess Williams. Claremont, Western Australia: University of Western Australia Press, 1999. 277–94.

Jacobs, Naomi. "Posthuman Bodies and Agency in Octavia Butler's *Xenogenesis.*" In Baccolini and Moylan. 91–111.

Jackson, H. Jerome. "Sci-Fi Tales from Octavia E. Butler." *Crisis* (April 1994): 4ff.

Johnson, Rebecca O. "African-American, Feminist Science Fiction." *Sojourner: The Women's Forum* 19.6 (1994): 12–14.

Keating, AnaLouise. "Octavia E. Butler." *Contemporary African American Novelists: A Bio-Bibliographical Critical Sourcebook,* ed. Emmanuel S. Nelson. Westport, CT: Greenwood, 1999. 69–75.

Mehaffy, Marilyn and AnaLouise Keating. "'Radio Imagination': Octavia Butler on the Poetics of Narrative Embodiment." *MELUS* 26 (2001): 45–76.

Merrick, Helen and Tess Williams, eds. *Women of Other Worlds: Excursions through Science Fiction and Feminism.* Claremont, Western Australia: University of Western Australia Press, 1999.

Melzer, Patricia. "'All that you touch you change': Utopian Desire and the Concept of Change in Octavia Butler's *Parable of the Sower* and *Parable of the Talents.*" *FEM-SPEC* 3.2 (2003): 31–52.

Miller, Jim. "Post-Apocalyptic Hoping: Octavia Butler's Dystopian/Utopian Vision." *Science-Fiction Studies* 25 (1998): 336–60.

Moylan, Tom. *Demand the Impossible: Science Fiction and the Utopian Imagination.* New York: Methuen, 1986.

———. "'The moment is here . . . and it's important': State, Agency, and Dystopia in Kim Stanley Robinson's *Antarctica* and Ursula K. Le Guin's *The Telling.*" In Baccolini and Moylan. 135–53.

———. *Scraps of the Untainted Sky: Science Fiction, Utopia, Dystopia.* Boulder, CO: Westview, 2000.

Peel, Ellen. *Politics, Persuasion, and Pragmatism: A Rhetoric of Feminist Utopian Fiction.* Columbus: The Ohio State University Press, 2002.

Pfeiffer, John R. "Octavia Butler Writes the Bible." In *Shaw and Other Matters: A Festschrift for Stanley Weintraub on the Occasion of His Forty-Second Anniversary at The Pennsylvania State University,* ed. Susan Rusinko. London: Associated University Presses, 1998. 140–52.

Potts, Stephen W. "'We Keep Playing the Same Record': A Conversation with Octavia E. Butler." *Science-Fiction Studies* 23 (1996): 331–38.

Rowell, Charles H. "An Interview with Octavia E. Butler." *Callaloo* 20 (1997): 47–66.

Sacks, Sheldon. *Fiction and the Shape of Belief: A Study of Henry Fielding, with Glances at Swift, Johnson and Richardson.* Berkeley: University of California Press, 1964.

Sands, Peter. "Octavia Butler's Chiastic Cannibalistics." *Utopian Studies* 14 (2003): 1–14. *Humanities Full Text,* 23 January 2004, http://0-spweb.silverplatter.com.opac.sfsu.edu/c10914.

Stillman, Peter G. "Dystopian Critiques, Utopian Possibilities, and Human Purposes in Octavia Butler's 'Parables.'" *Utopian Studies* 14 (2003): 15–35. *Humanities Full Text,* 23 January 2004, http://0-spweb.silverplatter.com.opac.sfsu.edu/c10914.
Suvin, Darko. "Theses on Dystopia 2001." In Baccolini and Moylan. 187–201.
Zaki, Hoda M. "Utopia, Dystopia, and Ideology in the Science Fiction of Octavia Butler." *Science Fiction Studies* 17 (1990): 239–51.

ALCENA MADELINE DAVIS ROGAN

Tananarive Due and Nalo Hopkinson Revisit the Reproduction of Mothering

Legacies of the Past and Strategies for the Future

In the United States, black women assume the burden of institutionalized sex/race discrimination, as well as sex discrimination within their own families and communities. A recurrent theme in black feminist intellectual work is the argument that the black woman's relationship to her self and her family must be constantly reevaluated, historicized as a relation degraded by the legacy of her slavery-era status as the literal site of the reproduction of white-owned property. In the case of the U.S. black woman, the status of the reproductive female body as the site of the reproduction of Oedipus is compounded by that body's historical relationship to the reproduction of capital. In the context of this relationship, the entire structure of Oedipus is rearranged, as the black man's role as father is supplanted by the white master: thus the black woman's relationship to the central formative trope of the culture in which she lives was, and continues to be, necessarily different from the white woman's.

Historian Paula Giddings documents evidence that black slave women fought to reject their position as brood stock for their white masters. The available evidence demonstrates that a large number of women were forced by this circumstance to abort; others killed their young children rather than allow them to grow up as property.[1] The legacy of this dreadful necessity can be seen in black and white women's quite different relationships to the feminist issue of abortion rights. In the twentieth and early twenty-first centuries, the practice of doctors performing tubal ligation on black women and women of color without their informed consent, as well as the vilification of black motherhood in politics and the media, has complicated the issue of reproductive choice.[2] In *Women, Race, and Class,* Angela Davis describes how the fight for safe and legal birth control—a cause universally central to the empowerment of women—is affected by the legacy of slavery and the rhetoric of racism:

> The abortion rights activists of the early 1970s should have examined the history of their movement. Had they done so, they might have understood why so many of their Black sisters adopted a posture of suspicion toward their cause. They might have understood how important it was to undo the racist deeds of their predecessors, who had advocated birth control as well as compulsory sterilization as a means of eliminating the "unfit" sectors of the population. Consequently, the young white feminists might have been more receptive to the suggestion that their campaign for abortion rights include a vigorous condemnation of sterilization abuse, which had become more widespread than ever. (215)

Although black and white feminists are generally equally concerned with the need to gain control over their own reproductive lives, the crucial differences in black and white women's experience of institutionalized control over the female body were seen as often not sufficiently accounted for by the Second-Wave feminist movement. Unfortunately, a cause with the capacity to unite women across race and class boundaries instead became an occasion for reinscribing the battle lines drawn by capitalist patriarchal institutions onto relations between and among women (see also note 3 below).

"The legacy of the past" that the U.S. black woman must contend with is her status within the slavery system both as an object of property and as the hypersexualized site of the reproduction of the slavery system. These roles continue to haunt black women, although they manifest themselves in different ways. We might read the overrepresentation of black women in low-paying, part-time work, as well as their position at the bottom of the wage gap scale, as indicators that the white capitalist patriarchy has not completely discontinued its slavery-era practice of exploiting black women's labor for economic gain. But, of course, the difference between slavery and the exploited laborer under capitalism is meaningful and multifaceted.

Marx addresses this difference in *Capital,* vol. 1, noting that "the slave works only under the spur of external fear but not for *his* [sic] *existence* which is *guaranteed* even though it does not belong to him. The free worker, however, is impelled by his wants" (1031). However, this change in what Marx calls "the relations of supremacy and subordination" (1031) wrought by the subsumption of labor under capital does not change the position of the black woman as subordinate. In her essay "Women and Capitalism: Dialectics of Oppression and Liberation," Davis illustrates the inevitability of the black woman's subordination under capitalism, demonstrating how this position is institutionally guaranteed:

> Within the existing class relations of capitalism, women in their vast majority are kept in a state of familial servitude and social inferiority not by men in general, but rather by the ruling class. Their oppression serves to maximize the efficacy of domination. The objective oppression of black women in America has a class, and also a national origin. Because the structures of female oppression are inextricably tethered to capitalism, female emancipation must be simultaneously and explicitly the pursuit of black liberation. (185)

Exacerbating the conditions of familial servitude is the state of black and working-class women's work outside of the home, whose features include the institutionalized gender and race wage gap, as well as the degrading nature of the work typically available to such women, especially single parents, who must find employment that does not interfere too much with their parenting responsibilities: often this means taking minimum wage jobs at inconvenient hours. Also, since such jobs are overwhelmingly service oriented—janitorial work, childcare, geriatric care, and the like—there is a sense in which the black female worker is often redomesticated as the "mother" in an oedipal configuration that, as Davis suggests, replaces the black man with the white man as "father." Thus, the master/slave dialectic can, in some senses, be seen to reinscribe itself in the relation of the black woman to capitalist patriarchy, for the black woman finds herself once again the victim of white male paternalism, only now she is victimized by institutionalized neglect rather than by the close scrutiny she bore as an object of property.

At the same time that black women are heavily marginalized in their role as participants in the U.S. economic system, they are also, ironically, rendered highly visible. Black feminist analyses of the influential 1965 Moynihan Report reveal that black women are scapegoated as the primary precipitators of the "dire" state of the black American family. The report cites the high numbers of households headed by black women as a cause, not a symptom, of blacks' social and economic disenfranchisement. According to the logic of the report, which we see repeated in the rhetoric of government welfare policies, the black American family suffers from an identity crisis, spurred not by such factors as wage inequity and the incipient racism of the prison industrial complex, but rather by black women's usurpation of black men's role as head of household. In this way, collective anxiety about black women's leadership role in the family is rationalized—her power within the black family is vilified, reconstructed as proof of her perverse desire to consolidate power and reproduce it in her offspring. Black women's status as the hypersexualized site of reproduction is reinscribed in myriad ways: in the language of political debates over welfare policies, by the news media's promotion of the image of the black mother as "welfare queen," and in the entertainment media's representation of the black woman a specifically *exotic* sex object. This status also manifests itself, with tragic results, in the history of black women's exploitation by reproductive healthcare providers.

The internalization of these forms of social and economic discrimination—specifically, how they become a particular sort of love/hate relationship to the self and to other women—is the subject of many works of theory and fiction by black women. In an essay about the destructive power of language and its deployment as mastery in the U.S. slavery system, Hortense J. Spillers describes the lasting effects of this brutal system on the black woman's subject formation. Spillers particularly underscores the sense in which kinship is a necessarily fraught issue for black women, whose relationship to their offspring under slavery was constantly threatened:

> In the context of the United States, we could not say that the enslaved offspring was "orphaned," but the child does become, under the press of a patronymic, patrifocal, patrilinear, and patriarchal order, the man/woman on the boundary, whose human and familial status, by the very nature of the case, had yet to be defined. I would call this enforced state of breach another instance of vestibular cultural formation where "kinship" loses meaning, since it can be invaded at any given and arbitrary moment by the property relations. . . . It seems clear . . . that "Family," as we practice and understand it "in the West"—the vertical transfer of a bloodline, of a patronymic, of titles and entitlements, of real estate and the prerogatives of "cold cash," from fathers to sons and in the supposedly free exchange of affectional ties between a male and a female of his choice—becomes the mythically revered privilege of a free and freed community. (68)

She traces the crisis of U.S. black women's identity to their founding role within the economic system both as property and as the unwilling reproducers of property. It is this role, Spillers contends, that guarantees the black family's marginality within a socioeconomic system that privileges a definition of family that is based on the inheritance of patronymic legitimacy and attendant property rights. The "Law of the Father" that dictates the structure of the "legitimate" family is thus not applicable to the black family, which has historically been denied the power to name and to own. The Moynihan Report seeks to locate the socioeconomic disenfranchisement arising from this historical inequity within the black family itself. According to this logic, the black man is disenfranchised by the aberrant psychology of his familial structure, wherein he is marginalized by the overweening presence of the black matriarch. Spillers notes:

> According to Daniel Patrick Moynihan's celebrated "report" of the late sixties, the "Negro Family" has no father to speak of—his Name, his Law, his Symbolic function mark the impressive missing agencies in the essential life of the black community, the "Report" maintains, and it is, surprisingly, the fault of the Daughter, or the female line. This stunning reversal of the castration thematic, displacing the Name and the Law of the Father to the territory of the Mother and Daughter, becomes an aspect of the African-American female's misnaming. (57)

The bourgeois white woman's daughter becomes an object of exchange in the perpetuation of patriarchal legitimacy, but the black woman's daughter guarantees the perpetuation of an aberrant, illegitimate bid for matriarchal power. It is within this context, argues Audre Lorde and bell hooks, that the American black woman's necessarily fraught relationship to her self and to the symbolic perpetuation of her self—her daughters—must be understood. I will explore the theme of the racialized "reproduction of mothering" in Tananarive Due's "Like Daughter" and in Nalo Hopkinson's *Brown Girl in the Ring*.

In "Like Daughter," Due presents one possible future of the black mother/daughter relationship. In the first scene the story's narrator, Paige, is asked by her best friend since childhood, Denise, to come and take her six-year-old child away from her. Denise's child, whom she has named after herself, is a clone, the product of a short-lived, near-future government initiative program to offer cloning services to acceptable candidates. Little Denise is one of only about 230 clone babies that were created before the U.S. Supreme Court reversed the country's cloning policy:

> In the end, I'm not sure how many copycat babies were born. I read somewhere that some of the mothers honored the Supreme Court's ban and were persuaded to abort. Of course, they might have been coerced or paid off by one of the extremist groups terrified of a crop of so-called "soulless" children. But none of that would have swayed Denise, anyway. For all I know, little Neecy might have been the very last one born. (96)

The story does not directly address the specifically racial dimension of

Denise's acceptability as a candidate for the cloning experiment. However, its narrative grounding in the issue of reproductive technologies and their control by the state must be contextualized within black women's historical relationship to reproductive technologies. Within such a contextualization, I read the cloning project's failure—the individual project of Denise's efforts to create a version of herself who is not mitigated or compromised by the Laws or Abuses of the Father—as an exposure and indictment of the lasting legacy of such Laws and Abuses in Denise's own life. As the story demonstrates, there is a dimension to the legacy of self-hatred that racist capitalist patriarchy produces which cannot be assuaged by simply removing the Father from the picture through the uses of technology. The Father's destructive capacity, in other words, is revealed to be a complex ideology that cannot be blamed on the individual man or alleviated through his removal from the site of reproduction. In this way, Due substantiates Davis's claim that black women suffer damage at the hands of the ruling class—a ruling class that is in large part constructed in terms of male supremacy but that cannot be reduced to the individual man. The reason is, of course, that maleness does not guarantee supremacy, although the ideology of the Law of the Father is an enduring trait of ruling-class supremacy.

Due's story reveals the tale of two inseparable black childhood friends (their friendship continues into adulthood), Paige and Denise. Although the girls grow up across the street from one another, they come from very different households. Paige's parents are able to provide her with a financially stable and emotionally loving environment. Denise, on the other hand, lives with her mother, who is an alcoholic, and her father, who beats both Denise and her mother. Denise is also sexually abused, from the time she is nine years old, by her young uncle. Even though they are contemporaries, Paige assumes a motherly role in their relationship. From the outset, Due's story is concerned with addressing questions of sameness, difference, and the impact of the past—childhood and young adult identity formation—upon the future of the self and succeeding generations. Although the girls are marked as quite similar in many ways—they wear the same clothes, enjoy the same games and books, share secrets—Denise's home life dictates that she will always be at a socioeconomic and psychic disadvantage in comparison to her friend. Paige burdens herself with a caretaking role that she, a child herself, cannot possibly fulfill.

As the story develops, it becomes heartbreakingly clear that Denise is not going to be able to overcome the huge obstacles that her abusive upbringing presents. With depressing inexorability, Denise acts out the consequences of her background while Paige observes, sympathetic but powerless to change the course of events:

What I didn't understand, as a child, was how Neecy could say she hated her father for hitting her and her mother, but then she'd be so sad during the months when he left, always wondering when he would decide to come home. And how Neecy could be so much smarter than I was—the best reader, speller, and multiplier in the entire fourth grade—and still manage to get so many Fs because she just wouldn't sit still and do her homework. And the thing that puzzled me most of all was why, as cute as Neecy was, she seemed to be ashamed to show her face to anyone unless she was going to bed with a boy, which was the only time she ever seemed to think she was beautiful. She had to go to the doctor to get abortion pills three times before she graduated from high school. (93)

"Like Daughter" can be read as a historical, materialist critique of the social conditions that all but ensure Denise's trajectory as a victim and replicator of the mistakes that her mother has made. Indeed, despite Denise's acute perception of how different her life could have been under different circumstances—a perception expressed in infrequent but poignant envy of Paige ("'Girl, you're so lucky,' Neecy told me once" [94])—she cannot seem to change. Paige also contemplates the differences that separate her from her friend, searching for a logic that would explain the blatant inequality of their positions: "I often asked myself what forces had separated us so young, dictating that I had grown up in my house and Neecy had grown up in the other"; "Was it only an *accident* that my own father never hit me, never stayed away from home for even a single night?"; "If only Neecy had been my real-life sister, not just a pretend one, I always thought. If only things had been different for her from the time she was born" (94). Due refuses to pigeonhole an "essential" black woman's experience, instead pointing to the ways in which black women's lives are shaped by the material conditions of institutional disenfranchisement and specific familial experience. However, Due's choice of the material influences that negatively shape Denise's life—poverty, physical and sexual abuse, the mother's survival strategy of denial and alcoholism—is not arbitrary but rather constitutes a critique of the most serious material inequities that black women face in the United States today.

In "Sick and Tired of Being Sick and Tired: The Politics of Black Women's Health," Davis contends that the political contextualization of U.S. black women's emotional and physical health is an important and often-overlooked component of black feminist praxis. Written in 1988, at the end of the Reagan presidency, Davis's essay assesses the damage wrought by that administration upon black women, the working class, and social welfare programs: the numbers are devastating. "Of all the groups in this country, Black women have the highest rates of admission to outpatient psychiatric services"; "Two out of three poor adults are women, and 80 percent of the poor in the United States are women and children" (56); "Afro-American women are twice as likely as white women to die of hypertensive cardio-vascular disease, and they have three times the rate of high blood pressure. Black infant mortality is twice that of whites, and maternal mortality is three times as high"; "This cycle of oppression is largely responsible for the fact that far too many Black women resort to drugs as a means—however ineffective it ultimate proves to be—of softening the blows of poverty" (58); "Black women . . . are twelve times more likely to contract the AIDS virus than white women"; "Four times as many Black women as white women die of homicide" (59). As the statistic concerning *all* women and children's poverty rates in comparison to men's demonstrates, none of these problems is specific to the Black community per se: they result from the vicious combination of poverty and patriarchy, and as such poor white women and children suffer from the same material constraints as black women and their children. However, just as women and children fare worse than men within any given U.S. socioeconomic group, blacks fare worse than whites within any given U.S. economic group. The compounded problems of patriarchy and racism guarantee that black women are overrepresented in any set of statistics concerning the impact of poverty.

Although Denise escapes her impoverished past by marrying into middle-class respectability, her fateful, desperate phone call to Paige is precipitated by her husband's departure—a turn of events that one can easily infer will lead to Denise's reentry into the working class. Denise also suffers from alcoholism and mental illness, ailments that she has inherited from her family. I read Denise as a product of her environment, which includes but is not limited to the inherited disease of alcoholism passed on to her by her mother. As Paige describes it, Denise's adulthood has been one long series of failed plans and unfulfilled expectations: each time a plan fails, a crisis ensues, and Denise scrambles to find a new scheme upon which to pin her hopes for the future. In the following passage, Paige describes her friend's decision to have a cloned child:

> She actually had the whole thing charted out. We were having lunch in a Loop pizzeria the day Denise told me what she wanted to do. She spread out a group of elaborate charts; one was marked HOME, one FATHER, one SCHOOL, all in her too-neat artist's script. The whole time she showed me, her hands were shaking as if they were trying to fly away from her. I'd never seen anyone shake like that until then, watching Denise's fingers bounce like rubber with so much excitement and fervor. The shaking scared me more than her plans and charts.
>
> "Neecy, please wait," I told her.

"If I wait, I might change my mind," Denise said, as if this were a logical argument for going forward rather than just the opposite. She still hadn't learned that *doubt* was a signal to stop and think, not to plow ahead with her eyes covered, bracing for a crash. (97)

Denise's decision is a bid to construct a version of herself who will not inherit the legacy of poverty and abuse that she suffered in her own family. Not surprisingly, Denise finds herself unable to continue to care for the child the moment that the latest trappings of stability she has constructed for her own life begin to fall apart. Her child becomes a mirror—exaggerated in this case because of its striking likeness (as Denise's clone) to her—in which her self-hatred is reflected: "Sean's gone. Come up here and get Neecy. Take her. *I can't stand to look at her*" (Due 91; italics added).

In her influential study of mothering and object-relations theory, *The Reproduction of Mothering,* Nancy Chodorow describes the consequences arising from the fact that social relations dictate that the mother typically acts as primary caregiver to infants of both sexes. Her thesis is that mother and daughter share a unique relationship of narcissistic identification that, unlike in the case of the male infant, remains unbroken. While the male child identifies early on with the father, thus precipitating an active attachment to the mother as an object of desire, the girl's oedipal drama comes later, and, because she shares the perceived lack of her mother, precipitates a passive, negative identification with the mother as a continuation of her self. According to Chodorow, the relationship between mother and daughter is both strengthened and complicated by the intense identification inspired by the sameness of their bodies. The strength turns into weakness when the daughter, because of her strong identification with the mother, fails to develop the same sense of individuation and autonomy that the son develops quite early. As a result, while the son goes on to define himself positively in relation to an appropriate mother-substitute, the girl, who identifies strongly with the perceived lack of the mother's body—and, later, with the perceived lack of her position within the symbolic order—goes on to define herself in negative relation to an appropriate father-substitute. Because of the cultural value placed on the male-identified model of development-as-autonomy, the reproduction of mothering guarantees that the typical girl child will grow up to define herself in a negative relation to her culture's privileged construction of selfhood: the reproduction of mothering becomes the reproduction of Oedipus. This configuration is, in several ways, complicated further in the case of the American black family.[3] First, little cultural value accrues to black male or female subjectivity in a racist society. Black men and women must contend with their historically skewed relationship to the oedipal configuration, wherein, as Spillers points out, the white master replaces the black male as father—whether literally or figuratively—and the black mother is forced into a reproduction of mothering that guarantees her own and her daughter's identification both in negative relation to the white male and as property of the white male. Thus, in the white, Western, propertarian sense of "family," the black family cannot be said to meaningfully qualify as family.

Chodorow concludes that the oedipal mother/daughter continuum of narcissistic identification produces a particularly fraught love/hate relationship wherein the daughter recognizes herself in the mother, and thus recognizes the position of negatively defined subjectivity that she herself can look forward to attaining. Lorde and hooks argue that this state of affairs produces an even more problematical relationship between black mothers and daughters, for the daughter recognizes in the mother not only the position of lack dictated by Oedipus, but also the position of lack dictated by her culture's racism. In "Eye to Eye: Black Women, Hatred, and Anger," Lorde writes of black women:

> We do not love ourselves, therefore we cannot love each other. Because we see in each other's face our own face, the face we never stopped wanting. Because we survived and survival breeds desire for more self. A face we never stopped wanting at the same time as we try to obliterate it.
>
> Why don't we meet each other's eyes? Do we expect betrayal in each other's gaze, or recognition? (155)

In Due's story, the issue of the recognition of self in the other is underscored by the fact that Denise's daughter is her physical replica. When Paige arrives in Chicago to take Denise's child, Due carefully sets a scene in which the gaze, the reflection, and eye contact are centrally featured. When Paige calls Chicago to let Denise know that she is coming, Denise refuses to turn on the video link that would allow her friend to make eye contact with her—at the same time, she assures her friend again that she cannot bear to look at her own daughter. In the following scene, Paige sees Denise for the first time since her breakdown:

> Denise looked like a vagrant in her own home. As soon as I got there, I knew why she hadn't wanted me to see her on the phone; she was half dressed in a torn T-shirt, her hair wasn't combed, and the skin beneath her eyes looked so discolored that I had to wonder, for a moment, if Sean might have been hitting her. It wouldn't be the first time she'd been in an abusive relationship. But then I stared into the deep mud of my friend's irises before she shuffled away from me, and I knew better. No, she wasn't

being beaten; she wouldn't have tolerated that with Neecy in the house. Instead, my friend was probably having a nervous breakdown. (97)

Denise avoids Paige's eyes because she fears that Paige will recognize her own failure in that of her friend's. After all, Paige has spent a lifetime trying, without much success, to "look after" Denise. The look of recognition and desire for obliteration which Lorde describes is not one that Paige and Denise share, but is rather the gaze that Denise casts upon her own daughter. This is a significant point because the "eye to eye" phenomenon that Lorde describes depends on a *mutual* self-hatred spawned by internalization of sexism and racism. Due reinforces the fact that this look is not an *essential* part of a black woman's experience of racism but rather is dictated by social and material circumstances that many, but not all, black women share. Due achieves this complexity by presenting two black female contemporaries, one whose material circumstances all but guarantee her disenfranchisement, and one whose careful upbringing and exposure to educational opportunities offer an escape from the cycle of self-loathing.

In "Revolutionary Black Women," hooks also addresses the problem of black women's internalized self-hatred, including how those feelings are passed on as violent behavior toward other women and girl children. Although hooks sees the same phenomenon in the mutual black female gaze that Lorde does, she is critical of Lorde's use of the word "we." She points out that not all black women are likely to experience this phenomenon or respond to it in the same way: "To some extent Lorde's essay acts to shut down, close off, and deny those black female experiences that do not fit the norm she constructs from the location of her experience" (43). [H]ooks appreciates Lorde's recognition that black women, like all other race, gender, and socioeconomic groups that are interpellated in U.S. culture as inferior, cannot avoid internalizing the hatred that the culture in which they live directs at them. However, she argues that more emphasis should be placed on the process of black women's recovery, and she calls on "revolutionary" black women to share their life stories as a means of conveying forms of praxis. It is in this context that Due's story is potentially praxis-oriented. Due shares a science-fictional representation of black women's life stories that strongly implicates, through Paige's rescue of Denise, new parenting practices as a practical mode of recovery for black mothers and daughters.

Due addresses the contradictory nature of black women's experience in two ways: first, as I discuss above, she presents two very different portraits of the future of black womanhood. Second, she ends the story on another note that contradicts our expectations of both Paige's and Neecy's future.

By assuming responsibility for Neecy, Paige has a second chance to save her friend:

> Tears found my eyes for the first time since I'd arrived. "Denise, what's this going to mean to her?"
>
> "I don't know. I don't . . . care," Denise said, her voice shattered until she sounded like a mute struggling to form words. "Look at me. I can't stand to be near her. I vomit every time I look at her. It's all ruined. Everything. Oh, God—" She nearly sobbed, but there was only silence from her open mouth. "I can't. Not again. No more. Take her, Paige." (99)

Again, Due chooses to focus on the power of the look. It is the act of looking at her child that scares Denise more than anything, for her child's face is a mirror that reflects her own internalized rage, fear, and hate. Arguing with Denise about Neecy, Paige recalls her promise to her own mother to care for Denise. As Paige contemplates Neecy, she understands for the first time what Denise's motivation was in having a clone, and she finds herself implicated. Due provides a socially realistic portrait of a woman caught in the trap that her socioeconomic and material background has set for her. Denise, we are told, has indeed been driven to madness through her failed project to instantiate a loved and loving version of herself. But Due also presents the potential for hope through young Neecy, who gives Paige a second chance to fulfill the doomed promise that she made to look after Denise. The legacy of the past, once its tragic social implications and consequences are adequately understood, has the potential to positively impact the future of black women's experience.

At the conclusion of "Revolutionary Black Women," hooks offers her prescriptive for the future of black feminist resistance: "The crisis of black womanhood can only be addressed by the development of resistance struggles that emphasize the importance of decolonizing our minds, developing critical consciousness" (60). Due articulates the future of the legacy of the past as the development of a critical consciousness that might allow black women to use the knowledge of their own oppression to shape a decolonized gaze toward the future.

I will begin my discussion of Nalo Hopkinson by briefly outlining two distinct yet interimplicated historical moments—colonization and U.S. slavery—in which race serves as an important mediating factor in women's experience of capitalist patriarchal domination. I have described women as Earth's "native aliens" in order to highlight the overdetermination at work in representations of women in the speculative alien space. Here, I reverse this formulation with regard to black women and women of color, who are interpellated as Earth's alien natives. The reversal is meant to highlight the different yet related overdeterminations that female racial "Others" bear in relation to their historical interpellation and oppression as "natives" in relation to white cultures. This has been true of both black women and women of color since the beginning of the European colonialist enterprise, and it becomes increasingly true of women who are located outside of the first-world socioeconomic matrix.

Fredric Jameson names postmodernism the "cultural logic of late capitalism": his celebrated work identifies the multinational corporation as the primary economic paradigm of late capitalism. However, in the time since this work was published in 1991, the multinational corporation has become part of—with the ever-increasing efficiency of which Marx warns us in *Capital,* vol. 1—*globalization,* an economic paradigm in which the multinational corporation is but one factor in the organization of the major countries of the globe into blocs. Although in strictly economic terms this practice has caused *consolidation*—the increasing hegemony of the "capitalist democracy" over all other forms of political and economic enterprise—it has also resulted in the reification of cultural multiplicity. The new international division of labor has, in other words, produced a dialectical expansion in cultural form: the international division of culture. By the logic of the *supplement,* the Oriental, Indian, or African female subject is impacted by the position of subservience that is necessarily accorded to her by her entry into the white-male-dominated nexus of global capital. This international division of culture—the patriarchal reification of the indigenous cultural space—is accompanied by the third-world female subject's unprecedented movement into the economic sphere, overwhelmingly as factory workers or prostitutes.[4] As in the years surrounding the expansions of the Industrial Revolution, when women's movement outside the home and into the economic public sphere was accompanied by an aggressive promotion of the feminized domestic sphere, the international division of culture has produced its own globalized, highly visible "angel in the house." Gayatri Spivak states, "When a cultural identity is thrust upon one because the center wants an identifiable margin, claims for marginality assure validation from the center. It should then be pointed out that what is being negotiated here is . . . an economic principle of identification through separation" (55). I extend this argument and note that women are used in this equation as the "place-holders" of cultural identity. In this way, the Western capitalist "democratic" hegemony effectively interpellates its nonwhite subjects as "colored" and emasculates them as depoliticized containers of the cultural sphere.

This state of affairs is complicated in the case of the *woman* of color, who finds herself relegated to the status of minority despite her formal statistical status as majority: both as woman and as person of color. At home, through the commodification of a depoliticized African-American identity, as well as abroad, through the gendered division of the international labor market, globalization spurs the reification of the cultural space, inspired by anxiety over the encroachment of economic homogenization and its attendant putatively democratic social ethic into the traditionally woman-dominated private/domestic sphere. Of course, such encroachment is inevitable, and it is therefore not coincidental that practices detrimental to women's dignity and freedom (such as female genital mutilation) are defended as traditional cultural practices, while the homogenization of that same culture's economic and political practices is not seen as a violation of cultural traditions. As the primary maintainers and vessels of the "cultural," then, women of color under globalization are both exploited for their low-paid labor and are at the same time increasingly pressured to conform to their culture's dictates of feminine normativity. The contradictory nature of these two positions has been well documented by critics of the Anglo-American ideology of "having it all," which dictates that (default-white, educated, middle-class, and married) women are now free to pursue their jobs or careers (for 30 cents less on the dollar than their male counterparts earn) and to continue to perform most childcare and housework.[5] I turn now to Hopkinson's *Brown Girl in the Ring* to investigate how the problem of cultural reification informs feminist science fiction.

The legacy of the past is not always a wholly negative force in black women's science fiction. Hopkinson explores the place of past cultural history in the future in both her short fiction and her novels. An Afro-Caribbean woman who moved to Canada during her teenage years, Hopkinson deploys the discourses of Afro-Caribbean culture; white, first-world, late-capitalist culture; and contemporary science fiction in her fiction. In *Brown Girl in the Ring,* she explores the racial and sexual politics of the uneasy relationship between margin and center that the integrated metropolitan space creates. Making specific reference to canonical black global literary traditions, particularly Afro-Caribbean magical realism, Hopkinson also carries out a revisionist critique of the international division of culture, specifically the issue of cultural translation that this dialectic presents. In this way, she redresses the racism and sexism of globalism's cultural reifications, which are represented in this novel as the practice of obeah. The most persistent theme of her novel, however, is women and children's survival in a postapocalyptic first-world setting, where survival depends on the ability to revise, adapt, and deploy disparate cultural epistemologies.

Hopkinson announces her revisionist project with the introduction of her Afro-Caribbean female protagonist, Ti-Jeanne, a feminization of the lead character's name in Derek Walcott's Afro-Caribbean magical realist play, *Ti-Jean and His Brothers.* In Walcott's play, Ti-Jean and his brothers each battle the "devil," an allegorical instantiation of colonialist forces who can be outwitted only by the title character. Ti-Jean's victory over the devil depends on the fact that he alone has mastered both the discourse of the white Western philosophical and intellectual traditions that inspire the devil's attempt to colonize the minds and bodies of his brothers, as well as the discourse of Afro-Caribbean culture's folkloric resistances to colonization. Ti-Jean's capacity to translate both of these knowledges into a survival strategy guarantees his victory over the devil: in Hopkinson's feminized version of this tale, the survival strategies inspired and necessitated by the protagonist's position as a single black mother in an apocalyptic urban setting are the ultimate means of her victory. Ti-Jeanne is a single black mother living in the near-future urban wasteland of Toronto with her "Mami" (grandmother). Hopkinson describes a situation of postindustrial urban blight brought on by the ruthless and shortsighted co-optation of the first-world landscape by global capitalist economic and political governance—the future of Tony Blair and George W.'s managerial or corporate-style politics:

> Imagine a cartwheel half-mired in muddy water, its hub just clearing the surface. The spokes are the satellite cities that form Metropolitan Toronto . . . the Toronto city core is the hub. The mud itself is vast Lake Ontario, which cuts Toronto off at its southern border. . . . Now imagine the hub of that wheel as being rusted through and through. When Toronto's economic base collapsed, investors, commerce, and government withdrew into the suburb cities, leaving the rotten core to decay. Those who stayed were the ones who wouldn't or couldn't leave. The street people. The poor people. The ones who didn't see the writing on the wall, or who were too stubborn to give up their homes. Or who saw the decline of authority as an opportunity. As the police force left, it sparked large-scale chaos in the city core: the Riots. The satellite cities quickly raised roadblocks at their borders to keep Toronto out. The only unguarded exit from the city core was now over water. . . . In the twelve years since the Riots, repeated efforts to reclaim and rebuild the core were failing: fear of vandalism and violence was keeping 'burb people out. (3–4)

From the outset, Hopkinson evokes the race- and class-based nature of the relationship between margin and center. The center—in this case the urban center of Toronto, "the Ring,"—depends for its existence upon a docile and marginalized class of urban poor—among whom, as in the United States, persons of color are extremely overrepresented. When markets for cheaper wage labor outside of the metropole are found, industry's wealthy white owners relocate, leaving the marginalized class in the city's core. Thus the margin moves to the center, and the asymmetrical power relations between margin and center become brutally apparent as the urban poor of "the Ring" shift their attention from survival under capitalist exploitation to simple survival. Although money and police protection are no longer in evidence in urban Toronto, the center still makes its presence felt, in much the same way as ex-colonialist forces still control the "new" national space through the installation of puppet governments. In the less formal arrangement described in *Brown Girl*, exploitative thugs control the two trades that the power structure deems as profitable in the Ring: drugs and organs.

The novel begins with a startling request from the controlling power structure: Canada's Premier Uttley requires a human heart. With public opinion running high against porcine donor farms, and with human volunteer donors at an all-time low, the Canadian Premier enlists the thugs of the Ring to procure a healthy human heart at any cost. The Premier's request for a heart from Toronto epitomizes science fiction's capacity to literalize the symbolic. Vonda McIntyre's *Superluminal* features a similar moment of symbolic estrangement. The opening line of the novel, in which space pilots must undergo extensive organ replacement surgery in order to survive interstellar travel, reads as follows: "She gave up her heart quite willingly" (1). This statement proves to be true not only literally but also in its familiar, symbolic sense, as the heroine "gives up her heart" in a love affair. In a similar linguistic/contextual maneuver, the Premier's request for a heart procured from within the Ring concretizes both the heartlessness of capitalist political and economic interests *and* the sense in which the life of the inner city is constantly threatened by the invisible power structures that contain it.

However, there is an opposing power structure within the Ring, one that does not rely on allegiance to the white capitalist patriarchal system that rules from the margins. Ti-Jeanne's Grandmother Mami exemplifies this power structure. Mami is a healer woman, the Ring's resident alternative healthcare provider, as well as a powerful practitioner of Caribbean-influenced religious rites. Although the rituals that she performs are closely related to what her granddaughter is tempted to name "obeah," Mami refuses the appellation of obeah-woman, preferring to ascribe her supernatural talents to the Western image of God: "Mami shook a finger in front of Ti-Jeanne's face. "Girl child, you know better than to call it obeah. Stupidness. Is a gift from God Father. Is a good thing, not an evil thing. But child, if you don't learn how to use it, it will use you, just like it take your mother" (47). The history of the relationship between colony and metropole is evoked in Mami's description of her powers: the idea of "God Father" as it was professed by white missionaries and colonialists in the eighteenth and nineteenth centuries did not replace Afro-Caribbean religious practice, but rather augmented it. As (a generalized set of) polytheistic practices, obeah or voodoo/voodun had the capacity to accommodate a Western God, thus enacting a subversive marginalization of the figure that Western colonial forces considered to be the center of their spiritual life. However, in case we romanticize Afro-Caribbean religious practices as the locus of the Ring's "traditional" or "authentic" spiritual life, a cultural antidote to the ways of the white man, Hopkinson references the hybridity of Mami's religion, its complex relationship to the socioeconomic forces that have historically attempted to control it. This hybridity becomes more apparent as the plot unfolds to reveal that Mami's religion does not operate exclusively in the interests of the marginalized. It can also be used to further the interests of the absent center. This fact underscores Hopkinson's project of problematizing the relationship between the legacy of the Caribbean colonial past and that legacy's translation to a future wherein the Diaspora is, ironically, recolonized in the first-world urban space.

In his essay on the missionary's problematic role as cultural and spiritual translator, "The Translation of Cultures," James Clifford concludes, "For the missionary, in any event, there were no final versions. Authenticity was a process—the *translation* of cultures, creatively and humanly indeterminate" (692; italics mine). *Brown Girl in the Ring*, a title that evokes Ti-Jeanne's alien/outsider status in relation to the first-world urban center, is about the process of cultural translation as a life-or-death matter. Ti-Jeanne serves as a sort of missionary for the international division of culture, one whose translation of obeah from its Afro-Caribbean roots to Toronto's inner city entails an implicit revision of its sexist and capitalist reifications at the hands of her thug grandfather, Rudy. Ti-Jeanne's supernatural powers first manifest themselves as dreams, and Ti-Jeanne's ability to successfully translate these dreams as moments of prescience will determine whether she controls her powers or descends into madness, like her mother. The cultural legacy of Afro-Caribbean religious practices, manifested within Ti-Jeanne's family as supernatural abilities, must be translated into survival strategies for the future, or they will become destructive forces. In this way Hopkinson postulates one vision of the future of the legacy of the past.

Another complicating factor of Mami's religion is the indeterminate relationship between her religious rites and science-fictional discourse. Mami's, and later Ti-Jeanne's, rites produce tangible results: Mami casts a spell, and Ti-Jeanne and her baby's father, Tony, are rendered invisible; Mami performs a ritual and is suddenly inhabited by the spirit of an ancestor; and Ti-Jeanne's battle with her Grandfather Rudy for control of her soul is waged on a battleground of supernatural powers. The text constructs these powers as real. But do they depend upon some effect of the future context in which the novel takes place? Are these seemingly "supernatural" powers (in other words, a function of this particular version of the future)? Or are they a continuation of the powers that have always been available to successful practitioners of "obeah"? Since these powers can influence people outside Ti-Jeanne's family, and since the active souls of the dead include people unrelated to the family, they cannot be explained as merely a "family affair." Hopkinson's choice not to provide an explanation for these phenomena is, I believe, a significant one: the result is a new hybrid of past and future discourses, one that challenges the traditional, preservationist spatiotemporal dimensions of the international division of culture through its *translation* into the future space. Just as Walcott's Ti-Jean becomes Hopkinson's Ti-Jeanne, Mami's gift from "God Father" translates into Ti-Jeanne's survival strategy for the future.

In the following scene, Ti-Jeanne must discern how to enlist help from her spirit ancestors in order to fight Rudy, the drug-dealing thug whom the Premier has hired to take a human heart from the Ring. Rudy, as it turns out, is Ti-Jeanne's grandfather (Mami's estranged husband). The man whom he hires to take the heart is Tony, the estranged father of Ti-Jeanne's baby and an addict of 'buff, the drug that Rudy peddles in the Ring. Tony chooses Mami as his victim, leaving Ti-Jeanne alone to avenge the death of her grandmother and save herself from destruction at the hands of her grandfather:

> She had to figure out how to stop Rudy herself.
>
> She remembered her grandmother's words: *The center pole is the bridge between the worlds.* Why had those words come to her right then?
>
> Ti-Jeanne thought of the center pole of the palais, reaching up into the air and down toward the ground. She thought of the building she was in. The CN tower. And she understood what it was: 1,815 feet of the tallest center pole in the world. Her duppy body almost laughed a silent *kya-kya*, a jokey Jab-Jab laugh. For like the spirit tree that the center pole symbolized, the CN tower dug roots deep into the ground where the dead lived and pushed high into the heavens where the oldest ancestors lived. The tower was their ladder into this world. A Jab-Jab type of joke, oui.
>
> She was halfway into Guinea Land herself. She could call the spirits to help her. She wouldn't have to call very loudly. (221)

This passage describes an act of translation, if not transubstantiation: the "spirit tree," which Mami has taught Ti-Jeanne to think of as the transporter of souls from one world to the next, is translated in the future, first-world urban context to a contemporary building that once held the promise of urban economic growth and expansion. Now deserted by the monied interests that owned and controlled it, the building serves, appropriately enough, as a conduit that translates the victims of the ruthless expansionism that the building itself emblematizes from their spirit world into a context of militant intervention on Ti-Jeanne's behalf.

Brown Girl describes many other instances of cultural translation, most memorably the Ellisonian underworld of the subway system, which has been co-opted by street urchins. The Invisible Man's pointedly political co-optation of power from the electric company—an enterprise of the white male power structure—serves, ironically, to illuminate for the reader the curious *invisibility* of black subjectivity in a white world: "I have been carrying on a fight with Monopolated Light and Power for some time now. I use their service and pay them nothing at all, and they don't know it. Oh, they suspect that power is being drained off, but they don't know where" (5). Similarly, the street urchins' co-optation of the abandoned subway system illuminates one of the most tragic consequences of this future-world's urban decay: its abandoned children. In a key scene the street urchins, whom Ti-Jeanne and Mami have previously fed and given medical attention, rescue Ti-Jeanne from Rudy and his thugs. They pull Ti-Jeanne into their underground world, whose labyrinthine obscurity allows them to create the illusion of power in numbers. Although the street children survive in small, fragmented packs, they appear, through innovations of their own ingenious design, to be as legion as the masses that once filled the subways of the city. In the following scene, Josée, the leader of her group of orphaned children, explains how the children create the illusion of power:

> "Josée," Ti-Jeanne asked, "is what all you do? To fool Rudy, I mean?"
>
> Josée's grin was feral. "That was Mumtaz," she replied.
>
> A girl of about twelve returned the grin, flicking a hank of black hair out of her eyes. Her brown face was difficult to see in the dark of the tunnel. Her teeth gleamed. Mumtaz was carrying some sort of jury-rigged electronic box, about the size of a loaf of bread, held together with patchy layers of masking and electric tape. Ti-Jeanne could just make out toggle switches bristling from the top of it.
>
> "Listen," said Mumtaz. She flicked a switch, and Ti-Jeanne jumped as the tunnel filled with the din of hundreds of children screaming. She could discern the words "Die!" "Fuckers!" "Kill you!"
>
> Mumtaz shut off the noise. "I layered all our voices. That way, it sounds like there's more of us than there are."
>
> "And the visuals?" Ti-Jeanne could have sworn there'd been a good forty kids.

> "Deeplight projector hooked up on the subway tracks. I rigged it myself a long time ago. Keeps people out of our space. It's a tape I made of all of us, dubbed on six waves so it looks like a lot more." (185–86)

Like the Invisible Man, the street children use stolen power to counter their own vulnerability and invisibility. As they reveal in this scene, the children are the regular victims of Rudy's thirst for blood, a thirst inspired by the capitalist and sexist uses of his powers of obeah. Unlike Mami, Rudy uses his abilities for personal gain. Rudy has kept himself alive and powerful beyond his years by keeping the soul of his daughter (Ti-Jeanne's mother, Mi-Jeanne) in limbo. Mi-Jeanne, unable to comprehend the special powers she has inherited from her mother, turned her soul over to her father in Ti-Jeanne's childhood to ensure its protection. Her contained soul, called a "duppy," requires a steady diet of human sacrifices in order to empower Rudy. As the least visible, least valued, and therefore most dispensable group in the Ring, the street children provide an ideal source for Rudy's duppy's diet. But, like Ellison's Invisible Man, the children find some strength in the position of dispensability accorded them by the absent center—embodied in their case by the figure of Rudy, the agent of the (literally) heartless Premier. As Ellison's hero puts it, "It is sometimes advantageous to be unseen, though it is most often rather wearing on the nerves" (3).

Rudy's translation of obeah into the future's urban wasteland provides Hopkinson with another occasion to illuminate science fiction's capacity to literalize the symbolic: for, as the Ring's primary drug dealer and pimp, as well as a powerful practitioner of black magic, Rudy both literally and symbolically co-opts the souls of the disenfranchised urban minority. Although the Premier is appropriately vilified for her greed at the expense of the people of the Ring, it is Rudy who stands head and shoulders above the Premier as the Ring's primary source of destruction. As a nominal member of the underclass he exploits, Rudy understands the desires and weaknesses of his community and is therefore able to infiltrate and control the Ring in ways inaccessible to the absent center, despite its considerable power. The insidious nature of Rudy's controlling capacities is exemplified by Tony, whose addiction to 'buff guarantees his ultimate allegiance to Rudy, at the expense of his own family and his own health. Under Rudy's command, Tony must procure a heart for the Premier: in desperation, he chooses the heart of Mami, the community's healer.

Brown Girl explores and critiques the impact of globalized patriarchy as it is often translated in the black urban population. Rudy, an ageless, physically powerful, and charismatic force, exemplifies the patriarchy's particular powers of manipulation and control over the family and the community. A wife-beater and a pimp, a child-killer as well as the controller of his daughter's life, Rudy's destructive potential is heavily informed by his maleness. Under the patriarchy's influence, even sympathetic black men such as Tony become pawns in a game of power consolidation, a game inspired by Rudy's thralldom to the absent center that he at once emulates and reviles. Rudy, with his immense power, his black magic, and his exploitative agelessness, recalls Doro, the charismatically masculine figure in Octavia E. Butler's *Wild Seed*. Through Doro, Butler describes the ways in which patriarchy and colonization—especially in terms of the figurative and literal deployment of rape—exist as mutually productive and mutually sustaining ideologies. It falls to Anyanwu, the novel's heroine, to find a way to destroy the seemingly indestructible Doro. Like Ti-Jeanne, Anyanwu discovers that her intelligence—in this case, her powers of mind control—is her key defense against the brute strength of her oppressor.

In both novels, a supernatural power is accorded to the male and the female protagonist. And in both novels, men's abuse of that power follows a depressingly familiar oedipal pattern, one that Frantz Fanon describes succinctly in *The Wretched of the Earth*: "The look that the native turns on the settler's town is a look of lust, a look of envy" (39). The crux of Fanon's first chapter, "Concerning Violence," includes a masculine version of Lorde's and hooks's theses regarding the mirrored internalized sexism and racism that black women sometimes tragically share:

> The colonized man will first manifest this aggressiveness which has been deposited in his bones against his own people. . . . The settler's world is a hostile world, which spurns the native, but at the same time it is a world of which he is envious. We have seen that the native never ceases to dream of putting himself in the place of the settler—not of becoming the settler but of substituting himself for the settler. This hostile world, ponderous and aggressive because it fends off the colonized masses with all the harshness it is capable of, represents not merely a hell from which the swiftest flight possible is desirable, but also a paradise close at hand which is guarded by terrible watchdogs. (52–53)

Such is the paradoxical nature of the relationship between the oppressed and the oppressor—the oppressor flaunts his power conspicuously, both at the expense of the oppressed, as well as in a manner calculated to inspire his respect and envy. However, as Spillers points out, the capitalist, patriarchal imperatives of legal property ownership and the transfer of that property through the development of kinship lines (which, of course, necessitates the female's status as property) are not available to black men. And disenfranchised men under patriarchy, of any race or nationality, are liable to act out their feelings of powerlessness through abuse of their own families, as well as through more-generalized bids for control within their own communities. Butler's Doro recapitulates his people's colonization by attempting—through force when necessary—to sire a kinship line that shares his supernatural abilities. Rudy reinscribes his people's marginalization in the first-world urban sphere by attempting to destroy the women in his own family and by holding sway over his community through his illicit drug trafficking. Both protagonists seem to engage in the same process of attempted "substitution" that Fanon describes, and in both instances the attempted substitution involves the subjugation of women: in Doro's case, through the use of women as breeding stock; and in Rudy's case through the murder and prostitution of women. Such is the eminently *translatable* nature of capitalist patriarchal ideology.

Ultimately, Ti-Jeanne attributes her ability to outwit Rudy to her skills of survival and bravery, and not exclusively to her supernatural power—which, after all, both she and Rudy possess. Like the children of the memorable underworld of the Toronto subways, Ti-Jeanne's most profound strength is her capacity to adapt, to translate the legacy of her past into a strategy for survival in the near-future dystopia of the first-world urban wasteland. Through Ti-Jeanne, Hopkinson illustrates how the survival skills of the single black parent, well-honed through her exposure to the tyrannies of institutionalized racism and familial sexism, might translate into her best hope for the future. In *Sister Outsider*, Lorde makes the now often-quoted observation that "the master's tools will never dismantle the master's house" (123). She describes how the alienated class must create its own strategies for change by drawing on its own strengths and abilities. By valorizing the strengths and abilities available to a single, black, inner-city-dwelling mother, Hopkinson strongly suggests that it may well be the present-day "survivor," as Lorde puts it, who will be best equipped to survive the future.

In closing, I return to the image of the "alien native" that I suggested as a figure for the overdetermination of sexual and racial "Othering." In her essay on the relationship between science-fictional aliens and race-based alienation, Octavia E. Butler mused fancifully on the impact that "real" aliens might make on our globally divided culture:

> New siblings to rival. Perhaps for a moment, only a moment, this affront will bring us together, all human, all much more alike than different, all much more alike than is good for our prickly pride. Humanity, *E pluribus unum* at last, a oneness focused on and fertilized by certain knowledge of alien others. What will be born of that brief, strange, and ironic union? (416)

The idea that a real alien presence might bring humanity together in opposition to the alien is at once liberating and sobering. By suggesting such a configuration, Butler highlights the arbitrary nature of the divisions that our oedipal sibling rivalry seems to instill continually within us. Despite the simplifying clichés that the sentiment "we're all the same, under the skin" seems to imply, Butler risks expressing just this sentiment in order to consider the awesome potential of challenging the divisions that have been thrust upon us. That's what I find liberating about this suggested configuration. The sobering quality of this configuration—us, as in Humanity, versus the Aliens—is Butler's suggestion that our unity as a human race will still be predicated upon the presence of an Other. Thus we can easily imagine a situation in which the human race configures the aliens as the new oppressed class. Given our track record in relation to using divide and conquer as a strategy of oppression, it might be just as imperative as it is fanciful to imagine humanity's "certain knowledge of alien others," if only to recognize the potential for a collective response on the part of the oppressed to all repressive ideological systems.

Notes

1. See Giddings, *When and Where I Enter: The Impact of Black Women on Race and Sex in America.* See especially chapter 2, in which Giddings documents extensive evidence of slave women's use of abortives, contraceptives, and, less frequently, child homicide as means to resist their use as sexual slaves.

2. Davis, in her article "Surrogates and Outcast Mothers: Racism and Reproductive Politics in the Nineties," states: "While poor women in many states effectively have lost access to abortion, they may be sterilized with the full financial support of the government. While the 'right' to opt for surgical sterilization is an important feature of women's control over the reproductive functions of their bodies, the imbalance between the difficulty of access to abortions and the ease of access to sterilization reveals the continued and tenacious insinuation of racism into the politics of reproduction. The astoundingly high—and continually mounting—statistics regarding the sterilization of Puerto Rican women expose one of the most dramatic ways in which women's bodies bear the evidence of colonization. Likewise, the bodies of vast numbers of sterilized and indigenous women within the presumed borders of the US bear the traces of a 500-year-old tradition of genocide. While there is as yet no evidence of large-scale sterilization of African-American and Latina teenage girls, there is documented evidence of the federal government's promotion and funding of sterilization operations for young black girls during the 1960s and 70s" (217).

3. Chodorow's work is often critiqued for its overly totalizing claims and its failure to describe the implications of race, class, and nationality in regard to her thesis. For

an overview of this issue as it relates to the charge of "essentialism" in white feminist theory, see Frye's article "Ethnocentrism/Essentialism: The Failure of the Ontological Cure." Frye sees the constructive critique of Chodorow as useful and necessary, and her rejection as "essentialist" as an oversimplification. See also Chodorow's Preface to the Second Edition of *The Reproduction of Mothering,* in which she critically addresses the totalizing aspects of her work, especially pertaining to race and class (xi; xvi).

4. In her analysis of the gendered division of the international labor market, Brine elaborates on Swasti Mitter's research on the sexism of the transnational corporation: "Mitter describes the late twentieth-century use of free trade zones and export processing zones within newly industrialized countries, and also the enterprise zone sweatshops and outworking systems of the increasingly deregulated industrialized countries. Common to both is the exploitation of working-women's labour, and their gendered economic, political, and sexual oppression. The occupational, physical, and sexual exploitation and abuse of women working in free trade zones has also led to early prostitution and drug dependency. . . . Women are the cheapest and most 'flexible' source of labour within the industrialized colonizing countries, and even more so within the newly industrializing postcolonized countries" (40).

5. See Hartmann's "The Family as the Locus of Gender, Class, and Political Struggle: The Example of Housework." Although her statistics are outdated (the article was originally published in *Signs* in 1981), her basic feminist analysis of the mutually reinforcing relationship between the sexual politics of the family and the state unfortunately has remained current.

) **Works Cited**

Brine, Jacky. *Undereducating Women: Globalizing Inequality.* Buckingham and Philadelphia: Open University Press, 1999.

Butler, Octavia E. *Wild Seed.* New York: Warner Books, 1980.

Chodorow, Nancy. Preface to the Second Edition. *The Reproduction of Mothering.* Berkeley: University of California Press, 1999. vii–xvii.

———. *The Reproduction of Mothering.* Berkley: University of California Press, 1978.

Clifford, James. "The Translation of Cultures." In *Contemporary Literary Criticism,* ed. Robert Con Davis and Ronald Schleifer. New York: Longman, Inc., 1998. 679–94.

Davis, Angela. "Sick and Tired of Being Sick and Tired: The Politics of Black Women's Health." In *Women, Culture, and Politics.* New York: Random House, 1989. 53–65.

———. "Surrogates and Outcast Mothers: Racism and Reproductive Politics in the Nineties." In *The Angela Y. Davis Reader,* ed. Joy James. Boston: Blackwell, 1998. 210–21.

———. "Women and Capitalism: Dialectics of Oppression and Liberation." In *The Angela Y. Davis Reader,* ed. Joy James. Boston: Blackwell, 1998. 161–92.

———. *Women, Race, and Class.* New York: Random House, 1981.

Due, Tananarive. "Like Daughter." In *Dark Matter: A Century of Speculative Fiction from the African Diaspora,* ed. Sheree R. Thomas. New York: Warner Books, 2000. 91–102.

Ellison, Ralph. *Invisible Man.* New York: Random House, 1989.

Fanon, Frantz. *The Wretched of the Earth.* New York: Grove Press, 1963.

Frye, Marilyn. "Ethnocentrism/Essentialism: The Failure of the Ontological Cure." In *Is Academic Feminism Dead? Theory in Practice,* ed. *The Social Justice Group* at The Center for Advanced Feminist Studies, University of Minnesota. New York: New York University Press, 2000. 47–60.

Giddings, Paula. *When and Where I Enter: The Impact of Black Women on Race and Sex in America.* New York: Bantam Books, 1984.

Hartmann, Heidi I. "The Family as the Locus of Gender, Class, and Political Struggle: The Example of Housework." *Signs* 6 (1981): 366–94.

hooks, bell. "Revolutionary Black Women." In *Black Looks: Race and Representation.* Boston: South End Press, 1992. 41–60.

Hopkinson, Nalo. *Brown Girl in the Ring.* New York: Warner Books, 1998.

Jameson, Fredric. *Postmodernism, or The Cultural Logic of Late Capitalism.* New York: Verso, 1991.

Lorde, Audre. "Eye to Eye: Black Women, Hatred, and Anger." *Sister Outsider: Essays and Speeches.* Trumansburg, New York: Crossing Press, 1984. 145–75.

Marx, Karl. (1867). *Capital.* Trans. Ben Fowkes. New York: Penguin Classics, 1990.

McIntyre, Vonda. *Superluminal.* Boston: Houghton Mifflin, 1983.

Mitter, Swasti. *Common Fate, Common Bond: Women in the Global Economy.* London: Pluto Press, 1988.

Moynihan, Daniel Patrick. "The Negro Family: The Case for National Action." Washington, DC: U.S. Department of Labor, 1965.

Spillers, Hortense J. "Mama's Baby, Papa's Maybe: An American Grammar Book." In *The Women and Language Debate,* ed. Camille Roman, Suzanne Juhasz, and Cristanne Miller. New Brunswick: Rutgers University Press, 1994. 56–77.

Spivak, Gayatri. *Outside in the Teaching Machine.* New York: Routledge, 1993.

Walcott, Derek. *Ti-Jean and His Brothers. Plays for Today.* Ed. Errol Hill. Burnt Mill, Harlow, Essex: Longman House, 1985. 21–72.

JENNIFER E. HENTON

Close Encounters between Traditional and Nontraditional Science Fiction

Octavia E. Butler's Kindred *and Gayl Jones's* Corregidora *Sing the Time Travel Blues*

The presence of women within science fiction (SF) coincides with the requirement that the genre must maintain a sense of humor. I do not necessarily mean hilarity but, rather, the kind of open-minded humor that facilitates strange or unruly discussions. SF, after all, enables uteruses mysteriously to float all over female bodies and fans the fires of female psychoanalytic frenzies. The humor I describe allows us unabashedly to look into our own consciousness. Both Freud and Lacan reveal how jokes and women provide insight into our own "working over" of issues. SF potentially covers fissures that reveal the Other to be ourselves and adopts the stodgy attitudes and stiff regulations that often accompany canonization—dead white men belong; living women of color need to die in poverty. Instead of traveling down this road again, SF must retain its sense of humor with the understanding that humor arises from confronting the pleasure/pain of our existence, our *jouissance*. Humor enables SF to bring to light a troubled view of our industrialized society. It is now time to boldly go further.

While Lacan's theory of psychoanalysis remains useful for elucidating many feminist readings, his psycholinguistic analysis is particularly pertinent to SF. "Science fiction" seems synonymous with "jouissance" if only because of its insistence on "working through" scientific ideals until the ends unravel the means. Attempts to reduce SF empirically in light of its canonization tend to flatten its sense of humor. Free to define and redefine itself, SF seems predisposed to resistance and diversity. Indeed, Gwyneth Jones notes that SF "involving human exploitation of newly discovered planets [has] often sided with the natives" ("Metempsychosis" 3).[1] SF naturally includes such perspectives and, equally naturally, reflects the anxieties of the Other. The thinly disguised alien as woman or nonwhite or both—recall *King Kong* (1933) and *Alien* (1979)—remains exemplary in relation to fiction (Meyers 86). Just as science and fiction are historically rooted in disallowance (excluding or sacrificing racial/ethnic, sexual, and gender marginalities), newly developed versions of the genre remain marked by Lacanian lack. In other words: "why are there still so few Black, Hispanic or Asian SF writers in the USA, never mind in the world in general?" (Jones, "Metempsychosis" 8). I concurrently ask why, in the presence of a new surge of nonwhite writers of science fiction (such as Walter Mosley, Steven Barnes, Maryse Conde, Nalo Hopkinson, and LeVar Burton) do strident moves toward defining the field seem like "refining" the field?

Instituting another type of "science,"—canonization or standards of greatness/validity—offers a new exactitude or a linguistic rigidity whereby SF becomes a genre that necessarily excludes all but somewhat Western voices. Alone, SF potentially plays within Lacanian resistance to exactitude. SF exposes the fissures in natural science: SF relies on a concept of the "real" or that which we know will always appear in the same place and yet remains impossibly situated outside of our control (Lacan, *Seminar Book II*; hereafter abbreviated *SII*; 298–99). Perhaps SF should remain analogous to the ego in Lacanian discourse, a process rather than a static entity. Attempts to define "valid" SF texts will necessarily solidify its nebulous Diaspora, elide disparities in the field that I view as being potential sites of cognitive dissonance which expose the hoax of scientific order/exactitude. SF potentially parallels the fantasy-structuring work of the ego—that is to say, the Western ego—inherent in exact science according to Lacan's discussion of cybernetics and psychoanalysis. My discussion will therefore err on the side of inclusiveness. First, I articulate a newly broadened understanding of SF that enables the genre to incorporate marginalized Other voices. Then, with my expanded conception of SF in mind, I exemplify the inclusiveness I intend by reading Octavia E. Butler's *Kindred* (1979), which is unquestionably a SF text, in terms of Gayl Jones's *Corregidora* (1975), now freshly positioned as SF. I make it possible for a black woman's traditionally science-fictional text to closely encounter a black woman's text that has never before boldly gone within genre SF. Butler and Jones are black SF ladies who sing the time travel blues.

◗ Opening the Borders of Science Fiction
Psychohistory as Time Travel

By further expanding the already burgeoning SF genre, we also make a joke of it. We make the field impossible to control or contain, to show where "science" functions in the "imaginary." SF reveals where it is possible to expose the ego; it circumvents our desire to organize and orchestrate our disjointed selves, histories, and beliefs into an identifiable framework. Blurring generic boundaries provides "time" and "space" for subjugated voices, that is, time and space for articulation via a different sense of order. I refer to the improvisation, disorderliness, and rhythm of the calculated structure called "the blues." Lacan destabilizes the privilege we assign to "exact" sciences and may loosen the myopic vision of productivity/life/future. Readers may not want to permanently adhere to an expansive view of SF. However, when doing so, they may glimpse a vision of what SF writers have tried to articulate: a wariness of Western values and a diverse and cooperative utopia.

For Lacan, exact science relies upon a rubric of psychological perception: "the exact sciences do nothing other than tie the real to a syntax" (*SII* 305). SF exposes science's connection to language, its "working through" of formulas and equations, exposing how our egos coordinate disunities and discrepancies. For my purposes, canonization of SF may mean neatly concealing this disruptive language. Canonization may mean hiding the potential in SF to expose desires toward the Other or the "radical Other" in Lacan's schema, which enables the symbolic order and human speech: "the human being has a special relation with his own image—a relation of gap, of alienating tension. That is where the possibility of the order of a presence and absence, that is of the symbolic order, comes in" (*SII* 323). Indeed, SF enables the novice to jokingly undercut what science seriously pursues in the name of "progress." With recent forays into cloning and genetic food production, the questioning nature of jokes is sorely needed.

Given leeway, SF works both backward and forward in a manner similar to Lacan's and Freud's discussion of jokes and dreams working both backward and forward in psychotemporal realms. If SF critiques the exact sciences for failing to admit their construct, canonizing SF stands poised to make the same mistake as science itself: defining true SF as that which enacts "exact" science as *the science* (i.e., progressive, linear, logical) upon which the literature must be based.

"From the moment man thinks that the great clock of nature turns all by itself and continues to mark the hour even when he isn't there, the order of science is born" (*SII* 298). According to Lacan, science may seem like an order differentiated from religion and superstition. He also comments upon the "hard" sciences: "And like the slave, [man] tries to make the master dependent on him by serving him well" (*SII* 298). "Science," strictly defined, holds linguistic bias toward Western epistemology. Darko Suvin, in *Metamorphoses of Science Fiction* (1979), reflects this Lacanian interpretation. "The world of a work of SF is not a priori intentionally oriented toward its protagonist, either positively or negatively; the protagonist may succeed or fail in their objectives, but nothing in the basic contract with the reader, in the physical laws of their worlds, guarantees either. SF thus shares with the dominant literature of our civilization a mature approach analogous to that of *modern science and philosophy*, as well as the omni temporal horizons of such an approach" (Suvin 11; italics mine). This "maturity" seems unconstructed and derived from the human frailty of desire, perhaps stemming from less "civilized" understandings of the world in which motives and fears seem more apparent. By virtue of this "maturity," SF admits constructs of Western objectivity into its purview—constructs that are so many tenets of "hard" science. Maybe people of color adhere to these laws in order to earn a place within the mature fields of science, philosophy, and literature (which now include SF literature). But the ideal still excludes Other sciences, sensibilities, and ways of knowing.

There are risks involved with opening SF to the broadest margins. On the one hand, Gwyneth Jones predicts that "as a result of the twenty-first-century folklore effect compounded by current literary theory, we will see a further blurring of the line between mainstream fiction and SF, to the extent that the fiction of the constructed world may even become as respectable as that other, more favored non-realist genre, 'magical realism'" (*Deconstructing* 7). On the other hand, for linguist Walter E. Meyers, even such a respected SF writer as Samuel R. Delany can be "just wrong" according to formal linguistic order (179).[2] Such criticism highlights disparate views of SF that range from loose manifestations to stringent adherence to exact order. Delany's *Babel-17* (1966) seems "wrong"—non-science-fictional— and Gabriel García Márquez' *One Hundred Years of Solitude* (1967) stands on the brink of inclusion within SF when we understand the discussion as grounded in language—that is, as definition. In the middle, falling between these borders, sit the peculiar contributions of oppressed groups who have manifested a *funny*, more in the sense of peculiar than humorous, relationship to the master discourse.

SF covertly masks the displacement of our own troublesome relation to women, people of color, nature, technology, and other groups by using extraterrestrial aliens to function as stand-ins for despised Others. Failed SF—transparent attempts to show science gone "native"—is usually expressed via the worry that extraterrestrial aliens will do to us what we have done to them.[3] I perhaps refer to what Ed Guerrero calls "the return of the repressed."[4] SF becomes the dream/nightmare that cradles our inner imaginings. The genre highlights unruly connections that science both makes and masks; SF can sabotage the order of things.[5] As Madelyn Jablon notes, black authors often "introduce history into genres that are often thought to be ahistorical" (165). Yet SF remains reflective: "Tell me what you think is going to happen tomorrow, and I'll tell you what is happening to you today" (Jones, *Deconstructing* 16). My version of Jones's comment: tell me what is happening to you today, and I will tell you what happened to you before. Jones best expresses the issue when she states, "Science fiction is never ahistorical" and "[i]nevitably, the cultures and landscapes annexed in imagination have been largely identical with the cultures and landscapes of those annexed, exploited territories known until recently as the Third World" ("Metempsychosis" 2–3).

The issue, then, becomes one that clarifies the terrain of Western psychology, a "space" where female, black, and subaltern identities have been carved out well before the time when technology became "sexy." Junior Viviane, a protagonist of Toni Morrison's *Love* (2003), possesses both "'Save This Child'" eyes (66) and "sci-fi eyes" (114). Morrison's descriptors reify the axiom where science and third-world/black women intersect. Since SF is so deeply connected to the Other, it is logical to widen its boundaries to include different voices. Broadly defining SF orders its disorder, privileges its relation to and dependency on exact or "natural" sciences—and makes the genre speak to us in the same old way. To be sure, Isaac Asimov sees SF (or, more exactly, the public's new "fascination" with science [88]) emerging after the inception of the use of poison gas during World War I (122). Asimov depicted this fascination in *The Roving Mind* (1983) when he imagined that people could travel in energy-saving vehicles.

Asimov's novel exemplifies Jones's notion that "[w]e write about 'our own' present, and other people's pasts" (Jones, "Metempsychosis" 6). Curiously enough, this view had always entailed the bulk of Western travel/exploits. If we wish to include black and subaltern identities within this Western perspective, we need to consider the raw material of technology that existed before machines remade mass productivity. When we do, we blur SF's definitive "invention." We could, alternatively, ask the alien how it feels. We could listen to the land before using it. And, we could think about the world before we invade it.

Mary Shelley's *Frankenstein* (1818), an example of pregenre "science fiction," depicts the "alien" in ways unparalleled by "pulp" SF.[6] Possibilities for marginalized groups to participate in SF spring from within this alternative viewpoint. The field could expand to include works such as Pauline Hopkins's *Of One Blood* (1903), Ishmael Reed's *Mumbo Jumbo* (1973), and

Toni Morrison's *Beloved* (1988). The genre can willingly "go native." Though SF at first gained popularity as a source of entertainment for young white boys,[7] it must be realized that blacks were writing SF—and humorous SF at that—as early as the Harlem Renaissance. In *Black No More* (1931), George Samuel Schuyler insists upon poking fun at both white and black America, as he did in "The Negro-Art Hokum" (1926). The joke currently continues whenever blacks engage SF discourse.

John Akomfrah's film *The Last Angel of History* (1996) connects African-American SF "stars"—such as Nichelle Nichols and Samuel R. Delany—to narratives linking pan-African, postcolonial funk music (I think of George Clinton) and experience to intergalactic travel. When doing so, Akomfrah articulates science and history as closely paralleling each other within the black Diaspora. Instead of duplicating the linear narratives of science which emerge from Western history (as is common in colonialist discourse), Akomfrah's film highlights the humorous nature of black experience, that is to say, its bizarre, irrational, illogical, and "already *out* there" traits. During the eighteenth and nineteenth centuries, the West used "science" to validate outrageous racial hierarchies and atrocious acts of domination—and Sheree R. Thomas stresses that Africa has long been a major source of speculation for Westerners (xiii).[8] Many nineteenth-century scholars have produced their own "science fictions" which emanate from their spurious constructs of blackness.[9] Science's erasure of the Other historically exposes "Western" scientific ideals as inventions, or constructs. Its discoveries become steeped in the black bodies used to get "there" (consider the Tuskegee Syphilis Experiment, for example). Science and fiction have clearly interacted within Western discourses even before the SF genre came to fruition.

SF opens rather than closes speculations: "magical realism," or voodoo/mumbo jumbo, functions as different ways of seeing and explaining the world by incorporating "scientific" knowledge derived from Other groups.[10] For example, Isabelle Allende's *The House of Spirits* (1985), Arundhati Roy's *The God of Small Things* (1997), and Gabriel García Márquez' *One Hundred Years of Solitude* (1970) portray fantastic events merging with historical and political turmoil. These works can be taught in conjunction with such traditional SF texts as H. G. Wells's *The Time Machine* (1895). SF critics might do well to heed the words of Ann duCille, who states that scholars should not ask texts to adhere to their own sense of "truth." According to duCille, "'[T]ruth' is generally held to be a false standard by which to evaluate a writer's work" (560). Every writer from every conceivable group has access to the imagination, and different cultural groups will determine different sciences and fictions to articulate their differing histories.

These differences cause "SF" to become a vacuous term, a designation that includes everything and, hence, signifies nothing. The gesture toward an inclusive SF might prove to be interesting, however. Is SF ready for a "working through"?[11] Are we ready to confront the way SF coordinates our disjointed selves? SF reveals the uneven nature of perceptions and psychic energy; the genre directs our ego toward accomplishing the hardest task—self-analysis.

A funny kind of discussion, then, risks stretching SF to the point of unrecognizability.[12] The parameters of this discussion will not be exclusively concerned with SF as it is presently defined. It is crucial to understand the scientific and historical as psychologically transient devices at work in the African-American imagination. Butler's *Kindred* and Jones's *Corregidora* illustrate a psychohistorical vehicle that underscores the importance of time travel in both stories. Both Jones and Butler write on the brink of the backlash against liberalism, near the close of a second Black Renaissance when black power movements created an atmosphere of realism and resistance. Their two novels access time travel via the psychohistorical device of black creation: the blues. An internal expression that becomes external, the blues made it possible for blacks to travel in the mid to late nineteenth century. These novels potentially lead SF into a speculative arena in which the genre opens to the past—perhaps the time it has longed for most fervently.

Lacan's notion that science itself is an organizing principle informed by the way humans narrate (organize) their internal perceptions can enable SF to open itself to new frontiers. My intent is not to apply Lacan—as if psychoanalytical theory "applies" to African-Americans or African-American culture.[13] Instead—following the late Claudia Tate's *Psychoanalysis and Black Novels: Desire and the Protocols of Race* (1998) and Hortense Spillers' "interior intersubjectivity"—Jones and Butler open the possibility for comparison within the unique African-American experience of time travel.

Jones and Butler diverge. In Butler's text, time travel is achieved by way of memory; Jones describes time travel occurring via dematerialization and materialization. They both situate time travel as the crux of subjectivity and interior space. As the protagonists narrate their "stories," time travel mediates their experience via their ancestors: Butler's Edana Franklin (Dana) of *Kindred* can time-travel because of her great-great-grandfather's force, and Jones's Ursula Corregidora (Ursa) experiences her great-grandmother's force similarly. The protagonists travel along the axioms of time, history, and self. Both *Kindred* and *Corregidora* insist upon establishing a connection to the past—or *sankofa* (a return to the past) (Mitchell 72)—as a requisite for the present and future's existence. Both do so within frameworks that recall the blues. *Kindred* and *Corregidora* become kindred through this link; a SF novel and a novel that has not been defined as SF have affinities. The generative power of this meeting opens SF to the recursive horror and humor of time travel, what I call black people's traveling blues.

Kindred as Science Fiction

Greg Tate says that "[t]hrough writing, I can verify my experience . . . I have put some of my ideas together from outside information . . . they're definitely about the larger relationships . . . to the moon, the tides, and you know, mystery cycles" (218). I turn to Tate to illuminate my point that it may seem funny or obvious to claim that Butler's *Kindred* is science fiction. Robert Crossley, in his Introduction to *Kindred*, observes that it is not typical SF in that "a psycho-historical force, not a feat of engineering motivates Butler's plot" (x). In this vein, Frederik Pohl writes that "science fiction is not, is *positively not*, fantasy" (11). Butler herself denied that *Kindred* is SF, referring to her work as fantasy (Kenan 495). But then again she said, "I don't like the labels, they're marketing tools, and I certainly don't worry about them when I'm writing" (qtd. in Kenan 495).

When defining *Kindred* as SF, many scholars are willing to forgive the absence of the traditional slew of SF qualifications. Tate points out where writing becomes a formula for self-retrieval, a literary device that functions as a "working through" of white Western forgetfulness; this device reminds the mad scientist of what he opportunistically forgot. Instead of excluding *Kindred* from definitions of SF, perhaps scholars should include this interior intersubjectivity subset of African-American letters and cultural expression which rely upon repeated connections to explicate a story that is all too elliptical and invisible in Western narratives. These connections are often "humored" because they don't follow scientific or linear trajectories. Adhering to this line of thought, Dana Franklin must make inferences—invisible, internal connections—to validate her experience. Like the blues, Dana's travels follow rhythm rather than linear/exact measurements: "The intervals between trips don't mean anything" (244)—but those intervals definitely adhere to Dana's narrative.

In *Kindred*, Dana lives during 1976. Her great-great-grandfather, Rufus Weylin, calls her back to a time span ranging approximately from 1815 to the early 1830s. Dana, an African-American woman, travels through time and space whenever Rufus's life is in danger. (He is a white American, and he calls her psychically, internally, and impulsively.) Dana literally becomes primitively bound and enslaved by a psychosomatic-like device that moves her to remember the miseries of slavery. As she travels back to antebellum Maryland, her narrative expands, growing in concentric circles until a final break between Dana and Rufus's strange bond occurs.

Dana's travels at first seem to be superficial; when she arrives in the past, she is only acting (98). A reversal occurs near the conclusion of her travels. Dana only play-acts during her own time period, and she feels a disconcerting commingling of pleasure/pain (or *jouissance*) when she travels back to the nineteenth century.

"The longer Dana lives on Rufus' plantation, the more she learns, empirically, about pain and suffering" (Govan 86). Crucially, fantasy is the only means to gain firsthand, empirical knowledge of antebellum America. Dana's slave past becomes her reality, displacing 1976 pseudoliberty. The ability to rationalize and make sense of Dana's two worlds becomes more fragmented and dismembered as she frequents the past and experiences its brutalities. Dana, as opposed to many other characters who travel through time, learns how much she can endure as a nonsubject.

Meanwhile, Dana's true mobility depends upon the dissemination of her time travel mobility. Rufus's death restores Dana's physical movement permanently: his death marks the end of her ability to circumvent time. She can again live as a normal, non–time traveling woman. Thus Butler enables readers to see the striking difference between travel for black women in the twentieth century and in the antebellum South. For people of color, travel holds special significance. The impossibility of time travel frees Dana—a striking refutation of time travel as techno-advancement. Not only have writers of color struggled with physical immobility in an oppressive environment, but, by way of immobility, their work also emerges from a tradition of disenfranchisement. As Angela Y. Davis points out, the blues enabled many place-bound postslavery blacks to "travel." For newly freed blacks, the blues enabled the present to eclipse the future for the sake of laying claim to virtual privileges within denigrating silences. Madhu Dubey calls this displacement "cultural disinheritance" (2). The inability to become owners and other conditions of racism plagued the few outlets open to blacks. Getting one's people "on the move," which blues "travel" often inspired, remained steeped in the difficulties inherent in mental and physical mobility.[14]

Blacks' place in America, mediated by literal and figurative transportations/rites of passage, takes its shape from the Middle Passage, Reconstruction, the Black Renaissance, and the civil rights movement. The process continues by way of the debate over slavery reparations and institutionalized racism. Struggles with the past remain a constant. The perpetual and repetitive regrouping of a past that is often marginally addressed or minimally acknowledged creates what Dubey calls the "tradition as a necessary fiction" (2). The persistence of the slave narrative into the twenty-first century attests to this necessity. This tradition, this interior intersubjectivity, can be understood to be a metaphorical device that moves black narrative logic between the present and the past in order to better understand the present and future.

On the surface, Dana's narrative occurs in the past tense: "I *lost* an arm" (1). "Kevin and I *had not planned*" (12). "I *was* working out of a casual labor agency" (52) (my emphasis). Dana narrates *Kindred* in retrospect, past perfect: she *had not* done. Even in the epilogue Dana says, "We flew to Maryland as soon as my arm was well enough" (262). *Kindred* disallows the present.

Kindred's "recall" format emphasizes that Dana's memory is integral to physical and emotional survival. Perhaps what is most striking about Dana's reminder to the young Rufus—"People don't learn everything about the times that came before them . . . Why should they" (63)—is that both Dana and Ursa remind readers about black women's long history and culture from which they speak as subjects.[15] "History" deems that Other sciences, discoveries, and events are uncivilized, primitive or—even worse—nonexistent.[16] Dana jars the reader's awareness—and so too for her husband, Kevin; for Rufus and his father; and for Alice and the other slaves. Dana's survival depends upon her telling the right person the right information at the right time—especially the reader.

For example, when Dana first begins to time-travel, she mentions twice that she must remember things for Kevin: "I *remembered* it for him in detail" and "I went back to the beginning, to the first dizziness, and *remembered* it all for him" (46, 15; my emphasis). The fact that it is Dana and not Kevin who can time-travel privileges her black female history and underscores the psychological "device" as reflective of how Western narratives of identity have elliptically annexed certain ethnic perspectives. Dana must educate Kevin and the reader, and this necessity may account for the text's didactic tone. Reluctantly, Dana "move[s] closer to him, relieved, content with even such grudging acceptance . . . He couldn't have known how much I needed him firmly on my side" (47).

Kevin's understanding remains tenuous. And, because Rufus's primary education is derived from the time period in which he resides, Dana can merely impart peripheral understanding to him. Her communications with both men deteriorates and merely echo each other. She can no longer talk to Rufus when he becomes an adult or to Kevin when her experience in the past deepens. Hence, her hopes of influencing the antebellum South dissolve. "He's no good," Dana regretfully explains to the slave woman Carrie. "He's all grown up now, and part of the system. He could feel for us a little when his father was running things—when he wasn't entirely free himself" (223). Rufus has too much power; Dana has too little. She suggests that he free his children and the other slaves and that he allow her to continue schooling the slave children. Only some of her suggestions are followed.

In the manner of a blues song, Dana's power to narrate represents the great divide separating black subjectivity from Western history's gaps and lacks and the privileging of mainstream American perception. On one occasion, Dana takes Kevin back through time where they observe slave children playing "slave sale." While Dana walks away in disgust, Kevin continues to watch. He accuses her of "reading too much into a kid's game." She responds: "You're reading too little into it" (100). Dana, reflecting the blues, mourns the cruelty of the game. Kevin, like history, remains *removed, objective, neutral*. His body is not at stake.

When Dana tries to tell Kevin what Rufus's potential rape of her would mean, she knows "[h]e didn't understand" (246). As a male, and as a white male, he does not have the capacity to understand *her* body politics. Unlike Dana, Kevin has not had to "pimp" a black woman's body to ensure his lineage. The threat of being enslaved or indentured does not touch him.

Most importantly, the blues cannot be taught: Dana's experience is not didactic. Her method of coming to terms with Rufus and Kevin blurs. She must confront and understand their striking similarity: "The words echoed strangely in my head" (213). Their *tone* parallels in *sound* to her, almost like synchronizing diverse instruments. *Corregidora* sings the blues too.

Corregidora's Blues as Time Travel

In *Black Skin, White Masks* (1967) Franz Fanon addresses how black subjectivity is attacked by presumptions of substandard existence—a present moment "freed" of self-conscious history: "When it comes to the case of the Negro. . . . [h]e has no culture, no civilization, no 'long historical past'" (34). Imagining one's own subjectivity in terms of history becomes a feat of science and fiction in the African-American Diaspora. Morrison's *Playing in the Dark* (1992) explores the ellipses-like knowledge that American letters foster. But early African-American literature remains marked by a lack—that is, by what could not be said, written, or sung. More modern works such as *Roots, Jubilee,* and *Beloved* reconstruct history by incorporating both fact and fiction. The ability to claim and write from historical subjectivity is both a recent and a futuristic design. This connection clarifies Butler's portrayal of time travel in terms of the blues and Jones's understanding of the blues as time travel. When Crossley notes that *Kindred* "looms behind every American slave narrative" (xi), he provides an appropriate means to begin to read *Corregidora* in terms of *Kindred*.

In *Kindred* and *Corregidora,* the time travel mechanism is interior— Dana and Ursa both use psychological device to literally and figuratively (respectively) time-travel. The protagonists' emotions and desires defy the orderly assumptions about the rigor and formality of science in Wells's *The Time Machine.* Adam McKible offers this observation about contemporary black women writers: "The 'privilege' of this marginalization is a consciousness that defies the purported truthfulness of History, a perspective that envisions *Truth* as a fictionalized assemblage and erasure of events rather than as a factual representation of actual social or historical relations" (224). History and subjectivity, two very tenuous spaces for blacks and women, lie at the core of their narratological voice. Dana and Ursa time-travel to the past in acts of self-discovery, which relate to their subjective history.

Corregidora simultaneously explores Ursa's slave ancestry and her marital past. The narrative describes Ursa's hysterectomy, her marriages, and her grandmothers' enslavement. This space of "many African American women's texts" insists upon "the contemporaneity of history" (McKible 229). Ursa narrates accounts of her life before and after her violent argument with her husband, Mutt Thomas. Like Dana, she uses the past tense to express herself. She, in fact, describes *everything* in the past tense.

Women become collective history in *Corregidora.* The process of remembering at once refutes the past as portraiture and both literally and figuratively gives birth to *Corregidora.* If the blues speaks that which is silenced or ignored, then *Corregidora* reinvents history. Corregidora, the surname of the man who owned Ursa's ancestors, eclipses the linguistic "spotlight." *Corregidora* repeats and highlights his barbarity in place of what he accomplished, owned, and conquered. The women's narrative creates the meaning of Corregidora; the man's horror becomes fully articulated. Although Corregidora's name is the title of Jones's novel, the female protagonists tell his story and, by doing so, undo the tradition of "his"tory. Although the text centralizes Corregidora's name, it remains excruciatingly difficult for readers to sympathize with him.

Ursa's great-grandmother (Dorita), her unnamed grandmother, and her mother (Irene), inscribe "her"story through "making generations." By giving birth to children who can bear witness, the women (with the exception of Ursa) do *their* thinking and remembering (22); they "leave evidence" (14) of Corregidora's atrocities. The women's experience plays out in a distinctly African-American tradition. Ursa's text is a blues novel (Sharpe 306) that comes into being because she sings to the reader, reproducing a chorus of her mothers' voices.[17]

Ursa's incessant repetition produces a text where there was none, just as her foremothers produced children where there was no "history."

Initially, Ursa's power to bear witness is removed when the doctors perform an emergency hysterectomy. She cannot bear witness by having children, and she initially feels as though she can't even "fuck" (90). Ursa breaks free by claiming the blues as her power to reproduce. This act enables her to express sexual desire with her mouth; she performs fellatio on Mutt at the end of *Corregidora*. "Ursa and Mutt perform the sexual ambiguity that the blues articulate" (Sharpe 323). The novel does more than reclaim "stolen property," however.

The blues is a tradition forged in the African-American experience, which is meant to speak the unspeakable. As Leon Forrest says when describing Billie Holiday, the blues lets black folks know that "your grief was being articulated and that the common plight of your ordinariness, and the commonness of your pain was being transformed into the uncommon" (357). Jones brilliantly affirms this quality when the unnamed mother becomes the key to the continuation of the women's narrative. Dorita's daughter or Irene's mother (Ursa's grandmother) is the one who enjoys the blues, a ritual/performance form that Ursa will grow up to practice in place of bearing children. Importantly, critics often overlook the grandmother's namelessness.[18] It is she, the nameless one, who is able to take pleasure from what Christina E. Sharpe calls the possibility of nonreproductive remembrance—the blues (307). Ursa thinks, "Mama's Christian songs, and Grandmama—wasn't it funny—it was Grandmama who liked the blues" (103). Ursa says that the blues "help me to explain what I can't explain" (56). Indeed, it is the grandmother who cannot express what Corregidora does to her: "Then he was raising me and doing you know I said what he did" (79).[19] The grandmother speaks only through possession; she is possessed when she articulates Dorita's experiences of rape and prostitution.

Dorita's story becomes the mouthpiece for the mass experience of Corregidora's monstrous behavior. Because the blues expresses the tradition of the inexpressible and gives voice to the masses, the grandmother remains appropriately unnamed. The grandmother, who does not sing the blues, listens to them—and introduces Ursa to them. The grandmother is the last family member to know Corregidora—and the first one to know freedom. She falls in between worlds in an immutable position of shame and passion. Truly embodying the blues, she emerges at a moment after the past has "burned" and before "utopia" arrives. Her passing evokes Ursa's strongest tie to the blues. Ursa and her grandmother decenter patriarchal norms by using their engagement with the blues to liberate themselves.

Forged in the tradition of speaking for that which is unspeakable, *Corregidora* marks the difference between its own expression of the past and written "factoid"-driven history in the West, where the winners are the writers and suppliers of history.[20] Deemed objective and honest enough to write and supply history to/for those who do not historicize in the same way, or to/for those who have been purposely silenced, *Corregidora* becomes a performative remembrance, a psychohistory of personal testifying and contesting. What is contested is precisely what R. Radhakrishnan calls the promise of "Science-Reason-Technology based internationalism (based on unilinear chronology of developmental time)" (756).

Corregidora cannot be defined as a time travel novel merely because it engages the past and the blues. Instead, Jones's novel can be understood as time travel because of the plurality of black subjectivity. More specifically, in *Corregidora*, the vocalization of the past incessantly repeats itself as three generations of women articulate their respective stories. This form of communication is as old as Africa—and therein lies its survival. The text reverses the outwardly ahistorical and apolitical façade surrounding the African-American experience. *Corregidora* forces us to travel and to hear the black women's experiences which have been "e-raced" and evaded for centuries. The blues makes possible an interior, intersubjective travel. The resulting text enables the minority voice to move from margin to center—and all in the name of the father. Lacan's notion that one speaks only when one has the time to do so is crucial for understanding *Corregidora* as science fiction. In Jones's novel, the past makes it possible for those who inhabit the present to have time to vocalize their essences. The past Other returns from repression through present voices.

Conclusion

Kindred and *Corregidora* become SF when the boundaries of SF do not adequately encompass the types of experience that qualify as extraterrestrial SF. Radhakrishnan writes that "teaching Conrad without teaching Chinua Achebe is as much bad faith as it is bad scholarship" (767). Perhaps the burgeoning SF field will not need such rejoinders. Instructors who bring *The Creature from the Black Lagoon* (1954) into the classroom can fruitfully illuminate it by referring to *Brother from Another Planet* (1984).

To be sure, SF should not become what it seeks to dismantle—that is, a set of rules or boundaries that limit human imagination and growth. My comparison of *Kindred* and *Corregidora* pushes that faulty boundary— admittedly perhaps too far. But why should SF writers have more fun than critics? Narrow constraints will cause SF to haunt its own ontological taxonomy. The idea that African-Americans have not been participating in SF is a joke that reveals the tendency to repeat old errors over and over again. Stodgy attitudes and stiff regulations were once responsible for perpetuating such wrong-headed notions as America has no literature and Africa has no civilization. The immutability of black women's experiences as slave subjects acquires reality-defying characteristics when *Kindred* and *Corregidora* insist that we must revisit the past in order to understand the present and imagine a future. We are not alone. Someone else *is* already here.

Notes

1. The Douen people (Hopkinson, *Midnight Robber* 2000) provide a good example.

2. Meyers at once lauds and finds fault with Delany's linguistic accuracy.

3. In *The Matrix* (1999) humans are "farmed" in the manner of plants, animals, and minerals. The matrix functions like the Western narratives (ideology) of science and history which cause participants to become complacent and complicit.

4. Guerrero argues in *Framing Blackness: The African American Image in Film* (1993) that reading the "monster in the horror, sci-fi, and fantasy genres [signals] the incessant return of those repressed fears and problems that society cannot articulate or cope with openly" (59).

5. See Lacan, *Seminar Book II.* Lacan considers exact sciences in "Psychoanalysis and cybernetics, or on the nature of language."

6. Butler explained that SF describes common precepts about space aliens that parallel immigrant aliens: "In earlier science fiction there tended to be a lot of conquest: you land on another planet and you set up a colony and the natives have their quarters some place and they come in and work for you. There was a lot of that, and it was, you know, let's do Europe and Africa and South America all over again" (Kenan 498).

7. Mchaffy and Keating note, in "'Radio Imagination': Octavia Butler on the Poetics of Narrative Embodiment," that for "many years, science fiction was written by, primarily, 'white' men for 'white' male adolescents. With very few exceptions, women of any color did not write science fiction, female characters were in general portrayed as sex objects, and men of color rarely wrote or appeared in science fiction novels or stories" (46).

8. See Gilman's discussion (*Difference and Pathology* 1985) of how race is scientifically validated. Moreover, "nineteenth-century racial scientists hoped to prove that the African race was inherently inferior" (Gotanda 261).

9. The remains of the Hottentot Venus, which can be understood as early colonial "science fiction," were released from "scientific purposes" in France in January 2002.

10. Hurston's *Tell My Horse* (1938) explores the religious facets of voodoo culture in Haiti. She discusses the scientific nature of "graveyard dust" and other roots and elements that at once "work" in voodoo culture and lack Western scientific validation. Similarly, Reed's *Mumbo Jumbo* (1972) simultaneously validates and disparages voodoo culture via futuristic talking androids and historical revisionism.

11. See Lacan, *Seminar Book I,* "Working through" (187). Lacan is useful here to denote the myriad possible ways that SF may emphasize what we think we know and the boundaries we consider to be established. According to Jones, "[t]he ideal language of science fiction can never be natural, it has to be worked over" (*Deconstructing* 10).

12. Lacan notes that "if planets and other things of the same order spoke, it would make a funny kind of discussion" (*SII* 240). His statement signals how science conforms to our own order in terms of our temporal fantasies of the real. Why don't planets speak? Because they haven't got the *time*. But this perception is derived from Western epistemology. Lacan's provocative question indicates the dependency of psychoanalysis on interstices of time and space—elements that inform science fiction.

13. Spillers states that "the Freudian and Lacanian fields of discourse are not only separated from each other by considerable disparity in time, conditions of material culture, and the narrative and conceptual modalities that would situate and explain them, but also, because they reach subject formation by an act of poetic faith that imagines subjectivity hermetically sealed off from other informing discourses and practices, both are foreign, if not inimical, to subject formations defined by the suppression of discourse" (142). Lacan indicates the limits of Western subjectivity; Spillers approaches Freudian and Lacanian analysis in terms of the need to derive influence from different groups and epistemologies.

14. Wheatley's "On Imagination" (173–74) provides a pertinent example. Even though Wheatley was enslaved, she was "free" to explore her apolitical subjectivity. Though deferred and displaced, her imagination claims mythical proportions and connections to timelessness. Freedom, though, crippled her poetic voice when her physical mobility became subject to social, financial, and psychological oppression. Similarly, Dana is "free" when she loses her ability to move through time and space while she is chained to the present moment.

15. In Kenan's interview, Butler mentioned that *Kindred* was meant to remind all readers in general and African-Americans in particular of that long history: "people were feeling ashamed of, or more strongly, angry with their parents for not having improved things faster" (496). Butler echoed the sentiment Hopkins expresses (*Of One Blood*) where the protagonist, medical student Reuel Briggs, wants to disassociate himself from his African past.

16. For example, in their recent film history textbook, Ellis and Wexman say this about Canadian film: "Canada's quest to develop a strong national cinematic identity has also been hampered by its history—*or lack of it*. Unlike the United States, which has endured the Revolutionary War in the eighteenth century and the Civil War in the nineteenth century, Canada has known only peace since the European settlement" (423; my emphasis). The authors problematically imply that "history" occurs only within the context of Western contact and violence.

17. Jones mentions in an interview that the text began as a "sort of song" (Harper 357).

18. Their names are not used often. In "Angry Arts: Silence, Speech, and Song in Gayl Jones's *Corregidora*," Gottfried notes that "the only formal name Jones gives these women is their rapist's surname" (560). In "These Are the Facts of the Darky's History: Thinking History and Reading Names in Four African American Texts," McKible focuses solely on Corregidora's name, not the names of the women.

19. Near the conclusion of *Corregidora* (172), Grandmama states that "he fucked her and he fucked me." In this one instance, Grandmama does articulate what Corregidora has done to her. However, the storytelling remains focused on Dorita's experi-

ence. Grandmama's failure to narrate her own horror stories is emphasized when Ursa fellates Mutt: "It was like I didn't know how much was me and Mutt and how much was Great Gram and Corregidora—like Mama when she had started talking like Great Gram" (184). Grandmama's story is mostly told when she, adhering to the blues, reiterates her narrative.

20. See Guinier and Torres, *The Miner's Canary: Enlisting Race, Resisting Power, Transforming Democracy* (2002).

▶ Works Cited

Allende, Isabel. *The House of Spirits*. New York: Bantam, 1985.

Asimov, Isaac. *The Roving Mind*. Buffalo: Prometheus Books, 1983.

Brother from Another Planet. Directed by John Sayles. With Joe Morton. A Train Films, 1984.

Butler, Octavia E. *Kindred*. Boston: Beacon Press, 1979.

Creature from the Black Lagoon. Directed by Jack Arnold. With Richard Carlson and Julie Adams. UI, 1954.

Crossley, Robert. Introduction. *Kindred*. By Octavia E. Butler. Boston: Beacon, 1979. ix–xxvii.

Davis, Angela Y. *Blues Legacies and Black Feminisms: Gertrude "Ma" Rainey, Bessie Smith, and Billie Holiday*. New York: Pantheon, 1998.

Dubey, Madhu. "Gayl Jones and the Matrilineal Metaphor of Tradition." *Signs* 20.2 (1995): 245–62.

duCille, Ann. "Phallus(ies) of Interpretation: Toward Engendering the Black Critical 'I.'" *Callaloo* 16.3 (1993): 559–73.

Ellis, Jack C. and Virginia Wright Wexman. *A History of Film*. Boston: Allyn and Bacon, 2002.

Fanon, Franz. *Black Skin, White Masks*. New York: Grove Press, 1967.

Forrest, Leon. "A Solo Long-Song: For Lady Day." *Callaloo* 16.2 (1993): 332–67.

Gilman, Sander L. *Difference and Pathology: Stereotypes of Sexuality, Race, and Madness*. Ithaca: Cornell University Press, 1985.

Gotanda, Neil. "A Critique of 'Our Constitution Is Color-Blind.'" In *Critical Race Theory: The Key Writings That Formed the Movement*, ed. Kimberlé Crenshaw, Neil Gotanda, Gary Peller, and Kendall Thomas. New York: New Press. 257–75.

Gottfried, Amy S. "Angry Arts: Silence, Speech, and Song in Gayl Jones's *Corregidora*." *African American Review* 28.4 (1994): 559–70.

Govan, Sandra Y. "Connections, Links, and Extended Networks: Patterns in Octavia Butler's Science Fiction." *Black American Literature Forum* 18.2 (Summer 1984): 82–87.

Guerrero, Ed. *Framing Blackness: The African American Image in Film*. Philadelphia: Temple University Press, 1993.

Guinier, Lani and Gerald Torres. *The Miner's Canary: Enlisting Race, Resisting Power, Transforming Democracy*. Cambridge: Harvard University Press, 2002.

Harper, Michael S. "Gayl Jones: An Interview." In *Chant of Saints: A Gathering of Afro-*

American Literature, Art, and Scholarship, ed. Michael S. Harper and Robert B. Stepto. Urbana: Illinois University Press, 1979.

Hopkins, Pauline. (1903). *One Blood (Of One Blood).* London: The X Press, 1996.

Hopkinson, Nalo. *Midnight Robber.* New York: Warner Books, 2000.

Hurston, Zora Neale. (1938). *Tell My Horse.* New York: Harper Perennial, 1990.

Jablon, Madelyn. *Black Metafiction: Self-Consciousness in African American Literature.* Iowa City: University of Iowa Press, 1997.

Jones, Gayl. *Corregidora.* Boston: Beacon Press, 1975.

Jones, Gwyneth. *Deconstructing the Starships: Science, Fiction and Reality.* Liverpool: Liverpool University Press, 1999.

———. "Metempsychosis of the Machine: Science Fiction in the Halls of Karma." *Science Fiction Studies* 24 (1997): 1–10.

Kenan, Randall. "An Interview with Octavia E. Butler." *Callaloo* 14.2 (1991): 494–504.

Lacan, Jacques. *The Seminar of Jacques Lacan Book I: Freud's Papers on Technique, 1953–54.* New York: Norton, 1975.

———. *The Seminar of Jacques Lacan Book II: The Ego in Freud's Theory and in the Technique of Psychoanalysis, 1954–1955.* New York: Norton, 1978.

The Last Angel of History. Director John Akomfrah. First Run Icarus Films, 1996.

Márquez, Gabriel García. (1967). *One Hundred Years of Solitude.* New York: Harper, 1998.

The Matrix. Directed by the Wachowski Brothers. With Keanu Reeves and Laurence Fishburne. Warner Bros., 1999.

Mchaffy, Marilyn and AnaLouise Keating. "'Radio Imagination': Octavia Butler on the Poetics of Narrative Embodiment." *MELUS* 26.1 (2001): 43–76.

McKible, Adam. "'These Are the Facts of the Darky's History': Thinking History and Reading Names in Four African American Texts." *African American Review* 28.2 (Summer): 223–35.

Meyers, Walter E. *Aliens and Linguists: Language Study and Science Fiction.* Athens: University of Georgia Press, 1980.

Mitchell, Angelyn. "Not Enough of the Past: Feminist Revisions of Slavery in Octavia Butler's *Kindred.*" *MELUS* 26.3 (2001): 51–75.

Morrison, Toni. *Love.* New York: Knopf, 2003.

———. *Playing in the Dark: Whiteness and the Literary Imagination.* Cambridge: Harvard University Press, 1992.

———. *Beloved.* New York: Knopf, 1987.

Pohl, Frederik. "The Study of Science Fiction: A Modest Proposal." *Science Fiction Studies* 24 (1997): 11–16.

Radhakrishnan, R. "Postcoloniality and the Boundaries of Identity." *Callaloo* 16.4 (1993): 750–71.

Reed, Ishmael. *Mumbo Jumbo.* New York: Bantam, 1972.

Roy, Arundhati. *The God of Small Things.* New York: Harper Perennial, 1997.

Schuyler, George Samuel. (1931). *Black No More: Being an Account of the Strange and Wonderful Workings of Science in the Land of the Free.* New York: Modern Library, 1999.

———. "The Negro-Art Hokum." In *The Norton Anthology of African American Lit-*

erature, ed. Henry Louis Gates, Jr. and Nellie Y. McKay. New York: W. W. Norton, 1997. 1171–74.

Sharpe, Christina E. "The Costs of Remembering: What's at Stake in Gayl Jones's *Corregidora.*" In *African American Performance and Theater History: A Critical Reader,* ed. Harry J. Elam and David Krasner. New York: Oxford University Press, 2001. 306–27.

Shelley, Mary. *Frankenstein.* (1818). New York: Signet, 2000.

Spillers, Hortense J. "'All the Things You Could Be by Now if Sigmund Freud's Wife Was Your Mother': Psychoanalysis and Race." *Boundary 2* 23 (Fall 1996).

Suvin, Darko. *Metamorphoses of Science Fiction: On the Poetics and History of a Literary Genre.* New Haven: Yale University Press, 1979.

Tate, Claudia C. *Psychoanalysis and Black Novels: Desire and the Protocols of Race (Race and American Culture).* New York: Oxford University Press, 1998.

Tate, Greg. "Narrative." In *Swing Low: Black Men Writing,* ed. Rebecca Carroll. New York: Carol Southern Books, 1994. 207–18.

Wells, H. G. (1895). *The Time Machine.* New York: Tor Books, 1995.

Wheatley, Phillis. "On Imagination." In Gates and McKay. New York: W. W. Norton, 1997. 173–74.

DE WITT DOUGLAS KILGORE

Beyond the History We Know

Nnedi Okorafor-Mbachu, Nisi Shawl, and Jarla Tangh
Rethink Science Fiction Tradition

I. New Reading Practices

The recent turn of a significant number of African-American writers to the fantastic raises an important question: is social realism the mode that best captures the texture and meaning of the black experience? The only sensible answer: certainly not. However, readers and cultural critics have faced significant odds against marshaling the evidence to support this position. African-American creative efforts in science fiction, fantasy, and horror have been notable, sometimes brilliant—and sparse. We have had to rely upon a handful of writers—most visibly Samuel R. Delany, Octavia E. Butler, and Steven Barnes, and lately Tananarive Due and Nalo Hopkinson. The issue that must be addressed is the range and depth of African-American involvement in fantastic fiction, not its representation or quality. In other words, in addition to the attention that significant, singular authorial voices receive, we should focus on experiments produced by emerging writers. This strategy helps reveal the rich play of influences, conversations, and movements that are remaking contemporary science fiction and fantasy.[1]

Establishing this critical agenda is no longer a vain hope. Indeed, now is the best time to survey speculative fiction and conclude that a diverse array of talented black writers are creating the exchanges necessary to successfully venture within new areas. The publication of two groundbreaking anthologies, Sheree R. Thomas's *Dark Matter: A Century of*

Speculative Fiction from the African Diaspora (2000) and Nalo Hopkinson's *Mojo: Conjure Stories* (2003), provides ample evidence for this claim. These ambitious collections broaden our view of how African-American women can enhance science fiction, fantasy, and horror (SF/F/H).

In this essay I focus on *Mojo: Conjure Stories*. I pay particular attention to the short stories that Nnedi Okorafor-Mbachu, Nisi Shawl, and Jarla Tangh contribute. I see their work as part of a feminist tradition in African-American literature that imaginatively engages mythic and historical pasts in order to describe livable futures. These pasts have been visible but marginal in relation to Anglo-American science fiction and fantasy. I argue that Okorafor-Mbachu, Shawl, and Tangh bring these pasts into contact with the conventions and expectations that fantastic literature fosters. Having no desire to erase the reading pleasures associated with speculative fiction, these authors use story-telling conventions inherited from the Anglo-American literary tradition in unintended ways. The writers venture beyond merely moving black female characters and their histories into previously white and male precincts to create "diverse" versions of familiar tales. Instead, they directly engage genre conventions to change what and how we read. Thus, fantastic literature's resources are used to tell stories that have been impossible to imagine.

Hopkinson has lately emerged as a significant force in science fiction and fantasy. Her 1998 award-winning novel, *Brown Girl in the Ring*, heralded her visibility within the science fiction community. *Mojo: Conjure Stories* signals that Hopkinson has become influential as well as notable. The anthology reads as a manifesto that opens new frontiers within the realm of the fantastic. It engages the field in a manner that makes it responsive to the long-neglected experience of the African Diaspora. Thus, it is as challenging as such famously groundbreaking SF anthologies as Judith Merril's *England Swings SF* (1968), Harlan Ellison's *Dangerous Visions* (1967), and Bruce Sterling's *Mirrorshades* (1988).

The authors whom Hopkinson chooses to represent the diasporic experience articulate a diverse array of black, white, male, and female experiences. Her choices indicate that race and gender present no barrier to understanding or imagining a confluence of minority group histories and experiences in relation to fantastic literature. With that said, however, my focus is on the American and Canadian women of color Hopkinson includes. Anthologizing their work imbues these writers with a collective influence, a critical mass that could potentially ignite a chain reaction. *Mojo: Conjure Stories* might be a catalyst to change the kinds of people and history considered to be normal in SF/F/H narratives.

Mojo: Conjure Stories is an unusual theme anthology that invites readers to sample black women's writing, irrespective of race, in conjunction with their male and female peers' contributions. Thus, we are allowed to consider their work less as isolated, special cases than as part of a community bound by a shared literary history and common generic commitments. This method, an example of editorial desegregation, spotlights black women as knowledgeable participants in fantastic literature who simultaneously subscribe to the field's initiatives and seek to expand its expressive frontiers. The writers are at once influenced by speculative fiction tradition and positioned to inform and change that tradition.

A sense of history is essential to understanding the kind and tenor of generic discourse about narrative codes and conventions. This understanding can be measured not only in terms of writers' generic knowledge but also by the political and social history from which they, knowingly or not, emerge. Hopkinson has, in fact, chosen writers distinguished by their conscious interest in history. Her contributors look back to identify what has been forgotten, overlooked, or suppressed. What they find, not surprisingly, is trauma. They view history rife with pride, prejudice, greed, and simple cruelty. The ambition that drives their desire for discovery coincides with that of revisionist historians. Their goal, however, is not accuracy or documentary truth. Rather, they strive to create fictions that change how we imagine and feel history. The effect is stark revelation, not consolation of the kind Tolkien theorized for fantasy. These writers, in essence, reveal the truth behind complacent histories or futurist fiction that presupposes white and/or male superiority.

Within this broad rubric, Hopkinson's contributors use three strategies to highlight previously invisible or marginalized histories. First, they engage the events, people, and concerns of the recent past by presenting stories that take place during the civil rights movement. Second, they imaginatively depict the time preceding slavery and segregation to evoke a mythic epoch when the people of the African Diaspora are whole and fully empowered by links to their natal lands and cultures. Their ambition is to provide the myths necessary to comprehend any sense of their cultural purpose and destiny.[2] Third, the authors devote attention to the lives of women who have been previously marginalized in majority discourse about the past and the future. They create black women who fit neither the places assigned to them in a Euro-American racial hierarchy nor the patriarchal fantasies that often authorize Afrocentric visions of precolonial Africa. Hopkinson's black female contributors employ these three strategies to engage the familiar concerns of science fiction, fantasy, and African-American literature. In this way they bring to life past and futures informed by nontraditional historical perspectives.

▶ II. New Literary History

The Africa depicted in Western popular fiction has been a place of mascu-line adventure, an exotic proving ground for white male virtue and black male impotence. Such authors as H. Rider Haggard, Elspeth Huxley, Ernest Hemingway, and Saul Bellow exemplify this approach to the continent in popular and literary fiction. These authors perpetuate, in no small mea-sure, Theodore Roosevelt's Africa, the white boy's playing field that the domination of "exotic" lands and peoples makes possible.

Science fiction authors have sometimes portrayed Africa as a place of interesting and even politically transcendent futures. Arthur C. Clarke, for example, provides the sunny scenario of a politically stable, wealthy con-tinent in *The Fountains of Paradise* (1979), and Mack Reynolds gives us the more radical *Black Man's Burden* series (written during the 1960s and '70s). More commonly, however, Africa is depicted as a place that cannot be understood. Thus, genre fiction writers can dismiss the entire continent from the future after, say, a regrettable but convenient holocaust occurs. Few writers have tried to grapple with the continent as a place where real people possess a respected past and a potentially interesting future. Mack Reynolds, Mike Resnick, Octavia E. Butler, A. M. Lightner, and Charles Saunders have described such fully realized African pasts and futures.[3] However, only in Butler's fiction do African women play a role in defining the shape of human destiny.

With this literary precedent in mind, Nnedi Okorafor-Mbachu accom-plishes two objectives: she engages the spirit of precolonial Africa and establishes that a powerful place for women is essential to its endurance. The focus of her narrative is colonial Africa and its mythic past. In her "Asuquo or the Winds of Harmattan" the past has been forgotten, delib-erately erased by a people whose understanding of their history has been corrupted by an invading culture (160). The foreigners who instigate the corruption never appear. Their presence, however, is evidenced by the tragic fate of Asuquo, the protagonist.

Asuquo is a Windseeker, "one of the people who could fly."[4] She repre-sents a group which once held high status, individuals whose powers were well-known and respected as integral to the regulation of social and phys-ical good (160). Okorafor-Mbachu demonstrates this history by describing Asuquo's close links to the natural world in terms of her abilities as a gar-dener, a healer, and a mother of extremely healthy sons. Within Asuquo's evidently fallen world, her gifts mark her as a witch, a conjure woman who poses a danger to the community and must be destroyed (160; 164–69).

Okorafor-Mbachu's imaginative vision is quite congruent with African-American literature written during the past thirty years. The story of Africans who can fly and do so to escape slavery has been told several times—most notably by Julius Lester in his collection *Black Folktales* (1969) and by Toni Morrison in her magical realist novel *The Song of Solomon* (1977). The former text presents a twice-told tale, a legend that teaches readers about the aspirations of a people. The latter text is rich in revelatory metaphors relevant to personal and family history. Lester's retelling of the African flight motif as folklore and Morrison's Todorovian hesitations situate their imaginative visions as social or personal myth. These ways of handling the tales either ignore or elide their relevance to historical reality. Okorafor-Mbachu, however, uses the realist strategies of modern science fiction and fantasy to position her story as a forgotten history that should change our view of past and future.

Okorafor-Mbachu presents Asuquo as a woman who, although she desires to be accepted by her village, is spurned because of her uncanny abilities. The protagonist's raw and untamed ability to "levitate" makes her an alien to common folk; she is also different in very familiar ways (157). As an undisciplined and sexually experienced girl, she is regarded as dangerous (155). She sexually attracts a man and satisfies him to the extent that he refuses to take another wife (160). She bears healthy children who incite envy (160–61). Although she is valued as a healer, the good she accomplishes incites superstitious gossip (161). Asuquo's inability to conform eventually becomes intolerable. With her husband's cooperation, she is condemned by the village elders and poisoned, a murder excused as justified punishment. When the community destroys Asuquo it also breaks its last link to a great past and to the land they inhabit (169).

Asuquo's tale ends not with her death but with her erasure from history. Her essence is erased; she is remembered as the predatory demi-god Ekong, a suitably male figure for patriarchy (169). Hence, the village community enforces the patriarchal imperatives it believes to be right and good. Okorafor-Mbachu emphasizes, however, that Asuquo's people are guilty of both murder and disregard for the natural order that sustains them. After Asuquo's death, the Harmattan winds that define the seasons and make the land fruitful fail to blow. When the winds eventually do return, life continues at an impoverished level.

Okorafor-Mbachu's text evokes the degeneration and corruption of African life during the colonial era. According to Okorafor-Mbachu, both the European-inspired slave trade and the hypocritical and patriarchal black culture are at fault (160; 165). Men are repelled by Asuquo: the institutional structures they control—the Epko society—have lost an older wisdom, the terms under which Asuquo could have been accepted. Her village is characterized by ugliness identical to the powerless black community Zora Neale Hurston depicts in *Their Eyes Were Watching God* (1937).

The fact that the slave trade has begun is the only historical marker present in Okorafor-Mbachu's story. Nisi Shawl's "The Tawny Bitch," in contrast, directly confronts our inadequate historical accounts and, therefore, our understanding of the past. Her tale is framed as a manuscript found during the demolition of a country house, the diary of a young heiress (named Belle) imprisoned by a greedy cousin who wishes to appropriate her fortune. Following the formula of Victorian potboilers, Belle has lost her liberty and is in danger of experiencing a fate worse than death. "The Tawny Bitch" reinvigorates that old form by engaging the social reality of race, class, and sex—figuring them through the material and emotional imperatives of science and magic.

Plots featuring imperiled heiresses usually focus upon the heroine's virtue and her oppressor's villainy. The claim on readers' attention is explicitly emotional, assuming a shared and bourgeois judgment of social rights and wrongs. Shawl veers away from this cliché by depicting a racially mixed heroine. Belle is "black but comely" (266), and she writes in an ornate, upper-class style. An intellectual committed to the rationalistic empiricism of her time, Belle is well acquainted with Royal Society debates (262–63). The wealth that her white father makes available funds her elite education and shields her from crude early-nineteenth-century racism. Belle is also a homosexual who lives during the inception of medical discourse about same-sex relationships. Her "irregular" relationship with a female schoolmate makes it possible for a male relative to abduct and imprison her in an abandoned country house (260).

Belle's commitment to science is tested when she is imprisoned. Her cousin employs a European scientist, Dr. Martin Hesselius, to diagnose her condition and to prescribe a remedy. It quickly becomes clear that the doctor is a quack for hire whose supposed knowledge masks sadism and oppression. In his judgment, Belle's race, sexuality, and intelligence are all psycho-physiological disorders which make her a candidate for institutionalization. The doctor declares Belle to be insane and prescribes a therapeutic regime that blurs the distinction between cure and rape. Thus, Shawl provides a brief fictionalized account of how nineteenth-century medical practice reflects and reinforces constraints placed upon blacks and women.

Belle's story is annotated by a historian who attempts to relate this newly (as of the late nineteenth century) discovered narrative fragment to the history we know. He (readers assume) notes that Dr. Hesselius "was well known during his professional career (1835–1871), and his presence would seem to vouch for the text's authenticity" (282). "Dr. Hesselius" evokes J. Sheridan Le Fanu's fictional character of the same name. Shawl's deliberate borrowing from Le Fanu makes it obvious that the "The Tawny Bitch" engages the late-nineteenth-century tradition of weird tales and ghost stories. Her text is, in part, a reconsideration of Le Fanu's "Carmilla," a tale of lesbian sexuality and vampiric seduction published in his story collection *In a Glass Darkly* (1886). Le Fanu's Hesselius prepares the reader for Bram Stoker's Abraham Van Helsing, a good doctor empowered to launch a religiously orthodox, science-authorized defense against the supernatural. Masquerading as a disciplined "layer of mental disturbances," Shawl's Hesselius is exposed as a champion of institutional racism and sexism (282). His agenda is to control female sexuality while claiming to defend it. Shawl reveals patriarchy's desire to contain the "New Woman" of the late nineteenth century. That the New Woman, placed in Shawl's hands, is presented as a black lesbian perhaps demonstrates how an oppressive narrative form might be used to argue for a subsequent generation's political hopes.

It is important to note that the knowledge and understanding that should protect Belle fails to do so. Science and medicine, as practiced by Belle's cousin, are tools of white male supremacy. Neither field supports antiracist hopes that later African-American scientists (such as chemist George Washington Carver and embryologist Ernest Everett Just) promote. It is, instead, the persistent power of past knowledge (represented in part by Belle's African nurse, Yeyetunde) that provides protection and escape. In other words, the social and supernatural violations that Le Fanu's Hesselius routinely defeats are, according to Shawl, benign. The author's terrible spirits are intent on freeing the marginal and the powerless. The rational, present-minded Belle, initially contemptuous of superstition, must finally embrace the marvelous as her only hope for survival and freedom.

Hence, we might read "The Tawny Bitch" as a reactionary statement against science. This potential reading is undermined by Shawl's closing move to establish that the story is a difficult-to-authenticate, historical fragment. Readers are drawn to our incomplete knowledge of past events and to the manner in which stories that could offer true accounts lie buried while half-truths become facts. Most importantly, Belle's escape cannot be explained by any record that either her cousin or Doctor Hesselius authors. Accepting her account requires readers to change perspectives that force them to define her story as being clearly observed and honestly recorded. The result is provocative within the general purview of science fiction, fantasy, and horror and the particular weird-tale tradition that Shawl engages.

III. New Primeval Horrors

A significant strand of Anglo-American story telling wrestles with a buried past from which its principal characters wish to escape. These stories contain shameful secrets that involve the most bestial aspects of human nature. They derive energy from secret history's eruption into the cool, sane, and socially respectable present. This emergence is most often represented as an invasion emanating from outside modern Western culture. Edgar Allan Poe, Arthur Conan Doyle, and H. P. Lovecraft established the conventions of this genre. Angela Carter's *The Bloody Chamber* (1979) follows in the wake of this tradition. According to the conventions these writers initiated, the threatening past always arises from Africa, Asia, or, in Doyle's case, the America described in his first Sherlock Holmes tale, *A Study in Scarlet* (1887). These places are stereotyped as culturally and racially Other, the continents that Joseph Conrad situated within the Western literary imagination as being the focal point of primeval horror. The rational explanations and technologies of the cosmopolitan West fail within these stories. Protagonists are in constant danger from beasts and beings that foster and sustain urban dangers and conflicts.

Jarla Tangh's "The Skinned" engages this genre tradition, carries it forward, and turns it on its head. "The Skinned" focuses upon Sinza Barantsar, a Rwandan who comes to the United States to escape his country's genocidal past. He settles into urban reality as an immigrant who finds much to fault in "wicked America" (128). As an accomplice to the Hutu devastation of the Tutsis, he carries with him the sin of his crimes and agonizing guilt. However, Barantsar, no burly black beast inherited from Poe or Lovecraft, has failed to incarnate the best attributes of his country and culture. What he confronts in America is a chance to redeem himself, to defend his American community from an evil it cannot understand because his neighbors "have lost—language, religion, a sense of place" (129).

Tangh's narrative combines the familiar with the new. Africa is familiarly depicted as a place of danger, a catastrophic land in which easy faith in human goodness or sanity is challenged. But Tangh's Africa is not Joseph Conrad's unknown and unknowable Africa. Her version of the continent contains languages and stories that allow Barantsar, a *nganga,* to make sense of what his African-American neighbors cannot understand. They have lost too much in the transition to an America full of "restless spirits" and "unclean things" (128). A streetwise boy dies because, failing to believe his mother's stories, he instead relies upon his gun to provide safety and symbolize his manhood. Nothing can defend him against the terror that haunts his street (126–27).

In accordance with fantasy and horror traditions, the evil that Tangh depicts also seems to be familiar. Within her narrative world, evil is represented by werewolves who prey upon anyone who violates arcane turf rules. Barantsar calls these predators "the Skinned." Like the displaced gods in Neil Gaiman's *American Gods* (2002), they could be inadvertent immigrants who reside in America merely because the people who believe in them do so. Or, they could be the ghostly remnants of aboriginal spirits who linger in this world to avenge long-dead supplicants. We discover, instead, that the Skinned are the creations of a powerful European shaman. It is he or she who, Dracula-like, invades the New World, leaving behind evidence of a deathless, malignant entity. Readers are informed that one "might think that the Native Americans, the original owners of the land, left them. But it does not feel like them. I do not think the juju of African slaves is responsible either. . . . No, The Skinned are something a white mind would imagine. I feel only admiration for what he or she has crafted" (133). Tangh uses the convention of horrific racial invasion and violation to designate Europe as the source of primal danger.

This decision illuminates the way Tangh ends her story. She does not allow Barantsar to redeem himself by defeating the enemy. Instead, Barantsar's himself becomes one of the Skinned. The history he hoped to escape marks him in that his failure in Rwanda becomes his failure in America. American corruption differs little from the corruption he finds within himself. Tangh engages the racial conventions of dark fantasy and holds them accountable for real-world evils.

IV. New Conjured Black Future Females

The fantastic histories collected in *Mojo: Conjure Stories* set the stage for new futures, elsewhere structured by previously hidden knowledge. Hopkinson's anthology presents a futurity which is markedly different from those that have inspired the popular historical imagination. The influential future histories of Heinlein, Asimov, Clarke, and others who follow their lead default to a benevolent industrial capitalism that white men control. No wonder, then, that Hopkinson gathers stories that just might result in the futures she imagines within her own contributions to science fiction. Black women who contribute to SF/F/H have reached the point where the history they recover can potentially become future history. It is now possible to identify a new pattern of expectation, one that emerges from long-suppressed voices.

Notes

1. Mosley notes that an important reason for writing science fiction is a need "to enter into a dialogue" with literature that has been important to him as a reader. Scifi.com Chat Transcript, Walter Mosley, 27 November 2001, http://www.scifi.com/transcripts/2001/mosely_chat.html.

2. The creation of new national myths is a very familiar feature of modern fantasy. Tolkien's fantasy writing is, of course, the paradigmatic exponent of this impulse. However, we can also trace this particular creative impulse in earlier as well as later writers. For example: the radical medievalism of Morris's "A Dream of John Ball" (1886); Kipling's *Puck of Pook's Hill* (1906), in which Britain is invested with the power of bringing Romans, Norsemen, Normans, Picts, and Anglo-Saxons together to form one people; and Cooper's *The Dark Is Rising* sequence (1965–77), which provides a history of the battle between good and evil in Arthurian terms. The fantastic recovery of premodern Europe, as Shippey has noted in reference to Tolkien, has been a significant part of fantasy's response to modern industrial capitalism. For more on this topic, see Shippey 2002. Note here that that response can be either progressive or reactionary.

3. Pertinent examples include Resnick's *Paradise: A Chronicle of a Distant World* (1989); Butler's *Wild Seed* (1988 [1980]); Lightner's *The Day of the Drones* (1970); and Saunders's *Imaro* series (1981–85). Naturally, these writers bring to their African stories very different interests and perspectives that are often incongruent.

4. Douglas and Thomas also refer to this popular African-American folktale in *Mojo: Conjure Stories* (320–34).

Works Cited

Butler, Octavia E. (1980). *Wild Seed.* New York: Popular Library, 1988.

Carter, Angela. *The Bloody Chamber.* New York: Penguin Books, 1979.

Clarke, Arthur C. *The Fountains of Paradise.* New York: Harcourt Brace Jovanovich, 1979.

Cooper, Susan. *The Dark Is Rising Sequence: Over Sea, Under Stone; The Dark Is Rising; Greenwitch; Grey King; Silver on the Tree.* New York: Simon Pulse, 1993.

Douglas, Marcia. "Notes from a Writer's Book of Cures and Spells." In *Mojo: Conjure Stories,* ed. Nalo Hopkinson. New York: Warner Books, 2003.

Doyle, Arthur Conan. *A Study in Scarlet.* New York: Oxford University Press, 1993.

Ellison, Harlan, ed. *Dangerous Visions.* New York: New American Library, 1967.

Gaiman, Neil. *American Gods.* New York: HarperTorch, 2002.

Hopkinson, Nalo, ed. *Mojo: Conjure Stories.* New York: Warner Books, 2003.

Hopkinson, Nalo. *Brown Girl in the Ring.* New York: Warner Books, 1998.

Hurston, Zora Neale. (1937). *Their Eyes Were Watching God.* New York: Perennial Library/Harper and Row, 1990.

Kipling, Rudyard. (1906). *Puck of Pook's Hill.* New York: Penguin, 1987.

Le Fanu, J. Sheridan. "Carmilla." In *In a Glass Darkly.* By J. Sheridan Le Fanu. London:

Richard Bentley and Son, 1886. 358–471.

———. *In a Glass Darkly.* London: Richard Bentley and Son, 1886.

Lester, Julius. "People Who Could Fly." In *Black Folktales.* By Julius Lester. New York: R. W. Baron, 1969.

Lightner, A. M. *The Day of the Drones.* New York: Bantam Books, 1970.

Merril, Judith, ed. *England Swings SF.* Garden City: Doubleday, 1968.

Morris, William. "A Dream of John Ball." In *News from Nowhere and Other Writings.* By William Morris and Clive Wilmer. New York: Penguin, 1993. 25–39.

Morrison, Toni. *The Song of Solomon.* New York: Alfred A. Knopf, 1977.

Mosley, Walter. Scifi.com Chat Transcript, 27 November 2001, http://www.scifi.com/transcripts/2001/mosely_chat.html.

Resnick, Mike. *Paradise: A Chronicle of a Distant World.* New York: Tor, 1989.

Reynolds, Mack. *Black Man's Burden.* New York: Ace Books, 1972.

———. *Border, Breed, Nor Birth.* New York: Ace Books, 1972.

———. *The Best Ye Breed.* New York: Ace Books, 1978.

Saunders, Charles R. *Imaro.* New York: DAW Books, 1981.

Shawl, Nisi. "The Tawny Bitch." In *Mojo: Conjure Stories,* ed. Nalo Hopkinson. New York: Warner Books, 2003. 259–82.

Shippey, Tom. *J. R. R. Tolkien: Author of the Century.* Boston: Houghton Mifflin, 2002.

Sterling, Bruce. *Mirrorshades: The Cyberpunk Anthology.* New York: Ace Books, 1988.

Tangh, Jarla. "The Skinned." In *Mojo: Conjure Stories,* ed. Nalo Hopkinson. New York: Warner Books, 2003. 124–40.

Thomas, Sheree R. "How Sukie Crosses de Big Wata." In *Mojo: Conjure Stories,* ed. Nalo Hopkinson. New York: Warner Books, 2003. 326–34.

———, ed. *Dark Matter: A Century of Speculative Fiction from the African Diaspora.* New York: Warner Books, 2000.

NISI SHAWL,
NNEDI OKORAFOR-MBACHU, &
JARLA TANGH

RESPONSES TO
DE WITT DOUGLAS KILGORE

⟩ Bubbling Champagne Power Trip
by Nisi Shawl

What a pleasure to read Kilgore's insightful analysis of the work my
sisters and I have created! His opinion that our joint inclusion in *Mojo:
Conjure Stories* "imbues these writers with a collective influence, a critical mass" strengthens and sweetens my resolve to tell my stories well.
Writing, I've always said, is a power trip; the idea that as a group we
might change the default settings for "normalcy" in science fiction, fantasy, and horror literature goes to my head like the bubbles in a glass of
champagne. It also helps to know that someone is picking up on much
of what I'm putting down.

Kilgore's critique of Tangh and Okorafor-Mbachu opens new vistas
for me. He situates their efforts in a landscape whose features are clearly
delineated and revealingly named. And I agree with most of what he
says about "The Tawny Bitch." There are, however, points where my
intentions, at least, differ from what I've achieved in his eyes.

My mixed-race heroine Belle, as I imagine her, does indeed initially reject the nonrational world of black religious tradition in favor
of rationalism, which the dominant paradigm of her time insists on
identifying as white. But when she is forced from her chosen terrain by
the machinations of white patriarchy (her cousin and Doctor Hesselius embody these machinations), Belle's "embrace" of the "marvelous"

comes at a price. Depending upon readers' interpretations, they may see Belle as mad when they reach the story's abrupt, incomplete, and deliberately inconclusive finish. Or perhaps she is more or less than human—a vengeful werebeast.

Losing either her sanity or her humanness, she accommodates herself to by no means entirely benign spirits. The ambiguity of these spirits' nature is meant to undercut any reactionary reading of my story as much as the ambiguity of its ending. Yet given the essentialism of the historical moment, this accommodation is the only circumstance that allows Belle to maintain her subjectivity.

I deeply appreciate Kilgore's interpretation of my references to Victorian ghost stories, in particular my use of Joseph Sheridan Le Fanu's protagonist Dr. Martin Hesselius. I also refer to Le Fanu's "Green Tea" and, via my title "The Tawny Bitch," to Wilhelm Meinhold's "The Amber Witch." Other influences include Charlotte Perkins Gilman's "The Yellow Wallpaper," that preeminent feminist redaction of the archetypal ghost story, and Louisa May Alcott's pseudonymous thriller, "A Whisper in the Dark."

▶ "Of Course People Can Fly"
by Nnedi Okorafor-Mbachu

Kilgore is right on point. Asuquo symbolizes things forgotten and the tragedy of forgetfulness. Not all traditions are meant to be or should be remembered. As human beings move forward in time, ideas and habits evolve. But some traditions and aspects of culture are especially valuable and timeless: they help to inspire hope, dreams, pride, freedom, and love. So does Asuquo.

To further expand Kilgore's argument beyond North America, I add that many African male authors also tend to portray African women and girls as being invisible, voiceless, or marginal. I was responding to this penchant when I created Asuquo.

Because I was born in the United States to two Nigerian immigrant parents, I am both a Nigerian writer and an American one. My dual cultural heritage partly accounts for why I was attracted to the myth of the flying Africans—a tale that connects North America and Africa. It is an African-American story of combined resistance, hopelessness, inevitability, and magic. In addition, it is an African story. The flying Africans were said to be Igbos. I too am an Igbo. I once told my uncle about the flying Africans myth.

His response: "Of course people can fly."

⬤ Carla Johnson/Jarla Tangh

A Close Encounter with My Pseudonym
by Jarla Tangh

It is heartening to think about one's own work being included in the context of a larger movement. I am delighted to acknowledge that some of my thematic objectives have been discussed in *Beyond the History We Know*.

I have no doubt that other writers such as Okorafor-Mbachu and Shawl have discovered for themselves that speculative fiction is a place where ideas about identity and the challenge of self-definition come to the fore.

Otherness has been an inescapable reality for me. Of course, I am responding to my experience of being marginalized. I am the product of two cultures: African-descended and North American. Neither culture defines me wholly.

I agree that I have attempted to engage the racial conventions of dark fantasy. One of my most influential sources of literary trauma is the portrayal of the black-skinned tribesmen and their terror regarding whiteness in Poe's *The Narrative of Arthur Gordon Pym of Nantucket*. My reflections on Conrad's *Heart of Darkness* would initiate a diatribe that is inappropriate for a short response. I tolerate the presence of Lovecraft in the genre even though I do not admire his fiction. I still consider Poe to be one of my most important influences. Nevertheless, I took offense when I read *The Narrative of Arthur Gordon Pym*.

"The Skinned" is, in part, a personal interaction with that work. Indeed, "the convention of horrific racial invasion and violation" cried out to me to be inverted. I deliberately chose an antihero when I created Sinza Barantsar and I alluded to Conrad's Kurtz. I longed to challenge my readers and myself to look askance at what lurks in the collective Western memory. The wonderful thing about dark fantasy lies in its recognition of the unspeakable.

Unspeakable fear and hate manifest themselves in "The Skinned." It might have been easier simply to dramatize, for example, that a long time ago there was a powerful white wizard who despised his nonwhite neighbors. So, he created "the skinned" to keep them in line. Then along comes an African equipped with the tools to combat these "projections," and he ends up succumbing to them. I will not even venture to comment upon the ramifications of my synopsis. Suffice it to say that I enjoyed my version of the telling. I hope that readers do too.

STORIES

Techno/Magic Sistahs
Are Not the Sistahs from
Another Planet

The Book of Martha

"It's difficult, isn't it?" God said with a weary smile. "You're truly free for the first time. What could be more difficult than that?"

Martha Bes looked around at the endless grayness that was, along with God, all that she could see. In fear and confusion, she covered her broad black face with her hands. "If only I could wake up," she whispered.

God kept silent but was so palpably, disturbingly present that even in the silence Martha felt rebuked. "Where is this?" she asked, not really wanting to know, not wanting to be dead when she was only forty-three. "Where am I?"

"Here with me," God said.

"Really here?" she asked. "Not at home in bed dreaming? Not locked up in a mental institution? Not . . . not lying dead in a morgue?"

"Here," God said softly. "With me."

After a moment, Martha was able to take her hands from her face and look again at the grayness around her and at God. "This can't be heaven," she said. "There's nothing here, no one here but you."

"Is that all you see?" God asked.

This confused her even more. "Don't you know what I see?" she demanded and then quickly softened her voice. "Don't you know everything?"

God smiled. "No, I outgrew that trick long ago. You can't imagine how boring it was."

This struck Martha as such a human thing to say that her fear diminished a little—although she was still impossibly confused. She

135

had, she remembered, been sitting at her computer, wrapping up one more day's work on her fifth novel. The writing had been going well for a change, and she'd been enjoying it. For hours, she'd been spilling her new story onto paper in that sweet frenzy of creation that she lived for. Finally, she had stopped, turned the computer off, and realized that she felt stiff. Her back hurt. She was hungry and thirsty, and it was almost five A.M. She had worked through the night. Amused in spite of her various aches and pains, she got up and went to the kitchen to find something to eat.

And then she was here, confused and scared. The comfort of her small, disorderly house was gone, and she was standing before this amazing figure who had convinced her at once that he was God—or someone so powerful that he might as well be God. He had work for her to do, he said—work that would mean a great deal to her and to the rest of humankind.

If she had been a little less frightened, she might have laughed. Beyond comic books and bad movies, who said things like that?

"Why," she dared to ask, "do you look like a twice-live-sized, bearded white man?" In fact, seated as he was on his huge throne-like chair, he looked, she thought, like a living version of Michelangelo's Moses, a sculpture that she remembered seeing pictured in her college art-history textbook about twenty years before. Except that God was more fully dressed than Michelangelo's Moses, wearing, from neck to ankles, the kind of long, white robe that she had so often seen in paintings of Christ.

"You see what your life has prepared you to see," God said.

"I want to see what's really here!"

"Do you? What you see is up to you, Martha. Everything is up to you."

She sighed. "Do you mind if I sit down?"

And she was sitting. She did not sit down, but simply found herself sitting in a comfortable armchair that had surely not been there a moment before. Another trick, she thought resentfully—like the grayness, like the giant on his throne, like her own sudden appearance here. Everything was just one more effort to amaze and frighten her. And, of course, it was working. She was amazed and badly frightened. Worse, she disliked the giant for manipulating her, and this frightened her even more. Surely he could read her mind. Surely he would punish. . . .

She made herself speak through her fear. "You said you had work for me." She paused, licked her lips, tried to steady her voice. "What do you want me to do?"

He didn't answer at once. He looked at her with what she read as amusement—looked at her long enough to make her even more uncomfortable.

"What do you want me to do?" she repeated, her voice stronger this time.

"I have a great deal of work for you," he said at last. "As I tell you about it,

I want you to keep three people in mind: Jonah, Job, and Noah. Remember them. Be guided by their stories."

"All right," she said because he had stopped speaking, and it seemed that she should say something. "All right."

When she was a girl, she had gone to church and to Sunday School, to Bible class and to vacation Bible school. Her mother, only a girl herself, hadn't known much about being a mother, but she had wanted her child to be "good," and to her, "good" meant "religious." As a result, Martha knew very well what the Bible said about Jonah, Job, and Noah. She had come to regard their stories as parables rather than literal truths, but she remembered them. God had ordered Jonah to go to the city of Nineveh and to tell the people there to mend their ways. Frightened, Jonah had tried to run away from the work and from God, but God had caused him to be ship-wrecked, swallowed by a great fish, and given to know that he could not escape.

Job had been the tormented pawn who lost his property, his children, and his health in a bet between God and Satan. And when Job proved faithful in spite of all that God had permitted Satan to do to him, God rewarded Job with even greater wealth, new children, and restored health.

As for Noah, of course, God ordered him to build an ark and save his family and a lot of animals because God had decided to flood the world and kill everyone and everything else.

Why was she to remember these three biblical figures in particular? What had they do with her—especially Job and all his agony?

"This is what you're to do," God said. "You will help humankind to survive its greedy, murderous, wasteful adolescence. Help it to find less destructive, more peaceful, sustainable ways to live."

Martha stared at him. After a while, she said feebly, ". . . What?"

"If you don't help them, they will be destroyed."

"You're going to destroy them . . . again?" she whispered.

"Of course not," God said, sounding annoyed. "They're well on the way to destroying billions of themselves by greatly changing the ability of the earth to sustain them. That's why they need help. That's why you will help them."

"How?" she asked. She shook her head. "What can I do?"

"Don't worry," God said. "I won't be sending you back home with another message that people can ignore or twist to suit themselves. It's too late for that kind of thing anyway." God shifted on his throne and looked at her with his head cocked to one side. "You'll borrow some of my power," he said. "You'll arrange it so that people treat one another better and treat their environment more sensibly. You'll give them a better chance to survive than they've given themselves. I'll lend you the power, and you'll do this." He paused, but this time she could think of nothing to say. After a while, he went on.

"When you've finished your work, you'll go back and live among them again as one of their lowliest. You're the one who will decide what that will mean, but whatever you decide is to be the bottom level of society, the lowest class or caste or race, that's what you'll be."

This time when he stopped talking, Martha laughed. She felt overwhelmed with questions, fears, and bitter laughter, but it was the laughter that broke free. She needed to laugh. It gave her strength somehow.

"I was born on the bottom level of society," she said. "You must have known that."

God did not answer.

"Sure you did." Martha stopped laughing and managed, somehow, not to cry. She stood up, stepped toward God. "How could you not know? I was born poor, black, and female to a fourteen-year-old mother who could barely read. We were homeless half the time while I was growing up. Is that bottom-level enough for you? I was born on the bottom, but I didn't stay there. I didn't leave my mother there, either. And I'm not going back there!"

Still God said nothing. He smiled.

Martha sat down again, frightened by the smile, aware that she had been shouting—shouting at God! After a while, she whispered, "Is that why you chose me to do this . . . this work? Because of where I came from?"

"I chose you for all that you are and all that you are not," God said. "I could have chosen someone much poorer and more downtrodden. I chose you because you were the one I wanted for this."

Martha couldn't decide whether he sounded annoyed. She couldn't decide whether it was an honor to be chosen to do a job so huge, so poorly defined, so impossible.

"Please let me go home," she whispered. She was instantly ashamed of herself. She was begging, sounding pitiful, humiliating herself. Yet these were the most honest words she'd spoken so far.

"You're free to ask me questions," God said as though he hadn't heard her plea at all. You're free to argue and think and investigate all of human history for ideas and warnings. You're free to take all the time you need to do these things. As I said earlier, you're truly free. You're even free to be terrified. But I assure you, you will do this work."

Martha thought of Job, Jonah, and Noah. After a while, she nodded.

"Good," God said. He stood up and stepped toward her. He was at least twelve feet high and inhumanly beautiful. He literally glowed. "Walk with me," he said.

And abruptly, he was not twelve feet high. Martha never saw him change, but now he was her size—just under six feet—and he no longer glowed. Now when he looked at her, they were eye to eye. He did look at her. He saw that something was disturbing her, and he asked, "What is it now? Has your image of me grown feathered wings or a blinding halo?"

"Your halo's gone," she answered. "And you're smaller. More normal."

"Good," he said. "What else do you see?"

"Nothing. Grayness."

"That will change."

It seemed that they walked over a smooth, hard, level surface, although when she looked down, she couldn't see her feet. It was as though she walked through ankle-high, ground-hugging fog.

"What are we walking on?" she asked.

"What would you like?" God asked. "A sidewalk? Beach sand? A dirt road?"

"A healthy, green lawn," she said, and was somehow not surprised to find herself walking on short, green grass. "And there should be trees," she said, getting the idea and discovering she liked it. "There should be sunshine—blue sky with a few clouds. It should be May or early June."

And it was so. It was as though it had always been so. They were walking through what could have been a vast city park.

Martha looked at God, her eyes wide. "Is that it?" she whispered. "I'm supposed to change people by deciding what they'll be like, and then just . . . just saying it?"

"Yes," God said.

And she went from being elated to—once again—being terrified. "What if I say something wrong, make a mistake?"

"You will."

"But . . . people could get hurt. People could die."

God went to a huge deep red Norway maple tree and sat down beneath it on a long wooden bench. Martha realized that he had created both the ancient tree and the comfortable-looking bench only a moment before. She knew this, but again, it had happened so smoothly that she was not jarred by it.

"It's so easy," she said. "Is it always this easy for you?"

God sighed. "Always," he said.

She thought about that—his sigh, the fact that he looked away into the trees instead of at her. Was an eternity of absolute ease just another name for hell? Or was that just the most sacrilegious thought she'd had so far? She said, "I don't want to hurt people. Not even by accident."

God turned away from the trees, looked at her for several seconds, then said, "It would be better for you if you had raised a child or two."

Then, she thought with irritation, he should have chosen someone who'd raised a child or two. But she didn't have the courage to say that. Instead, she said, "Won't you fix it so I don't hurt or kill anyone? I mean, I'm new at this. I could do something stupid and wipe people out and not even know I'd done it until afterward."

"I won't fix things for you," God said. "You have a free hand."

She sat down next to him because sitting and staring out into the endless park was easier than standing and facing him and asking him questions that she thought might make him angry. She said, "Why should it be my work? Why don't you do it? You know how. You could do it without making mistakes. Why make me do it? I don't know anything."

"Quite right," God said. And he smiled. "That's why."

She thought about this with growing horror. "Is it just a game to you, then?" she asked. "Are you playing with us because you're bored?"

God seemed to consider the question. "I'm not bored," he said. He seemed pleased somehow. "You should be thinking about the changes you'll make. We can talk about them. You don't have to just suddenly proclaim."

She looked at him, then stared down at the grass, trying to get her thoughts in order. "Okay. How do I start?"

"Think about this: what change would you want to make if you could make only one? Think of one important change."

She looked at the grass again and thought about the novels she had written. What if she were going to write a novel in which human beings had to be changed in only one positive way? "Well," she said after a while, "the growing population is making a lot of the other problems worse. What if people could only have two children? I mean, what if people who wanted children could only have two, no matter how many more they wanted or how many medical techniques they used to try to get more?"

"You believe the population problem is the worst one, then?" God asked.

"I think so," she said. "Too many people. If we solve that one, we'll have more time to solve other problems. And we can't solve it on our own. We all know about it, but some of us won't admit it. And nobody wants some big government authority telling them how many kids to have." She glanced at God and saw that he seemed to be listening politely. She wondered how far he would let her go. What might offend him. What might he do to her if he were offended? "So everyone's reproductive system shuts down after two kids," she said. "I mean, they get to live as long as before, and they aren't sick. They just can't have kids any more."

"They'll try," God said. "The effort they put into building pyramids, cathedrals, and moon rockets will be as nothing to the effort they'll put into trying to end what will seem to them a plague of barrenness. What about people whose children die or are seriously disabled? What about a woman whose first child is a result of rape? What about surrogate motherhood? What about men who become fathers without realizing it? What about cloning?"

Martha stared at him, chagrined. "That's why you should do this. It's too complicated."

Silence.

"All right," Martha sighed and gave up. "All right. What if even with accidents and modern medicine, even something like cloning, the two-kid limit holds. I don't know how that could be made to work, but you do."

"It could be made to work," God said, "but keep in mind that you won't be coming here again to repair any changes you make. What you do is what people will live with. Or in this case, die with."

"Oh," Martha said. She thought for a moment, then said, "Oh, no."

"They would last for a good many generations," God said. "But they would be dwindling all the time. In the end, they would be extinguished. With the usual diseases, disabilities, disasters, wars, deliberate childlessness, and murder, they wouldn't be able to replace themselves. Think of the needs of the future, Martha, as well as the needs of the present."

"I thought I was," she said. "What if I made four kids the maximum number instead of two?"

God shook his head. "Free will coupled with morality has been an interesting experiment. Free will is, among other things, the freedom to make mistakes. One group of mistakes will sometimes cancel another. That's saved any number of human groups, although it isn't dependable. Sometimes mistakes cause people to be wiped out, enslaved, or driven from their homes because they've so damaged or altered their land or their water or their climate. Free will isn't a guarantee of anything, but it's a potentially useful tool—too useful to erase casually."

"I thought you wanted me to put a stop to war and slavery and environmental destruction!" Martha snapped, remembering the history of her own people. How could God be so casual about such things?

God laughed. It was a startling sound—deep, full, and, Martha thought, inappropriately happy. Why would this particular subject make him laugh? Was he God? Was he Satan? Martha, in spite of her mother's efforts, had not been able to believe in the literal existence of either. Now, she did not know what to think—or what to do.

God recovered himself, shook his head, and looked at Martha. "Well, there's no hurry," he said. "Do you know what a nova is Martha?"

Martha frowned. "It's . . . a star that explodes," she said, willing, even eager, to be distracted from her doubts.

"It's a pair of stars," God said. "A large one—a giant—and a small, very dense dwarf. The dwarf pulls material from the giant. After a while, the dwarf has taken more material than it can control, and it explodes. It doesn't necessarily destroy itself, but it does throw off a great deal of excess material. It makes a very bright, violent display. But once the dwarf has quieted down, it begins to siphon material from the giant again. It can do this over and over. That's what a nova is. If you change it—move the two stars farther apart or equalize their density, then it's no longer a nova."

Martha listened, catching his meaning even though she didn't want to. "Are you saying that if . . . if humanity is changed, it won't be humanity any more?"

"I'm saying more than that," God told her. "I'm saying that even though this is true, I will permit you to do it. What you decide should be done with humankind will be done. But whatever you do, your decisions will have consequences. If you limit their fertility, you will probably destroy them. If you limit their competitiveness or their inventiveness, you might destroy their ability to survive the many disasters and challenges that they must face."

Worse and worse, Martha thought, and she actually felt nauseous with fear. She turned away from God, hugging herself, suddenly crying, tears streaming down her face. After a while, she sniffed and wiped her face on her hands, since she had nothing else. "What will you do to me if I refuse?" she asked, thinking of Job and Jonah in particular.

"Nothing." God didn't even sound annoyed. "You won't refuse."

"But what if I do? What if I really can't think of anything worth doing?"

"That won't happen. But if it did somehow, and if you asked, I would send you home. After all, there are millions of human beings who would give anything to do this work."

And, instantly, she thought of some of these—people who would be happy to wipe out whole segments of the population whom they hated and feared, or people who would set up vast tyrannies that forced everyone into a single mold, no matter how much suffering that created. And what about those who would treat the work as fun—as nothing more than a good-guys-versus-bad-guys computer game, and damn the consequences. There were people like that. Martha knew people like that.

But God wouldn't choose that kind of person. If he was God. Why had he chosen her, after all? For all of her adult life, she hadn't even believed in God as a literal being. If this terrifyingly powerful entity, God or not, could choose her, he could make even worse choices.

After a while, she asked, "Was there really a Noah?"

"Not one man dealing with a worldwide flood," God said. "But there have been a number of people who've had to deal with smaller disasters."

"People you ordered to save a few and let the rest die?"

"Yes," God said.

She shuddered and turned to face him again. "And what then? Did they go mad?" Even she could hear the disapproval and disgust in her voice.

God chose to hear the question as only a question. "Some took refuge in madness, some in drunkenness, some in sexual license. Some killed themselves. Some survived and lived long, fruitful lives."

Martha shook her head and managed to keep quiet.

"I don't do that any longer," God said.

No, Martha thought. Now he had found a different amusement. "How big a change do I have to make?" she asked. "What will please you and cause you to let me go and not bring in someone else to replace me?"

"I don't know," God said, and he smiled. He rested his head back against the tree. "Because I don't know what you will do. That's a lovely sensation— anticipating, not knowing."

"Not from my point of view," Martha said bitterly. After a while, she said in a different tone, "Definitely not from my point of view. Because I don't know what to do. I really don't."

"You write stories for a living," God said. "You create characters and situations, problems and solutions. That's less than I've given you to do."

"But you want me to tamper with real people. I don't want to do that. I'm afraid I'll make some horrible mistake."

"I'll answer your questions," God said. "Ask."

She didn't want to ask. After a while, though, she gave in. "What, exactly, do you want? A utopia? Because I don't believe in them. I don't believe it's possible to arrange a society so that everyone is content, everyone has what he or she wants."

"Not for more than a few moments," God said. "That's how long it would take for someone to decide that he wanted what his neighbor had— or that he wanted his neighbor as a slave of one kind or another, or that he wanted his neighbor dead. But never mind. I'm not asking you to create a utopia, Martha, although it would be interesting to see what you could come up with."

"So what are you asking me to do?"

"To help them, of course. Haven't you wanted to do that?"

"Always," she said. "And I never could in any meaningful way. Famines, epidemics, floods, fires, greed, slavery, revenge, stupid, stupid wars. . . ."

"Now you can. Of course, you can't put an end to all of those things without putting an end to humanity, but you can diminish some of the problems. Fewer wars, less covetousness, more forethought and care with the environment . . . What might cause that?"

She looked at her hands, then at him. Something had occurred to her as he spoke, but it seemed both too simple and too fantastic, and to her personally, perhaps, too painful. Could it be done? Should it be done? Would it really help if it were done? She asked, "Was there really anything like the Tower of Babel? Did you make people suddenly unable to understand each other?"

God nodded. "Again, it happened several times in one way or another."

"So what did you do? Change their thinking somehow, alter their memories?"

"Yes, I've done both. Although before literacy, all I had to do was divide them physically, send one group to a new land or give one group a custom that altered their mouths—knocking out the front teeth during puberty rites, for instance. Or give them a strong aversion to something others of their kind consider precious or sacred or—"

To her amazement, Martha interrupted him. "What about changing people's . . . I don't know, their brain activity. Can I do that?"

"Interesting," God said. "And probably dangerous. But you can do that if you decide to. What do you have in mind?"

"Dreams," she said. "Powerful, unavoidable, realistic dreams that come every time people sleep."

"Do you mean," God asked, "that they should be taught some lesson through their dreams?"

"Maybe. But I really mean that somehow people should spend a lot of their energy in their dreams. They would have their own personal best of all possible worlds during their dreams. The dreams should be much more realistic and intense than most dreams are now. Whatever people love to do most, they should dream about doing it, and the dreams should change to keep up with their individual interests. Whatever grabs their attention, whatever they desire, they can have it in their sleep. In fact, they can't avoid having it. Nothing should be able to keep the dreams away—not drugs, not surgery, not anything. And the dreams should satisfy much more deeply, more thoroughly, than reality can. I mean, the satisfaction should be in the dreaming, not in trying to make the dream real."

God smiled. "Why?"

"I want them to have the only possible utopia." Martha thought for a moment. "Each person will have a private, perfect utopia every night—or an imperfect one. If they crave conflict and struggle, they get that. If they want peace and love, they get that. Whatever they want or need comes to them. I think if people go to a . . . well, a private heaven every night, it might take the edge off their willingness to spend their waking hours trying to dominate or destroy one another." She hesitated. "Won't it?"

God was still smiling. "It might. Some people will be taken over by it as though it were an addictive drug. Some will try to fight it in themselves or others. Some will give up on their lives and decide to die because nothing they do matters as much as their dreams. Some will enjoy it and try to go on with their familiar lives, but even they will find that the dreams interfere with their relations with other people. What will humankind in general do? I don't know." He seemed interested, almost excited. "I think it might dull them too much at first—until they're used to it. I wonder whether they can get used to it."

Martha nodded. "I think you're right about it dulling them. I think at first most people will lose interest in a lot of other things—including real, wide-awake sex. Real sex is risky to both the health and the ego. Dream sex will be fantastic and not risky at all. Fewer children will be born for a while."

"And fewer of those will survive," God said.

"What?"

"Some parents will certainly be too involved in dreams to take care of their children. Loving and raising children is risky, too, and it's hard work.

"That shouldn't happen. Taking care of their kids should be the one thing that parents want to do for real in spite of the dreams. I don't want to be responsible for a lot of neglected kids."

"So you want people—adults and children—to have nights filled with vivid, wish-fulfilling dreams, but parents should somehow see child care as more important than the dreams, and the children should not be seduced away from their parents by the dreams, but should want and need a relationship with them as though there were no dreams?"

"As much as possible." Martha frowned, imagining what it might be like to live in such a world. Would people still read books? Perhaps they would to feed their dreams. Would she still be able to write books? Would she want to? What would happen to her if the only work she had ever cared for was lost? "People should still care about their families and their work," she said. "The dreams shouldn't take away their self-respect. They shouldn't be content to dream on a park bench or in an alley. I just want the dreams to slow things down a little. A little less aggression, as you said, less covetousness. Nothing slows people down like satisfaction, and this satisfaction will come every night."

God nodded. "Is that it, then? Do you want this to happen?"

"Yes. I mean, I think so."

"Are you sure?"

She stood up and looked down at him. "Is it what I should do? Will it work? Please tell me."

"I truly don't know. I don't want to know. I want to watch it all unfold. I've used dreams before, you know, but not like this."

His pleasure was so obvious that she almost took the whole idea back. He seemed able to be amused by terrible things. "Let me think about this," she said. "Can I be by myself for a while?"

God nodded. "Speak aloud to me when you want to talk. I'll come to you."

And she was alone. She was alone inside what looked and felt like her home—her little house in Seattle, Washington. She was in her living room.

Without thinking, she turned on a lamp and stood looking at her books. Three of the walls of the room were covered with bookshelves. Her books were there in their familiar order. She picked up several, one after another—history, medicine, religion, art, crime. She opened them to see that they were indeed her books, highlighted and written in by her own hand as she researched this novel or that short story.

She began to believe she really was at home. She had had some sort of strange waking dream about meeting with a God who looked like Michelangelo's Moses and who ordered her to come up with a way to make humanity a less self-destructive species. The experience felt completely, unnervingly real, but it couldn't have been. It was too ridiculous.

She went to her front window and opened the drapes. Her house was on a hill and faced east. Its great luxury was that it offered a beautiful view of Lake Washington just a few blocks down the hill.

But now, there was no lake. Outside was the park that she had wished into existence earlier. Perhaps twenty yards from her front window was the big red Norway maple tree and the bench where she had sat and talked with God.

The bench was empty now and in deep shadow. It was getting dark outside.

She closed the drapes and looked at the lamp that lit the room. For a moment, it bothered her that it was on and using electricity in this Twilight Zone of a place. Had her house been transported here, or had it been duplicated? Or was it all a complex hallucination?

She sighed. The lamp worked. Best to just accept it. There was light in the room. There was a room, a house. How it all worked was the least of her problems.

She went to the kitchen and there found all the food she had had at home. Like the lamp, the refrigerator, the electric stove top, and the oven worked. She could prepare a meal. It would be at least as real as anything else she'd run across recently. And she was hungry.

She took a small can of solid white albacore tuna and containers of dill weed and curry powder from the cupboard and got bread, lettuce, dill pickles, green onions, mayonnaise, and chunky salsa from the refrigerator.

She would have a tuna-salad sandwich or two. Thinking about it made her even hungrier.

Then she had another thought, and she said aloud, "May I ask you a question?"

And they were walking together on a broad, level dirt pathway bordered by dark, ghostly silhouettes of trees. Night had fallen, and the darkness beneath the trees was impenetrable. Only the pathway was a ribbon of pale light—starlight and moonlight. There was a full moon, brilliant, yellow-white, and huge. And there was a vast canopy of stars. She had seen the night sky this way only a few times in her life. She had always lived in cities where the lights and the smog obscured all but the brightest few stars.

She looked upward for several seconds, then looked at God and saw, somehow, without surprise, that he was black now, and clean-shaven. He was a tall, stocky black man wearing ordinary, modern clothing—a dark sweater over a white shirt and dark pants. He didn't tower over her, but he was taller than the human-sized version of the white God had been. He didn't look anything like the white Moses-God, and yet he was the same person. She never doubted that.

"You're seeing something different," God said. "What is it?" Even his voice was changed, deepened.

She told him what she was seeing, and he nodded. "At some point, you'll probably decide to see me as a woman," he said.

"I didn't decide to do this," she said. "None of it is real, anyway."

"I've told you," he said. "Everything is real. It's just not as you see it."

She shrugged. It didn't matter—not compared to what she wanted to ask. "I had a thought," she said, "and it scared me. That's why I called you. I sort of asked about it before, but you didn't give me a direct answer, and I guess I need one."

He waited.

"Am I dead?"

"Of course not," he said, smiling. "You're here."

"With you," she said bitterly.

Silence.

"Does it matter how long I take to decide what to do?"

"I've told you, no. Take as long as you like."

That was odd, Martha thought. Well, everything was odd. On impulse, she said, "Would you like a tuna-salad sandwich?"

"Yes," God said. "Thank you."

They walked back to the house together instead of simply appearing there. Martha was grateful for that. Once inside, she left him sitting in her living room, paging through a fantasy novel and smiling. She went through the motions of making the best tuna-salad sandwiches she could. Maybe effort counted. She didn't believe for a moment that she was preparing real food or that she and God were going to eat it.

And yet, the sandwiches were delicious. As they ate, Martha remembered the sparkling apple cider that she kept in the refrigerator for company. She went to get it, and when she got back to the living room, she saw that God had, in fact, become a woman.

Martha stopped, startled, then sighed. "I see you as female now," she said. "Actually, I think you look a little like me. We look like sisters." She smiled wearily and handed over a glass of cider.

God said, "You really are doing this yourself, you know. But as long as it isn't upsetting you, I suppose it doesn't matter."

"It does bother me. If I'm doing it, why did it take so long for me to see you as a black woman—since that's no more true than seeing you as a white or a black man?"

"As I've told you, you see what your life has prepared you to see." God looked at her, and for a moment, Martha felt that she was looking into a mirror.

Martha looked away. "I believe you. I just thought I had already broken out of the mental cage I was born and raised in—a human God, a white God, a male God. . . ."

"If it were truly a cage," God said, "you would still be in it, and I would still look the way I did when you first saw me."

"There is that," Martha said. "What would you call it then?"

"An old habit," God said. "That's the trouble with habits. They tend to outlive their usefulness."

Martha was quiet for a while. Finally she said, "What do you think about my dream idea? I'm not asking you to foresee the future. Just find fault. Punch holes. Warn me."

God rested her head against the back of the chair. "Well, the evolving environmental problems will be less likely to cause wars, so there will probably be less starvation, less disease. Real power will be less satisfying than the vast, absolute power they can possess in their dreams, so fewer people will be driven to try to conquer their neighbors or exterminate their minorities. All in all, the dreams will probably give humanity more time than it would have without them."

Martha was alarmed in spite of herself. "Time to do what?"

"Time to grow up a little. Or at least, time to find some way of surviving what remains of its adolescence." God smiled. "How many times have you wondered how some especially self-destructive individual managed to survive adolescence? It's a valid concern for humanity as well as for individual human beings."

"Why can't the dreams do more than that?" she asked. "Why can't the dreams be used not just to give them their heart's desire when they sleep, but to push them toward some kind of waking maturity? Although I'm not sure what species maturity might be like."

"Exhaust them with pleasure," God mused, "while teaching them that pleasure isn't everything."

"They already know that."

"Individuals usually know that by the time they reach adulthood. But all too often, they don't care. It's too easy to follow bad but attractive leaders, embrace pleasurable but destructive habits, ignore looming disaster because maybe it won't happen after all—or maybe it will only happen to other people. That kind of thinking is part of what it means to be adolescent."

"Can the dreams teach—or at least promote—more thoughtfulness when people are awake, promote more concern for real consequences?"

"It can be that way if you like."

"I do. I want them to enjoy themselves as much as they can while they're asleep, but to be a lot more awake and aware when they are awake, a lot less susceptible to lies, peer pressure, and self-delusion."

"None of this will make them perfect, Martha."

Martha stood looking down at God, fearing that she had missed something important, and that God knew it and was amused. "But this will help?" she said. "It will help more than it will hurt."

"Yes, it will probably do that. And it will no doubt do other things. I don't know what they are, but they are inevitable. Nothing ever works smoothly with humankind."

"You like that, don't you?"

"I didn't at first. They were mine, and I didn't know them. You cannot begin to understand how strange that was." God shook her head. "They were as familiar as my own substance, and yet they weren't."

"Make the dreams happen," Martha said.

"Are you sure?"

"Make them happen."

"You're ready to go home, then."

"Yes."

God stood and faced her. "You want to go. Why?"

"Because I don't find them interesting in the same way you do. Because your ways scare me."

God laughed—a less disturbing laugh now. "No, they don't," she said. "You're beginning to like my ways."

After a time, Martha nodded. "You're right. It did scare me at first, and now it doesn't. I've gotten used to it. In just the short time that I've been here, I've gotten used to it, and I'm starting to like it. That's what scares me."

In mirror image, God nodded, too. "You really could have stayed here, you know. No time would pass for you. No time has passed."

"I wondered why you didn't care about time."

"You'll go back to the life you remember, at first. But soon, I think you'll have to find another way of earning a living. Beginning again at your age won't be easy."

Martha stared at the neat shelves of books on her walls. "Reading will suffer, won't it—pleasure reading, anyway?"

"It will—for a while, anyway. People will read for information and for ideas, but they'll create their own fantasies. Did you think of that before you made your decision?"

Martha sighed. "Yes," she said. "I did." Sometime later, she added, "I want to go home."

"Do you want to remember being here?" God asked.

"No." On impulse, she stepped to God and hugged her—hugged her hard, feeling the familiar woman's body beneath the blue jeans and black T-shirt that looked as though it had come from Martha's own closet. Martha realized that somehow, in spite of everything, she had come to like this seductive, childlike, very dangerous being. "No," she repeated. "I'm afraid of the unintended damage that the dreams might do."

"Even though in the long run they'll almost certainly do more good than harm?" God asked.

"Even so," Martha said. "I'm afraid the time might come when I won't be able to stand knowing that I'm the one who caused not only the harm, but the end of the only career I've ever cared about. I'm afraid knowing all that might drive me out of my mind someday." She stepped away from God, and already God seemed to be fading, becoming translucent, transparent, gone.

"I want to forget," Martha said, and she stood alone in her living room, looking blankly past the open drapes of her front window at the surface of Lake Washington and the mist that hung above it. She wondered at the words she had just spoken, wondered what it was she wanted so badly to forget.

ANDREA HAIRSTON

Double Consciousness

> You see what you think you see. You find what you look for. If you can't imagine it, it won't happen for you. Imagine the impossible, imagine the spirit of your enemies, imagine miracles, imagine the last moment of your life, imagine eternity. Imagine what you can't imagine.
> —Vera Xa Lalafia, Healer Cosmology, The Final Lessons

They say, Celestina died once, but had to come back to life. Death didn't want her storming his domain. For citizens of New Ouagadougou this was no quaint urban legend, but poetic truth. They longed to know the story behind the story. Who would tell them, now that Celestina had gone on to dance with the ancestors? Elleni should write a suite for the fifty-string Kora. *Daughter of my mind and spirit, do you hear what I say? Sing my song, Elleni. Dance my struggle.*

The sun drifted below the hills surrounding *Seelenwald,* the forest of souls. Celestina was two people again, Thandiwe and Robin, seventy-five years ago, just moments before she poisoned herself. Alora blossoms unfurled in the twilight, splashes of color popping open in the shadowy cathedral tree forest. Enchanted by their florescent glow, Robin leaned against a slippery tree trunk and slid to the ground.

Forty years of sun and wind, of unanswered questions and hard living, had mapped deep lines in Robin's forehead and around her hazel eyes and inward-turned mouth. Bad gene art had thinned her wavy brown hair, so she'd cropped the sparse tresses to a downy skullcap. Thandiwe ran her fingers through this elegant buzz cut while plucking alora blossoms. Robin rarely smiled, but this evening, savoring Thandi's touch and gazing up through branches and vines, she grinned so hard her jaw ached. Fearless weaver ant sentries spit venom at the giant intruders as their younger sisters repaired a storm-ravaged nest.

"Old lady weaver ants are fierce about protecting their homeland," Thandiwe remarked.

Robin didn't hear her. She was on another track. "I can't believe you just sashayed into Council and snatched the Healers' top-secret holiest of holies from the shrine." Robin pointed a teak and ebony corridor staff at the flurry of life above her. Warriors worn smooth from years of handling cavorted around the wood. Femi's staff was almost as old as the Barrier. "Nobody in Paradigma has ever gotten their hands on an artifact from another dimension. Hell, people don't know these corridor staffs exist."

"It's a secret in New Ouagadougou as well. Only Council, only those initiated in the Final Lessons know about opening the corridors."

"We're about to change everything! Vera Xa Lalafia's final wisdom belongs to the world. No more retro secret society politics, no more holding truth hostage, no more barriers keeping us from one another, no . . . Ow!" Robin sliced her hand on the red orange crystals above the warriors. "That's sharp!"

"Can you see the new world we're making? What does it look like?"

Robin sucked a bloody finger. "I don't know, but I'd like to hurry up and get to it. When do we cut a corridor and get the hell out of Dodge?"

"They'll be watching the Barrier for miles, checking everyone. We couldn't get close enough to make a corridor. But Council won't look here. People come to *Seelenwald* to speak to the dead or die. We're safe for a few days, then we can leave." Thandiwe hovered above the renegade scientist. Spidery robes clung to her sweaty skin, but concealed nothing. An ordinary, middle-aged brown woman with gentle eyes, plump cheeks, and an expressive jaw, she whispered prayers in the twilight. She asked the universe to forgive them both in a language Robin did not speak.

"I thought most Healers didn't believe in God, so why are you always praying?" Robin asked.

"We believe in *prayer,* in the power of words to transform reality," Thandiwe replied. "The mind feasts on metaphors." Deadly alora vines filled her arms and she showered them down on Robin. "The alora bloom only one night."

The spicy fragrance of the blossoms and Thandiwe's earthy scent intoxicated Robin. Although she was loath to let Femi's staff slip from her grasp, she leaned it against the tree and pulled her beloved to the ground, kissing at raisin nipples through the spidery robes. "I could die right now," Robin murmured.

"What?" Thandiwe's body stiffened.

"Don't Healers say that in one of your multitude of languages?" Robin sat up and gazed at Thandi who was framed by black marbled roots arching out of the ground. "God, you look so serious. That's my dour face, not yours."

"We don't play with death," Thandi snapped. Her eyes filled with tears. "I never understand you."

Robin brushed the back of her hand across Thandi's cheeks and lips. "Figure of speech. Doesn't mean anything, just, I'm on the threshold of the greatest adventure of my life. You and I, my sweet, about to go down in history. I'd like to hold this moment, forever."

Thandiwe pulled Robin between her thighs. Their skin stuck together. Robin's shorts had crawled up to her crotch.

"Alora leaves sharpen the mind, chase away madness." Thandiwe broke poisonous leaves off the vines. "Chew slowly, it's like a veil lifted, like a moment of forever."

Robin hesitated. "Are they all right to eat, straight from the wild—without washing? How do they taste?"

"Sweet," Thandiwe said. "And the rain has washed them clean."

"For you, my love, anything." Robin opened her mouth and closed her eyes. Thandiwe balled up a fist of leaves, but brought it to her own lips instead. Robin, her mouth still gaping open, peeked at Thandiwe with one eye. "What are you doing?"

Thandiwe placed the lethal leaves on Robin's tongue with shaking hands.

"You're not having any?" Robin chewed slowly and swallowed. "Forever tastes pretty good. Something in this mimics neurotransmitters?" She jumped at a branch snapping in the woods. "What's that?"

"The wind, an animal, some spirit moving in the twilight." Thandiwe looked toward the sound. "Not a posse chasing us down for our crimes. Not yet."

Robin stared into the gathering darkness. "Do Healers really believe *Seelenwald* is haunted?"

"Of course not. Our imaginations are haunted, not a grove of trees." Thandiwe turned back to Robin, tears blurring her eyes. "You still can't see who we are, can you?" She fed herself leaves and wilted flowers, a nonlethal combination.

"Second thoughts? Don't worry, I have you to guide me through ignorance." Robin pressed her mouth against Thandi's belly and enjoyed the quivering that radiated from her lips. At a loud gasp of passion, Robin felt triumphant. "I'm stealing you and his corridor staff, Femi will certainly be jealous, when he finds out."

"Indeed. He is *der Geistesvater*," Thandiwe said tonelessly.

Robin's lips went dry against Thandiwe's trembling stomach. "The 'father of my mind and spirit.' You won't tell me, what does that mean, you were lovers . . . what?"

Thandiwe sighed. "More than lovers. Femi is my teacher, mentor. We . . ."

"What?" Robin asked, feeling something awful flicker across Thandi's skin.

"No. I cannot explain to the uninitiated."

"Not even to me?"

"It is a question of experience, not words. An experience that I desecrate by . . ."

Robin squeezed her. "It's okay. You'll initiate me to all of your secrets, in time. Going against Femi feels like betrayal but we can't stand by and do nothing as he wages a secret war on *Vermittler.*"

"Stop," Thandiwe said.

"It's genocide. Rank and file Ouagadougians wouldn't go for it, if they knew the truth, I don't care what Femi says about evil empires threatening the future of New Ouagadougou . . ."

"What he does is wrong . . . yet, if your whole future is under assault, there's sometimes nothing else but the wrong thing to do. But let's not talk of this." Thandiwe pressed one hand on Robin's mouth and gestured in the air with the other as if to ward off bad spirits, but it was too late. They both conjured images of Femi: a bull of a man, short and stocky, reddish-brown skin, bushy eyebrows that met a little off center. For an instant he took up all the room in their minds.

"It's as if he watches us now." Thandiwe squinted through trees and bushes.

"Femi's a warped genius, thinks your thoughts before you do. Kinda makes my heart race," Robin confessed. "But he's not right. Am I so evil, that I've ruined you?"

"Perhaps I am ruining you," Thandiwe said.

"Ha!" A wave of dizziness blurred Robin's vision and shuffled her stomach about. "This alora kicks in fast."

"Hmm," Thandiwe grunted. Her mind was very clear.

"Hmm," Robin repeated. She pressed her face between Thandiwe's warm breasts and savored the musky odors. "I'm rambling. What're you so quiet about?"

"No matter what, I love you." Thandi rested her cheek in the swirl of hair on top of Robin's head. "This is a moment we will always have."

"Romantic." Robin leaned against the tree trunk to gaze at Thandiwe. The rise and fall of breath, breast, and belly through spidery iridescence was hypnotic. The spicy aroma of their mutual arousal forecasted a night of sweet coupling. Optimism claimed her spirits. "Council's not all against us. The lady with the white blond hair . . . practically down to her knees . . . fierce."

"Awa." Thandiwe ripped dead blossoms from a vine and thrust them at Robin.

"I bet we could persuade Awa not to kill *Vermittler* too. What? They're a little wilted, honey." Noting Thandiwe's clenched jaw and scrunched eyes, Robin took the droopy flowers and stuck them behind her ears. "Think what we can learn from *Vermittler*. They're not just hunks of wood and crystal with a few set operations, albeit miraculous. *Vermittler* are a living conduit to another . . . dimension. Why would Femi want to exterminate a biological treasure?" Robin's eyes welled up with tears. "Symbiogenesis—a new species formed by genetic recombination and co-evolution."

"Vera Xa Lalafia was a great shaman to work with the Barrier. . . ."

"A hell of a gene artist, a biological revolutionary. . . ."

"Your passion carries you away, you forget the threat the Barrier poses. . . ."

"No, what Vera did, the Final Lessons, it's incredible!"

"You don't know the half of it."

"So why don't you tell me about it?" Robin's tongue seemed to swell and fill her mouth. "Do I sound funny? Drunk or something?"

"No." Thandiwe gathered Robin into her arms with such a grand gesture, Robin felt weak in the knees like a teenager at first love.

"Femi hates me." Robin's mind was clear as glass, just as Thandi promised. If she shook herself too hard though, these moments might shatter. "But I understand."

"Do you?" Thandiwe looked directly in her eyes. "He hates us both."

"He thinks I'm stealing your precious Barrier secrets and desecrating sacred mysteries for profit, for SCIENCE, for power."

"Aren't you?"

"No, you know that." Robin laughed. "Sharing secrets, busting the Barrier open won't be the end of the world. New Ouagadougou won't get swallowed up by Paradigma."

"History argues against you."

"History didn't have us to, what is that old Yoruba saying—*Mo so awon enia mi po*—I tie all my people together?"

"I want to believe you, but. . . ." Thandiwe looked up to the stars.

Robin tried to lift her arm, but it was too much effort. She nuzzled Thandi's neck with her nose and lips. "Yeah, okay, so at first I was coming to steal, to desecrate, whatever, but that was before I got to know you, before I fell in love with you, your whole way of life in New Ouagadougou. What'd I know before?" Thandiwe glanced at the corridor staff she'd stolen from the shrine. "Come on, Healers don't believe in God, so how could Femi claim we're desecrating anything?"

Thandiwe pressed Robin against her. "Honoring the sacred has nothing to do with God. It's a crime, what we've done, what I've done. I am gambling my homeland on the word of a stranger who acts without clear vision."

"What do you mean? Okay, I don't throw colored sand into images, my mandalas are questions." Robin kissed Thandi's salty skin and whispered, "It's like a fairy tale, a miracle. The wicked scientist comes to paradise to seduce the fair maiden. . . ."

Thandiwe groaned.

"All right, seduce the dark, mature Healer woman and steal her world," Robin continued. "But instead of betraying the mighty wizards of the land, the wicked scientist goes native. She and the mature Healer woman PROMISE to work together, to create a bright new world, as yet unseen, undiscovered. There they will live happily ever after."

Sparklers spit light all around *Seelenwald*. For a moment Robin thought dead souls had come to chase them from paradise and she would have to shout them back down to their subconscious realm. . . . But she couldn't remember how to shout or what she just thought or how she'd lost her feet her hands her back her breasts her mouth. . . .

Thandiwe rocked Robin's almost lifeless body.

"You must be careful with fairy tales. There are always many stories behind the one story." Femi's mellow bass filled Thandi's ears. Councilors in funeral regalia, carrying white rayon banners and sparklers, stepped from the cathedral tree shadows. Femi retrieved his corridor staff as they surrounded Thandiwe and Robin. He kicked aside wilted blossoms, his eyes blazing, fire dripping from his lips. "Thandiwe Xa Femi, alora leaves are lethal without the flowers. You know the punishment for murder."

"If you take a life, then it is yours." Awa quoted Council law. Thandiwe's beloved friend stood beside Femi shaking her head, white blond hair glowing in the dark.

Other Councilors moved in close to hear Thandiwe's response.

"I did what you told me, Femi, to save the world from catastrophe. Our secrets are now safe." Thandiwe pressed against Robin and refused to let Femi take up all the room in her imagination. "I betrayed Council, I betrayed Robin, giving her knowledge that she could not bear. *That was my crime;* this is my sacrifice. I knew it would mark my spirit as I put poison in her mouth, but how could I think of saving my own soul when the world was at stake."

A few Councilors clicked their tongues and sucked in whistling breaths.

"So, this is your trap, Femi, to be rid of them both," Awa said. She doused her sparkler in the dirt and stepped away from him. "I must walk away from your circle."

Before other Councilors could break ranks, Femi whirled through them, touching uncertain shoulders, glaring into guarded eyes, pounding Awa's objection into the dust. "Those who betray us to the uninitiated condemn themselves. Only a murderer would get snared in such a trap. Thandiwe did not find another way to save the future. Playing on the enemy battlefield, you are the enemy. We must proceed before it's too late. Robin will not linger among the living. Our justice must be swift." He gave the Councilors no time to disagree. "Thandiwe Xa Femi and Robin Wolf, you stand condemned to Double Consciousness." Calling to the Barrier, he sang low notes almost beyond the range of human hearing and pounded the ground with his staff. The Earth was his drum, the stars his witnesses. Who could walk away now?

"Promise you won't leave me alone," Thandiwe whispered in Robin's ears as she laid her on the ground. "Your way would destroy us, but I promise never to betray myself or our dreams again. Don't leave me now and I'll initiate you to all my secrets. I'll find another way."

Awa turned away from the circle and before Thandiwe could blink, Femi slashed her head with the red orange crystals on his corridor staff. The pain was so loud and dense, she slumped down against an unconscious Robin, gasping and drooling. A shaft of Barrier energy split the night sky. It arced over cathedral trees, passed through Robin, then flowed into the corridor staff. The crystals turned black, like a massive collapsed star. The last thing Thandiwe saw was Femi snorting ashes and sculpting a corridor between her and Robin. In a terrible instant, Thandiwe was engulfed by an alien presence and everything that she had been seemed lost forever.

The sweet song of dolphins chased away the lingering pain and. . . .

Celestina floated in a magenta sea on the Barrier starship, clutching the soggy roll of parchment that Elleni had tossed in the ocean at her funeral. Elleni was here with her. Elleni was a witness.

Sing my song, daughter.

Femi and the other Councilors never expected Robin and Thandiwe to survive more than a few moments in the same skin, never expected them to keep all their promises. How they managed life imprisonment together for seventy-five years was quite a sordid story, *ein Wunder,* but surely Thandiwe and Robin's debt to society had been paid in full. As architect of the Interzonal Treaty, Celestina had kept all her promises, brought peace to the world. Robin and Thandiwe's suffering should be over now. Why couldn't she die?

Dynamo Hum

"There are those," said Lara Godolphin, as she drove us along the country road, "who maintain that the human mind is nothing more than a great big chemical stew." Lara, as my therapist insisted I call her, sparkled and fluttered as she spoke, with the metallic glint of multiple bangle bracelets and the snap of several long silk scarves borne on the wind of our passage. I watched the scarves with some anxiety, as one or two seemed long enough to catch an axle, with results all too easy to anticipate. But it is my long-standing policy not to interfere in the personal lives of crazy white ladies, so I said nothing.

Lara gestured with one arm, unconcerned. "I decline to dispute this theory," she continued, "but what I do ask is this: If our bodies are a vat, and our hormones, blood, lymph, and all that the ingredients of this stew, who is the cook? *Who,* my dear Doris," she repeated for emphasis, "*is the cook?*"

"DNA?" I ventured, *sotto voce.*

"Electricity!" she exclaimed, slapping the steering wheel with one large, be-ringed hand. She appeared not to have heard me, caught up as she was in expounding her theory. "Electricity is the cook, and he follows the recipe book of the geophysical field."

"Stop sign ahead," I pointed out.

"Yes, of course, I see it," she said, applying the brakes. We came to a halt and the wind dropped to a gentle, summer-morning breeze. We rested at the top of a gradual slope, a soft morainic rise. To our left, the land dropped away to reveal a gravel pit. Distance reduced the noise of two or three trucks to a pleasant grumble. To our right, on a sort of miniature prairie, a blocky concrete building loomed, surrounded by fences. A long drive led to it from the road our path had just intersected, marked at either end by small yellowish-beige buildings—security checkpoints, I guessed. Lara turned right. Soon my guess was confirmed, as we stopped abruptly beside the first. A young man whose uniform matched the paint leaned out through an open doorway. His face registered recognition and faint but undeniable disapproval. "Dr. Godolphin?" he asked rhetorically.

"And client," she replied, waving one glittering arm in my direction. "I know we're a little early, but they're predicting thunderstorms this afternoon, and I want Doris' first balancing session free of atmospheric galvaniza—"

"One moment, and I'll phone up Mr. Lodi," the young man interrupted. He disappeared into the beige-ish booth. Lara cut the motor, and his voice floated back out to us, a murmur inconstant as the buzzing of a bee which stops at the mouth of flower after flower.

Several moments passed, and Lara glanced at me with amusement as I endeavored to sit up straight in the bucket seat. My feet were planted flat on the floor, my loafers lined up in careful parallel. My right hand toyed with the winding stem of my antique wristwatch, a move we had established in earlier sessions as synonymous with my frustration at being unable to control the current situation.

The young man reappeared and gave us the go-ahead. "What would have happened if they denied us access?" I asked as we drove past the second guard.

"Oh, you know. Tire shredders, I guess. Maybe some rubber bullets. Knute hasn't been too forthcoming about their antiterrorist devices, and I haven't unleashed my Wonder-Child self on him with all her questions. Those bureaucrats he works for aren't so sure it's a good idea to donate space to our Institute in the first place."

We drove past a low, dirt-colored sign, barely visible against the woodchip mulch surrounding a clump of bushes. "Midwest Electric Power Coordination Center," it announced discreetly. But anyone who had gotten this far already knew that.

There was no space in the parking lot. Lara made a couple of circuits, then pulled off onto the grass. She led me up a flight of narrow, shallow, concrete steps. "Let's hope our security badges are ready," she said, waiting with one hand on the door. "Step closer, Doris, so they can scan you. So foolish, this reliance on material means of protection." With a click, the black glass door swung open.

The lobby was surprisingly small, about the size of a large bathroom. It held a white Formica workstation, a Norfolk pine, two semipadded, metal-legged chairs joined at the hip by a white plastic magazine rack, a slender receptionist, and a good deal of overly conditioned air. I shivered, glad of my suit jacket and stockings.

The receptionist thought at first that our badges were ready, but of course they weren't. She began making calls and we settled into the two chairs to wait. Lara seemed eager to recapitulate the theory behind today's treatment. "All the electrical energy in a five-state area is controlled through here," she explained. "All the artificially generated energy, that is."

"Mmm-hmm," I replied, picking through the magazines: *Southeast Michigan Contractor,* mostly.

"This control is the highest manifestation of power—not the electricity itself, but its purest semiotic essence. So within the Crystal Cave, enormous energies will be focused on you, and your chakras will be enabled to retrieve their full dynamism—"

Baptists and business majors don't believe in Hindu religious concepts like locations on your body called chakras, I wanted to tell her. I was raised as the first one, and converted in college to the second, and the only reason I was here was Rick, my fiancé. He was gorgeous; brilliant, too, but a little more forward-thinking than me. Degrees in Sociology, Philosophy, and Anthro. After much discussion, he'd convinced me that premarital sex would strengthen our relationship.

Embarrassment heated my face, and I pulled a magazine at random from the rack, pretending instant absorption. I was dark enough not to blush, but Lara was all too apt at reading the subtleties of my expression. Rick's attempts to "fulfill" me had been disturbing enough to experience. Subsequent tellings and retellings, even to a nominal member of Rick's family like Lara, grew more and more painful. I didn't think I could bear to bring that evening to light once again here in this chilly, tiny room.

The magazine I was hiding behind was so close to my eyes that the letters swam in a disorderly blur. I held it at the proper distance and started reading an interview with the woman who provided the nonslip strips for the ramps in Illitch Stadium. A photo showed her looking self-assured and successful, leaning against the edge of her desk. She probably had earth-shattering climaxes. What was wrong with me? I'd read about orgasms; why couldn't I have one?

"Dr. Godolphin?" The receptionist's timid voice rescued me from my reverie. "Mr. Lodi will be down directly to see you. He said he'd bring the badges here himself."

"Fantastic," said Lara, turning to me excitedly. "You'll get to meet Knute. Perhaps he can provide some insight into your difficulties."

I was immediately furious. "You mean you discussed my case with your boyfriend, Lara? I know your methods of treatment are unorthodox, but that's just plain unprofessional of you!"

My therapist held up one bejeweled hand and made soothing, petting motions in my direction. "No, no, no, dear, of course I wouldn't do that. But Knute is the most discerning man I know. He has these eyes . . . he just seems to cut through to the heart of things with one look. But you'll understand when you see him."

I realized I was standing and sat down again, somewhat shaky in the wake of my receding anger. I took several deep breaths, attempting to calm myself.

The door behind the receptionist opened, revealing a large, shaggy-looking man wearing a cardigan over a sweater vest and a tweedy tie. Waves of white hair cascaded about his ears, in sharp contrast to his dark, neatly trimmed beard. He had a nose like a rosy ski-jump and his eyes were a quiet yet soul-piercing blue.

"Sorry about the delay, Lara. Welcome," he added to me, nodding. He removed his cardigan and offered it to Lara. "'Fraid the AC's on the fritz again. SNAFU. We're on a waiting list for a service man. I tell 'em, let me take a crack at it, but I'm a coordinator, they say, and I better stick to my coordinating."

He spoke from the doorway, not attempting to enter the little lobby, which would have been hard-pressed to hold him. "Here's the badges." He handed them to the receptionist, who passed them on to us—laminated yellow cards stamped with our names and the date, probably magnetically coded with more important information in the strip along the bottom. I fastened mine to my lapel. Lara threaded a scarf through the pin on the back of hers and knotted the end.

"Time for a tour first?" asked Knute as we crowded through the door. I brushed against him and felt my skin tingle. Odd. "I've got that new, experimental Relegator Display to show off." Apparently he had noticed nothing. He stood calmly on the landing of a staircase, awaiting Lara's answer.

"Oh, no," she said, explaining about the thunderstorm. "And anyway, we can't detain you from your work like this, sweetheart. Go on, we've got our badges. I'll meet you for lunch after I get Doris all set up. Maybe she can see the place when she's done."

That arranged, the two kissed, and Lara and I headed down the stairs, while Knute climbed ponderously up.

We descended two flights. Lara used her card to open the door at the bottom. "Why no elevators?" I asked.

"Oh, there are," she replied, waving vaguely. "In other parts of the building. But I'm not cleared to use them." We walked down a long, dim, gray-carpeted corridor. Brown metal doors faced each other off in pairs. Lara stopped at one of these and used her card again to enter.

I stepped in behind her and wondered if the people who ran this place were so security conscious that they key-carded their broom closets. But though the size was right, the contents were all wrong. The shelves contained not cleaners and solvents but glass jars filled with different-colored stones. And the sticks standing in the corner weren't broom or mop handles but actual sticks—wands, Lara had called them when she described the treatment during our last talk.

Light leaked from beneath a door in the opposite wall.

"OK," said Lara. "I'll wait in the hall while you strip. Then just go on in the Cave and lie down, and I'll come in with the stones in a few minutes."

Fervently hoping that the Crystal Cave's vents were shut off, or that Lara had thought to equip it with a space heater, I removed my clothes. I had barely finished folding my pantyhose when the outer door began to open. "Not yet!" I squeaked, somewhat illogically. I was no more naked now than I would be a few minutes later. Still, I was relieved when the door swung quickly closed. I took off my wristwatch, set it squarely on top of my stack of clothes, and entered the Crystal Cave.

I was in an eye. A cat's-eye, made of gems. Every surface sparkled with cut and glittering stones, except for a small slit in the center, shaped like a cat's iris. It was black and velvety-looking. I picked my way slowly across the shining jewels and sank into that darkness. It gave beneath me with a sloshing sound—a water bed. Filled, no doubt, with Our Precious Essences. Anyway, at least it was heated.

Lying on my back, I gazed up at the ceiling. Like stars, the stones twinkled and shone with their own light. The whole room, Lara had told me, was encaged in filaments of incandescing wire. These, in turn, were connected with the displays the controllers used to monitor and switch the region's electrical loads. The crystals focused and directed the light from the filaments, and thus the information represented by that light. And thus, of course, the power represented by that information. She said.

It was pretty. The door opened. I concentrated on how pretty it all was while Lara placed cool round things on me. Some of them wound up in quite intimate places.

I was supposed to be emptying my mind, releasing my, well, my something. Inhibitions, maybe.

It was indescribably boring. When she placed two amethysts on my eyes, I couldn't even see the pretty lights anymore. Soon after that she left, and I bathed uninterrupted in the beneficent effects of electrodynamism, courtesy of several privately owned utility companies and my kooky therapist's boyfriend.

At the thought of Knute, I experienced once again that odd tingle. It was so strange . . . where was it coming from? I couldn't quite place it—it seemed all-pervasive, yet definitely directed. Waves, spreading out from—from there? Oh, god, it was getting stronger, a buzzing like a dentist's drill, vibrating my entire being, a throbbing violence that shook my very core. I couldn't bear it, couldn't stop it, couldn't move, transfixed by this primal power. The therapy was a success, I thought hysterically, as the current built and built within me, one intolerable crescendo followed swiftly by another, and another, and another. The therapy was a success, but the patient died. The sound, the sensations pounding me, intensified, and I cried out, a high scream, wonderfully thin—about a molecule in width, I judged. It broadened and descended till it felt more like a Neolithic axe head, smashing through my invisible restraints. A mighty convulsion ran along my spine, and I was free.

The spasm had dislodged the stones. I opened my eyes, but that made no difference in what I could see. The Crystal Cave was filled with darkness. The filaments must have all burnt out, I decided.

I felt my way to the anteroom. According to my wristwatch I had another half-hour of treatment left till Lara came back and did her rigmarole with the wands. Well, I had had enough. Whatever was supposed to happen next could wait till another session. I threw my clothes on, added a white lab coat hanging on a hook there for warmth, and left to find Lara and share the exciting news of my cure.

Only I got lost. I must have been a little loopy from all that electrodynamism, but it was a big place. It could have happened to anyone. I went back up two flights; or was it three? Probably I took a different staircase. I wound up not on the landing behind the receptionist but on this big, glass-walled internal balcony overlooking a dark pit. The balcony was full of people who looked like they knew exactly what *they* were doing and had no time for anyone who didn't. I should have asked for directions, but I didn't want to get thrown out, and I was positive I could find my own way to the cafeteria. And I might have, too, if they'd had one.

I circled around the balcony a few times. More and more people appeared there, with less and less the look of having some legitimate excuse. They gathered in small, muttering groups. I nodded to those who met my eyes, half-hearing remarks about tying into the new system, about Lodi's Relegator and the possibility of cutbacks once it came fully on line.

A tall, light-skinned man with a head like Charlie Brown scowled at me and told his weedy-looking companion to watch out for the union-buster. Feeling a little unwelcome, though glad of the cover, I decided to try my badge on the next door I passed.

But it opened as I got to it, and a short, ginger-haired woman strode out, arms swinging, jaw clenched. "Look at it!" she shouted, pointing down to the pit. "Just look! I've turned it on so you can see exactly what we're discussing." A crowd gathered by one of the more distant windows. I wandered over, too. It certainly was worth seeing. Sort of like a giant, phosphorescent, rectilinear jellyfish. Or an illuminated, animated, Etch-a-Sketch fountain. Yellow jets of light mounted in one corner, then spread in concentric oblongs, fading. A red river throbbed, deepening, dammed at its square mouth.

"Now you tell me," yelled the woman, "how one controller is going to operate *that!* Sure, this virtual set-up is designed to be more precise. That doesn't mean it's going to be any easier to run! We're going to have to expand staffing, not lay people off!"

A spray of periwinkle shot up from the top of the Relegator. "What the *hell*—" It climbed gradually, gracefully, till it was level with our faces. The shouter's voice dropped to a frightened whisper. "What does *that* mean?" She seemed to be asking me.

I shrugged, then said quite honestly, "I'd like to take a closer look."

As we stepped into the elevator, it occurred to me that she thought there was something wrong with the Relegator. And that I could fix it. "You know, perhaps Knute—"

"Oh, yes, quite," she said, her hand hesitating above a bank of controls. "He should be back in his office by now. I'll get him. Think you can find your way?"

"No," I admitted, reflecting on the elusive cafeteria.

"All right." She looked a little annoyed, but showed me into the pit and left without a fuss.

A roomful of tangled rainbows. A growing, glowing jungle gym—at first I only wanted to watch. But the spout of periwinkle beckoned and I came slowly closer. Then, right in front of me, one rippling pool of turquoise blue drained suddenly from its invisible basin, and my hand cupped to catch it. The warm light tingled through my fingers as I poured it back.

I found the tiny red river and sat down by its banks, slipping off my loafers. Off with the panty hose, as well, I thought, flinging them toward the dim edges of the room.

The red light was good. It pooled up around my feet, sharp and cool, like canned tomatoes. I waded forward, releasing the dam. We flowed intensely on, to the tower of periwinkle which glowed brighter and brighter at our approach. It was twisted now with spirals of blazing white that pulsed and burned and shot off hissing, trilling sparks. I lifted my arms, laughing, and caught them as they flew: sweet birds, fresh jewels of the queenly science of electrodynamism, come to adorn my hands and hair, to spill their splendor in living strands along my shoulders, pouring out in robes of pure, free, progressive light.

I spun once in a wide, slow circle, sparks and fingers fanning, and stopped to orient myself again against the twisting tower. Suddenly, I noticed a disturbance in the field. Knute and Lara burst through the door, seeming unusually distraught.

"My Relegator!" shouted Knute, lunging unsteadily toward me.

"Knute! No!" screamed Lara. "You don't know what kind of charge she's picked up! Stop! I didn't use the *wands* yet, Knute! SHE ISN'T GROUNDED!" But Knute didn't hear her, or didn't care.

He tackled me low, grabbing my waist in a bear hug. His considerable momentum thrust us straight into the spiraling shaft, and it began to blossom into a golden brilliance. Honey and ginger-ale bubbled up between us, washing through our bones, expanding outward as we fell.

With my eyes closed I could still see it all, the incredibly potent light changing the Center's structurals into a sugar-dripping comb, the workers into bees in amber. Blooming petal upon petal, the power opened out: surged, and spread, and surged and spread some more. And surged. And spread. And surged. And spread and spread and spread . . . and faded and faded off into the darkness, crumpling away.

When I recovered, it was hard to tell that anything out of the ordinary had happened. I lay curled comfortably on the floor, bathed once more in the Relegator's many-colored glow. I sat up and crossed my legs, yoga-style. It seemed easier than it should be. The Relegator's twisting tower was gone, and the building around it appeared to be intact. The gallery was empty, but behind me I heard an opening door and the jangling, tinkling step of my therapist as she reentered the pit.

"Glad to see you up and running again, Doris," she said.

"What happened?" I asked. "What'd I do? Where's Knute and everybody?"

"The storm hit."

"What?"

"You know, the one I was so concerned about. Oh, and Knute's just changing his pants. He got pretty excited there, you little Salome, you! Everyone else is off trying to rationalize what happened. I've kept the authority addicts away from you by waggling my medical license at them, but there's no doubt going to be a pretty tense Q-and-A as soon as you feel sufficiently centered to face it."

I reached up and pulled out the loose pins hanging from the remains of my French twist. "Was anyone hurt?"

"Well, not from an Orgonian point of view," Lara temporized. "All you *really* did was give the workers here a well-deserved break, *and* a first-hand example of how good it feels to maximize your full human sexual potential. Oh, and it looks like possibly at some of the generating plants, too . . ."

As it turned out, with the help of the Relegator and a local thunderstorm, I'd somehow managed to share my cure with Knute and a few thousand strangers. I was a little embarrassed.

But apparently the effects were much more diffuse for the others than for Knute. And Rick's not really the jealous type, so there was no harm done to our relationship, in the end. Quite the reverse.

It's just too bad we can't invite everyone to our wedding.

The Ferryman

He lingered in the moist afternoon, pulling fish from the water. Nothing on his line but a hook. Under the blossom tree, there on the bank where the river narrowed, he brought the boat to a rest and stared into the water. *What was it?* He allowed his paddle to nudge the surface, the dugout clung to stillness. *There,* something in the reeds. He reached for it, *shining, luminous,* the silver chain of that girl swallowed up by river, links like silver fishes nipping at the breeze. His body went still. He imagined Dusa rising from the river's floor, thrashing water torn up by its roots. But he laughed. The girl was just a spirit, some haint tale told to scare off children. It was his eyes tripping over light. Overhead the sun bore down on him, standing on his shoulders, making him sweat. He leaned over, *careful now, careful,* conscious of his weight, one hundred fifty-nine pounds reaching with steady hands and breath, *quick, light. Almost,* reach again, *almost,* reach, *al*—got it.

It was then a huge shadow passed over him, some great winged creature catching the light. High on the wing, it held his eyes and a fear came on him.

He'd have to fetch wooden boards, wire, and reeds before night.

She moved like a snake, coiling and uncoiling, the sign of power. Down the road she moved, an ancient road, now dirt and gravel, once a hunting path, trail of those that come before the Speights and the Reynolds, the English and the Spanish, the French and their Africans, a trade route that began in the East and twisted like the wind gathering, returning, receding, returning again, through the heart of the island, past the leaning wood, seven hundred acres then, now only a shadow of itself, until it reached the middle of sacred ground where Those that Come Before once gave blood offerings to the deer and the bull, the wild turkey and the legendary bird with wings as wide as this island, she moved, barefoot, hard-bottomed toes kicking up ditch dust, heels flattening seashells, down to the Double Moon where we sat on mismatched barstools and drank black drink and prayed.

"When she come through the door, everybody got silent," Richard was saying. "Whatn't like she was from the church or nothing. No, it was worse. The old folk say the last time the Bonecarver crossed them floorboards, was right after they kilt her daughter. Said her hands and her arms was all burnt up, the skin white and peeling, shiny even, like she'd dipped her whole arm in fatback grease. Say she raised her hand and that's when Lincoln over there liked to broke his neck cutting that jukebox off."

Link just grunted, stacking red Dixie cups in a corner, trying to look busy like he wasn't listening. Richard laughed, a rum-and-coke laugh, then his voice got low, serious.

"She come all that way, barefoot now, arms all burnt up, not even begun healing, and she come with a terrible story and this is what she say: They call her Simma Down. Call her that because her pot stay full of meat, the fat simmered down so good, make you sweat. Seem like nobody come to her went hungry, not if she had a hand in it. The women come with they bellies swole and they babies on they back, crying from hunger or the croup. She put her bony fingers in that pot and come up with a healing, something to tide them over 'til another feeding come. That's what she do. And that's why Mineral, old Speight's black mistress, didn't like her one bit. Mineral was the midwife, birthed all the black babies on the island, and the other ones, too, even birthed every one of Speight and The Miss Mistress children. Mineral thought the conjure gal was cutting in on her shade, splitting the folks' loyalties, and loosening Speight's grip on the slaves."

"But where she come from, this Simma Down?"

"Listen, girl," Richard said, annoyed. "Don't nobody rightly know. Same place as everybody else, cross them waters. All we know is that Mineral turned Speight's hand against her. And Simma Down was pregnant when he had Tuck put her down in that bellyhole, down on Mourner's Beach. Tuck was her man, daddy to the child she was 'bout to born. Made him dig it deep, deep enough to cover her up and protect her baby. 'Cause no matter how much Old Speight hated the mama, he wasn't 'bout to let no whooping harm or hurt the child. Whether girl or boy, Simma Down's new life would turn a profit, just like all the rest.

And Tuck was trembling so, his anger turned his slanty eyes red/black. They say Tuck mama was Indian, a Creek from the mainland, that he could hardly hold the big shovel gripped in his hand. Seem like he want to take that shovel and lay it upside his master's head, but he knowed if he done that, time over time, there'd be more than Speight's blood on his hands. In them time, not much word come back to those that lived on the islands, only that what come with the ferry and the ferryman. The island folk was close knit on themselves, but folk remembered what happened at Mourner's Beach and they knew, no matter how long the tide came and went, them salt waters would never wash away the blood living and spilt in that man's name.

So when Tuck's neck and back shoulders was slick with heartache and sweat, Speight handed him the tasseled bullwhip and took a step. He leaned over Simma, silent in the bellyhole, and he whispered something in her ear.

Now, don't nobody know what he say. There are all kinda lies, and I'm telling you a true one. Some say he warn her 'bout messing in white folk business, some say he tell her she so black and evil, the devil whatn't gone want her when she come and heaven whatn't gone have her when he got through neither, but she still better not step foot or spirit on his island again.

All I know is that Speight was so greedy, they say he even bonded them first Africans' soul. Say, after they birthed the whole island, all our grandmamas and papas from way back when, say he wouldn't even let them first nine spirits rest. Say he tie them to the blade, that great big ole machete Dusa got from Willie J to tote around. Say he tie them with his word and they been bound here ever since.

But some words so harsh, so cold, they don't have to travel far to be remembered. They go straight from the ear, to the spirit's head, and they stay there, burning into the mind. They say Simma start speaking in spirit tongue, let out a cry so loud, sound like haints hollering in the woods. Say whatever she say, didn't none but Speight understand, and when he heard her words, he turn pale like whatn't no mo' blood in him. He stumbled back, while Tuck held the whip limply in his hand, then he motioned for Simma's man, the one she'd dared to call her own, to whip her and that's what he did.

He whipped her 'til he killed her dead.

And Simma died, but not 'fore she saw her baby born. They say the child they named Sukie, after her mama spiritsong, come out that bellyhole on her own, the navelstring still steaming. And that's when Simma Down curse Speight's land, from the north island all the way to Mourner's Beach, and that's how Sukie, her daughter, come to be, and it whatn't long after that the black folk on this island come free.

And that night, when she come, the Bonecarver keep on talking like that, them old stories we already heard time and time again, but something 'bout the way she told that story that night made me want to get up out of here, pointing that crooked finger at everybody, like pointing was gon' make her grandbaby, whatever they call that child, get up from the ocean floor."

"Who was in here?"

"Well, me and Link, for sure, and Younger."

"Naw, Younger whatn't here," Link said running soapy water in the sink. "That was his brother, Tatum and that ole frog face boy, what his name?"

"Donnell!"

"Yeah, Donnell. Never did have no sense."

"And that's all she did. Walk all that way, barefoot, just to tell you some story you already know?"

They looked at each other, as if trying to decide what to say and what to leave back under the bar that long night ago. Finally, Link spoke. "She say Simma Down's curse."

"But don't nobody believe in that no more," Richard added quickly.

Link arched his brow and kept talking like I ain't never said nothing.

". . . say it on all the people that let her grandbaby die. Say Dusa whatn't gone rest—and she whatn't either—'til them that drowned her come to justice and whoever stole the Bonecarver bring it back home."

When he mentioned the bone blade, I felt a chill, wet shivers that shook down my spine, made me want to shake loose my skin.

Pepper piped in. "She done the same thing at First African, too." I turned to look at him, watched him gulp some watered down cola. I could do for some gin, myself. "Boy, I tell you, I ain't never seen a church empty out so fast," he said, chuckling. "Usually they be in there, standing around jaw jaggin'. After you been done sat through fifty songs and a service, thirty announcements about this and that, then you gat to sit through the Benediction, and you know them old folk gon' stand up to testify, every single last one of them. That's a whole 'nother sermon, there. That's why I don't go but two, three times a year. Easter, Christmas, and Anniversary. Sometimes I don't go to that. I don't know why, but that Anniversary, seem like I couldn't go nowhere but to church."

"This happened on Anniversary?"

"Yeah, I didn't tell you that?"

I shook my head. Link's jukebox was playing an old Lionel Ritchie song I ain't heard in a million years.

"Yeah, it was Anniversary, and you know how the Mother Board cook up all that good food, baked and fried chicken, biscuits and country gravy, sweet potato pies and macaroni and cheese, dumplings and honey ham, collard greens and pound cake. Girl, I was ready to eat. But the thing is, usually I just stop by, after the ushers gone home, and pick up me a plate they stashed for me, but this time, everywhere I call myself gone go, look like I was heading to church. Even put on my good shoes that day, and was there when the children was still in Sunday school, before they even started passing out the programs." Pepper looked bewildered.

"So what you trying to say, that Willie J put the root on you and *made* you go to church?" Richard's lips was all pursed up, like he smell something.

"That's what I'm saying."

Another man I didn't know, who'd been sitting at a table, minding his business the whole time, looked like he wanted to say something but hadn't made up his mind yet to do it. Link leaned over and told me that this was Stick Daddy's son, the gravedigger.

"What his name?" I asked.

"Stick Daddy."

I laughed.

"Naw, he named after his daddy, but I can't call they family name now," Link said, glancing over at him. "Wait a minute, it's Blackshear, but we ain't never called him or his papa nothing but Stick Daddy."

"'Course, if you don't feel comfortable, with you being a stranger and all," Richard nudged me, "then you can call him Mr. Shade. Stick Daddy Shade dig all the graves. You ain't expecting to do no business with him, are you?"

His question caught me by surprise. I must have looked at him real crazy 'cause he held up his hands.

"Girl, I'm just messing with you. Usually, folk coming back like this mean trouble, a burying or a birthing kind. Which one you planning?"

"I ain't planning on nothing but finishing this drink."

"Well, let me get you another one."

I shook my head.

"Geneva's granddaughter used to be married to him, you know her?" he asked. "No? Guess she come and gone before your time."

"Who else done come and gone?" I asked.

I watched Stick Daddy sip his drink as Richard caught me up on the news, mentioning every birth and marriage he could think of. I noticed how he carefully avoided Booker, and I started to call him on it when Stick Daddy finished his drink and motioned for Link to make him another one.

"You know, I been digging graves going on forty years," he said, getting up to get his cup. Richard turned around in his seat, winking at me. "Started up right 'longside my daddy. This a small enough place. Ain't like we got a heap of folk to be burying no way. Maybe one or two a year, mostly old ones been here a time and sometime folk pass on the mainland and they kin send 'em right back here, where they come from. But I ain't never buried nobody down near Mourner's Beach, and far as I know, nobody buried Willie J's granddaughter."

He was talking about the Bonecarver, though few folk had the nerve to call her by her given name. She owned Mourner's Beach and most of the land around it, because didn't nobody else dare to live down there with her. They say that's where the first ship docked that brought them first nine Africans and all the ones that was stole and sold here ever since. Say the slaveholders didn't want the new flesh settling near the ocean, said it might make them think too much of home and they feared another Ibo Landing. Story go, when the Africans at Ibo Landing off one of them South Carolina islands saw their future on these shores, they decided to just walk back cross the waters and go on home back to Africa. Other folk say the people flew away, something about some magic beans or black-eyed peas, whatever it was, the first slaveholders here were mighty careful not to let no black folk take root down near Mourner's Beach, but everytime there was a tragedy, seemed like that's where the path led.

But that's where the Bonecarver and all the women in her family before her chose to be, right there near Mourner's Beach, the last burying place of their most famous kin, first Simma, then Dusa.

"Scene of the crime."

"Scene of more than one damn crime."

"Were you there when they killed her?"

Stick Daddy shook his head, didn't even look offended. "I heard about it later, but you could tell that whole day that nothing but wrong was going on."

"You ain't never lied about that," Link said, leaning on the bar. "Clayborn never should have call himself gone marry that girl. You know whatn't no good gone come of it."

"Right," Stick Daddy said. "And I ain't putting the blame at her doorstep either, not like the rest of 'em. Truth is, Dusa didn't mean nobody no harm. Never bothered anybody, minded her own business, and would have been alright if it whatn't for her grandmama mixing her up in all that hoodoo. You could tell her heart whatn't in it."

"But I heard she had more power than her mama or Willie J."

Stick Daddy didn't say nothing. This time Link spoke up. "I don't know 'bout all that—her mama didn't live long enough for nobody to know, but that's what they say."

"That's what I heard, too, but how folk know that?" I asked.

"Serina Bell's child," Stick Daddy said. Richard lowered his eyes, sipped air from an empty cup while Link ran a damp washcloth over the counter.

Nobody said a word or even acknowledged that Stick Daddy had spoken until he started again.

She shook like a fish drowning in air, her hair braided with reeds and marsh. He looked down at her and bowed his head, webs where her hands should be. No way to treat a child, even if it ain't a natural-born daughter. Willie J had loved that girl, more than most folk love their bloodbone kin. Common sense told him to throw her back, let her rest, but pity changed his heart, he would have to take her in. Wouldn't be no good if somebody saw him, mess around and have it all start up again. Mourner's Beach had been quiet, deserted ever since they call theyself gon' burn down the church. Nobody talked about that, or the storm that split the island, nor the fact that they had tried to lock the Bonecarver in. The Ferryman knew the river was a jealous goddess, and unlike the sea, some of her secrets were best left kept.

Herbal

That first noise must have come from the powerful kick. It crashed like the sound of cannon shot. A second bang followed, painfully, stupefyingly loud; then a concussion of air from the direction of the front door as it collapsed inward. Jenny didn't even have time to react. She sat up straight on her couch that was all. The elephant was in the living room almost immediately. Jenny went wordlessly still in fright, horror, disbelief. She lived on the fifteenth floor.

The elephant took a step forward. One of its massive feet slammed casually through the housing of the television, which, unprotesting, broke apart into shards of plastic, tangles of colored wires and nubbins of shiny metal. So much for the evening news.

The elephant filled the close living room of Jenny's tiny apartment. Plaster crumbled from the walls where it had squeezed through her brief hallway. Its haunches knocked three rows of books and a vase down from her bookshelf. The vase shattered when it hit the floor.

The elephant's head brushed the ceiling, threatening the light fixture. It crowded the tree trunks of its two legs nearest her up against the couch. Fearing for her toes—well, her feet, really—Jenny yanked her own feet up onto the couch, then stood right up on the seat. It was only the merest advantage of height, but it was something. The phone was in the bedroom, on the other side of the elephant.

The elephant *smelled*. Its wrinkly, gray-brown hide gave off a pungent tang of mammalian sweat. Its body looked ashy, dry. Ludicrously, Jenny found herself thinking of how it might feel to tenderly rub bucketsful of lotion into its cracked skin, to feel the hide plump and soften from her care. Elephants were hairier than she'd thought. Black, straight bristles, thick as needles, sprung here and there from the leathery skin.

The elephant reached out with its trunk and sniffed the potted plant flourishing on its stand by the window—a large big-leaf thyme bush, fat and green from drinking in the sun. Fascinated, Jenny watched the elephant curl its trunk around the base of the bush and pluck it out of its pot. The pot thudded to the carpet, but didn't break. It rolled over onto its side and vomited dirt. The elephant lifted the plant to its mouth. Jenny closed her eyes and flinched at the rootspray of soil as the animal devoured her houseplant, chewing ruminatively.

She couldn't help it; didn't want to. She reached out a hand—so small, compared!—and touched the elephant's hide. Just one touch, so brief, but it set off an avalanche of juddering flesh. A fingertipped pod of gristle with two holes in it snaked over to her, slammed into her chest and shoved her away; the elephant's trunk. Jenny felt her back collide with the wall. Nowhere to go. She remained standing, very still.

She smelt a new smell then, one that pulled her eyes toward its source. The elephant had raised its tail and was depositing firm brown lumps of manure onto her carpet. She could see spiky threads of straw woven into each globule. The pong of rotted, fermented grass itched inside her nose, made her cough. Outraged, hardly knowing what she did, she leapt forward and slapped the elephant, hard, on its large, round rump. The vast animal trumpeted, and, leading with its shoulder, took two running steps through the rest of her living room. It stuck briefly in the open doorway on the other side. Then more plaster crumbled, and it popped out onto her brief balcony. With an astonishing agility, the pachyderm clambered out over the cement wall of the balcony. "No!" Jenny shouted, jumping down off the couch, but it was no use. Ponderous as a walrus diving from an ice floe, the elephant flung itself over the low wall. Jenny rushed to the door.

The elephant hovered in the air, and paddled until it was facing her. It looked at her a moment, executed a slow backwards flip, then trundled off, wading comfortably through the ether as though it swam in water.

The last thing she saw of the beast, in the crowding dark of evening, was the oddly graceful bulk of its blimp body, growing smaller, as it floated toward the horizon.

Jenny's knees gave way. She felt her bum hit the floor. A hot tear rolled down her cheek. She looked around at the mess: the scattered textbooks for the course she was glumly, doggedly failing; the crushed vase in a color she'd never liked, a grudging gift from an aunt who'd never liked her; the destroyed television with its thousand channels of candied nothing. She wrinkled her nose at the smell of elephant dung, then stood again. She fetched broom and dustpan from the kitchen and started to clean up.

A month later she passed the Web design course, just barely, and sold the books. She felt lighter when she exchanged them for crisp bills of money. At the pharmacy, she used most of the money to buy all the lotion they had, the type for the driest skin. After he'd helped her repair her walls, her father had given her another big-leaf thyme cutting, which, sitting in its jar of water, had quickly sprouted a healthy tangle of roots. She'd told him once about the elephant. He'd raised one articulate brow, then said nothing more.

Jenny lugged the tubs of skin lotion home, then went to the hardware store. With the remaining money she bought a bag of soil. Back home again, she transferred the cutting into the pot that had held the old plant. She stood it on the balcony. Two more months of summer. The plant grew quickly, and huge.

She got hired to maintain the question-and-answer page for the local natural history museum. The work was interesting enough, and sometimes people asked about the habits of elephants. Jenny would pore over the curators' answers before putting them up on the Web page. It must have been an Indian elephant; an African one would never have fit. For the rest of the summer, every evening when she got home, she would go out onto the balcony, taking a container of the skin lotion with her. She would brush her hands amongst the leaves of the plant, gently bruising them. The pungent smell of the herb would waft its beckoning call out on the evening air, and Jenny would lean against the balcony railing for an hour or so, lotion in hand, hopefully scanning the darkening sky.

COMMENTARIES

Kindred Spirits

On Octavia E. Butler

Even for writers, words can fail us. It has taken me twenty-four hours to find the words.

In speculative black fiction, we are a very small family. Our matriarch has died.

Sunday morning, when a magazine reporter sent me word that Octavia E. Butler had died, I didn't want to believe it. I saw nothing in the news or on the Web. I called Octavia's home number and listened with a pounding heart as her phone rang. Once. Twice. Three times. I delighted—for just a bare instant—when the ringing stopped and I heard her voice.

On her answering machine. Already distant, clearly a recording. But Octavia's voice.

I stammered a message. *What to say? Are you alive or dead?* "I've . . . heard something . . . and I was hoping to speak to Octavia. . . ." I stopped, nearly sobbing. In that instant, I understood the futility of the act. We cannot call the dead on the telephone.

I thought of the other times I had called her—never enough, it turns out—when I tried to make our conversations brief, never able to fight the certainty that I was pulling her away from a stream of brilliant thoughts. Once, she apologized for the loud music playing in the background. It turned out that Octavia, like me, enjoyed listening to music while she wrote. How many times did I hesitate to dial her number simply because I didn't want to disturb her?

I was introduced to the works of Octavia E. Butler when a friend of mine, a writer and columnist named Robert Vamosi, insisted I must read her. I read *Kindred,* her time travel story of a contemporary black woman who is periodically flung back into the antebellum slavery period, and I was floored. I often say that between Alex Haley's *Roots,* Toni Morrison's *Beloved,* and Butler's *Kindred,* we can come no closer to experiencing slavery, and its legacy, in America.

I advise people to read *Kindred* first, because it serves as such a wondrous bridge to speculative fiction. After that, some readers will insist it should be *Wild Seed* and the *Patternist* series. But I often suggest *Parable of the Sower.* In it, Butler creates her own religion—a religion that embraces change:

> *All that You touch / You Change.* [You touched us, Octavia]
> *All that you Change / Changes you.* [You had to know how much we loved you]
> *The only lasting truth / Is Change.* [It was inevitable that we would lose you]
> *God / Is Change.*

I met Octavia in person in 1997, when Clark Atlanta University sponsored a conference entitled "The African-American Fantastic Imagination: Explorations in Science Fiction, Fantasy and Horror." There, I also met a science fiction writer named Steven Barnes, who would soon become my husband. Steve had known Octavia for years. That conference at Clark was a remarkable family reunion.

At the time, I had published only one novel, *The Between.* I floated on air as I was asked to pose in a photo with such prolific writers as Octavia, Steve, Jewelle Gomez, and Samuel R. Delany. In 2000, visiting Octavia's home with Steve to interview her for a piece we wrote for *American Visions* magazine, I was surprised to see that photo from Clark hanging on her wall.

"My other family," she explained.

Octavia was well that day. She would not be well in subsequent meetings.

She was fighting a cold when I saw her in Seattle at the "Black to the Future" science fiction conference in June of 2004, when she was happy to meet our new baby, Jason, but she didn't want to give him germs. She was sick again when I saw her in New York for the Yari Yari Pamberi International Conference of Literature by Women of African Ancestry in October that same year. I cautioned her to be careful about too much travel. Subsequently, I have learned that Octavia was far more ill than I knew. The *New York Times* reported Monday that she could only walk a few steps without having to stop to catch her breath.

Like most people, I cannot say that I knew Octavia well. But in the too-brief time I knew her, I saw many sides of her. Her fierce disappointment with mankind's worst habits. Her girlish side. Her goddess side. Her insecure side.

Last summer, Octavia asked me to write a quote for her upcoming novel, *Fledgling.* I was on my own deadlines, trying to juggle the jobs of new mother, novelist, and beginning screenwriter. But I said *YES.* I was honored even to have been asked. Octavia sounded almost apologetic, as if the book embarrassed her. She explained that her medication made it difficult to write. "I'm sure it's brilliant," I assured her. (I don't regret leaving too much unsaid, at least.)

This past Christmas, we sent Octavia a photo of Jason on Santa's lap and said we hoped she was feeling better. Octavia could not have been feeling well when she sent out her own cards this year, but hers were always among the first to arrive. She wrote to us: *Have a creative, prosperous New Year down there in California where it's WAY too warm.*

I must call her soon, I thought many times these past two months. I must call Octavia.

But what if she is writing?

Can a Brother Get Some Love?

Sociobiology in Images of African-American Sensuality in Contemporary Cinema: Or, Why We'd Better the Hell Claim Vin Diesel as Our Own

As often happens in life, I have to go backwards in order to go forward.

About fifteen years ago I was sitting in my living room watching a movie called *Hell Up in Harlem,* starring Fred Williamson and Gloria Hendry. I was having a good time watching the two of them in a love scene, when I suddenly realized I felt oddly uncomfortable. It took some time for me to figure out "why," but I finally realized that it had been almost twenty years since I'd seen a black man and a black woman having sex in a movie. I just flat wasn't used to seeing it.

Recently the movie *Dream Catcher* opened, and before the feature, there was a seven- or eight-minute animated short subject called *The Animatrix.* It was a teaser for the *Matrix Reloaded* sequel coming in a couple of months. There is a sequence in *Animatrix* when the black ship captain leans over to kiss an Asian woman. They are both computer-generated characters. The primarily white audience's tension had palpably increased as the sexual tension between these two cartoon characters grew thicker. When he kissed her, a white kid sitting in front of us said "yuck" rather loudly.

On Sunday night, March 23, 2003, at the Oscars, Adrian Brody accepted his Best Actor Award and grabbed Halle Berry and laid a twelve-second big wet smackeroo on her. Does anyone doubt that if, say, Wesley Snipes had done this to Nicole Kidman the audience would not have rebelled? That critics wouldn't have been saying, "Oh, this is a terrible thing" or "What presumption—it has nothing to do with race of course. It's simply inappropriate"?

Of course, it *never* has anything to do with race.

The value of a theory is its explanatory and predictive capacity, its simplicity, and to a certain degree its universality. It's easy to look at some phenomenon of human behavior—especially a negative one—and simply take the position that the perpetrators are knaves or fools. The more difficult response is to ask: What universal human behaviors, what simple principles of human behavior, might, in emergent form, lead to complex and sometimes profoundly unpleasant results? What explanation helps me to understand humanity better? In other words, the question: Where am I in the issue of the behavior I abhor? Whether correct or not, it is valuable to look at things that way.

Let's take a look at sociobiology, a discipline that says that most human behaviors are things that tend to promote either reproduction of human beings or reproduction of social memes.

In understanding what has happened in American cinema, it is important to search for universal principles, and not say something as absurdly reductionist as "white people are evil and bigoted." One of the most important reasons not to think this way is that this is the way bigots think. The very racists we abhor think this way, and it is dangerous to use the enemy's mindset. But I will say that as I started to take a look at that question of Fred Williamson and Gloria Hendry in *Hell Up in Harlem,* I asked: Is there any way to integrate what I'm seeing and feeling here into some sort of pattern, so that I can predict future events?

One of my specialties is science fiction (SF) movies. And black people, traditionally, have not been present in SF movies unless they died protecting white people. Poor Paul Winfield (1939–2004) made an entire career out of dying protecting white people. Whether you're talking about *Terminator,* or *Serpent and the Rainbow,* or *Wrath of Khan,* or the absolute worst one, *Damnation Alley.* In this most painful of films, Paul Winfield, Jan-Michael Vincent, and George Peppard are traveling across a nuclear-devastated wasteland in an atomic-powered Winnebago. They go, I think, into Salt Lake City or Las Vegas—I forget which. Out of the ashes of the city comes the last woman in the world (as far as they know), and she's white. I remember turning to my girlfriend at the time and saying: "Oh, my God. They're going to kill Paul Winfield." She was incredulous. "Why would you think that?"

"It's simple," I replied. "They're not going to pretend he's not interested, and they won't let him compete for her. The only remaining choice is for them to kill him."

She clucked at my cynicism and turned her attention back to the movie. Five minutes later, Winfield was eaten by giant cockroaches.

So. The theory I came up with is that black people in action-adventure/ SF movies exist to help the white guy survive and/or get laid, often at the cost of his own life.

The "Hero" in an American film is almost always a lean-bodied, hetero-sexual male between the ages of 20 and 50 who survives the film. There-fore, if black people exist in movies, up until the last ten years (when things started changing a little bit), they will generally be too young, too old, too fat, too gay, or too dead to have sex. In the last ten years we've seen another trope: they can already be married. With extremely few excep-tions, married people don't have sex in movies. The point is that the "rogue male" who competes for the desirable female lead is almost never black or Asian. White males, on the other hand, can seek—and win—women of all groups.

Given this idea, I could begin to predict what I was going to see in movies. It got a little worse than this. Over the last few years, people have started noticing and whispering about the fact that black actors in major studio films never have sex in their movies. (This has finally started to become "almost never.") Black women are another matter. Almost every single black actress of any stature, on the other hand, is doing love scenes or is positioned as a sex object—as long as she is with a white man. For example: Halle Berry (*Monster's Ball, Die Another Day*), Beyonce Knowles (*Goldmember*), Thandie Newton (*Mission: Impossible, The Truth About Charlie*), Whitney Houston (*The Bodyguard*), Whoopie Goldberg (you pick), Rosario Dawson (*25th Hour*), Queen Latifah (*Bringing Down the House*), Gloria Hendry (*Live and Let Die*), Aliyah (*Queen of the Damned*), Vonetta McGee (*The Eiger Sanction*), etc., etc.

Asian men have it as bad as or worse than black men. In fact, there has never been a film earning over $50 million in which an Asian male has a love scene—with the single exception of *Crouching Tiger, Hidden Dragon*, which wasn't an American film. And there has never been a film earning over $100 million in which a black man has had sex—with the single exception of *Fast and the Furious*, if one chooses to consider Vin Diesel black. (If we do, then we simply define the limits of negritude: i.e., how much black blood does someone have to have before the audience's hind brain kicks in and says, "Eek! We're watching a Negro!" The answer seems to be: not much. Apparently, Dwayne "The Rock" Johnson is exotic enough to confuse white males. Good for him!)

Why is the question of "box office" so important? Because it reveals what white audiences are actually comfortable with. They are voting with their dollars, not making public statements about how liberal and open-hearted they are. In the privacy of the darkened theater, tens of millions of Americans are telling us quite clearly what they do and don't want to see.

In fact, you can go down to $70 million, and the only case you'll see of a movie in which a black man is frankly sexual is *Boomerang* with Eddie Murphy. That's just about it. There is one other interesting exception that I'll get to, but do the math for yourself. Go to the Internet Movie Database (www.imdb.com) and look up the 400 most profitable films of all time. Break them up into movies with white and nonwhite stars. You'll find out something interesting.

White actors participate in love scenes in 30% to 35% of these successful movies, including the movies that make $50, $75, or way above $100 million. Black actors have sex in about 2% to 4% of the movies they are in on this same list. In other words, a predictive theory can be formulated: If a movie is to appeal to a white audience, the black actor must be neutered. If a movie earns over $40 to $50 million, that means it has broken out of the "black market" and become a crossover film. And the truth is that white males, specifically, will not go to see those movies.

But isn't this assertion harsh? Well, let's take a look at the exception I have just mentioned. A few years ago there was a film called *Save the Last Dance*. I remember seeing the coming attractions, realizing it was an interracial love story, and turning to my wife, saying: "Boy, I hope they didn't spend three nickels on this flick, 'cause it's going to bomb!"

The movie opened on the same weekend as a film called *Anti-Trust,* a computer thriller. I went to see *Anti-Trust* and noticed a big line at the theater. It turned out that the big line was for *Save the Last Dance!* Two days later, I took my daughter to see the movie, and, when the lights went up, she was smiling and the audience was applauding.

Now understand this fact: I live in a very white town in a very white section of the country, the Pacific Northwest. I noticed something interesting: 90% of the audience comprised white females. I went to the restroom, and there were a couple of white guys there. They didn't see me, and

I overheard their conversation. Basically it was: "Jeeze, I don't know why they make crap like that."

On the way out of the theater, I asked my daughter why she liked the film. Her answer: "It was about a girl who had a dream, and she finds a guy who supports her in that dream, and that's what every girl wants!"

The movie went on to earn about $80 million. According to statistics gathered at the time the film came out, 78% of the people who went to see that movie were women. Which means that hardly a single white guy went to see it.

I think that this point and a lifetime of observation have led me to the conclusion that, in general, racism is about 80% a male domain. It is the warriors of the opposing tribes shaking spears at each other. Typical male behavior is to want access to all the females in the vicinity, while denying access to other males. This is not something confined to the white community by any means. I think it would be reasonable to say that 10% of human beings are mean-spirited, nasty, bigoted folk. Unfortunately, because black people are outnumbered almost ten to one in America, that means that there is one mean-spirited, nasty black bigot for every 100 white people. And there is one white bigot for every black man, woman, and child in America. Ouch.

If you are bigoted, one of the last things in the world you want to watch is reproductive behavior in members of another group. This becomes more offensive if the "Other" is impregnating one of *your* women. Billy Bob Thornton boffing Halle Berry, on the other hand, is peeing in the other guy's gene pool. Perfectly acceptable.

That aforementioned "yuck" factor means that box office drops approximately 25% if a black actor has sex. White males will avoid the film. Although they never say why, by some odd coincidence all of the films in which Denzel or whoever gets nookie just happen to be perceived as "below average." How interesting. I wonder how one would explain that phenomenon? Why would every movie in which a black actor drops trou just happen to be bad? Not true of white actors. Nor of other films starring the exact same actors if they keep their clothes on. Or films by the same directors. Just go to the IMDB and compare what happens when white actors get sexy—box office remains stable, or rises. Black or Asians? Box office drops like a paralyzed falcon.

Usually, people try to blame this on "Hollywood." Nonsense. Hollywood is no more bigoted than any other section of the country. They will make the movies, and the television shows, that America supports with its dollars. Over time, they are conditioned just as you condition a German Shepherd with positive and negative rewards: they stop trying, because they don't want to lose money.

Specifically, what we have here is white American males voting with their wallets for what they feel comfortable watching

This is the kind of thing that one might need to actually check for oneself, but fortunately the information is readily available. Go to the IMDB, or to www.variety.com, and look at the list of movies that have earned over $70 to $100 million. I'm not making this observation up: it's right there in black and white for anyone who wants to look at it.

If you define broadcast-medium success as the ability to last more than two seasons, not a single majority black or Asian dramatic series in history has *ever* been successful on broadcast television. There have been a few (very few) ensemble shows with a black lead (the lead is the actor or actress whose name appears first in the credits). This becomes starkly apparent when you look at the vast flood of successful comedies starring minorities. Laugh at us, yes. Seriously identify with us, no way.

When *Star Wars* came out, SF icon Samuel R. Delany wrote an essay saying that he thought it was a wonderful movie, but wouldn't it have been nice if there had been a black character in there somewhere? He was rewarded with a stack of hate mail from white readers. How dare he intrude on their fantasy—and their world? "When we see black people," they said, "it means trouble."

Now, it is my belief that if the situation were reversed, if America were primarily black instead of white, we'd treat them and respond to them exactly the same way: this isn't a problem with white people, it's a problem with people. It's the way human consciousness is wired—and the way hierarchical, competitive, male testosterone-driven behavior works. I'm not saying that the world's problems are caused by men, either. There are upsides and downsides to both male and female psychology. This happens to be one of the less fabulous aspects of Guy Think.

But what do you do with this information once you've found it? How do you deal with this information? For instance, the film *Blade* provides an interesting case. Note the majority of comic-book movies: *Batman, Superman, Spiderman, Daredevil,* etc. There is always a woman involved. In fact, the opening of *Spiderman* says it: "This, like all good stories, is about a woman." *Blade*—no women. Not a single kiss, let alone a love scene. Perhaps it's the vampire element you say? Look at that movie again. The vampire world is hypersexualized. All the other vampires are getting laid. Where is Blade? Apparently lurking in the shadows, marveling at how incredibly sexy those white folks are, and wishing he had a penis.

Wesley Snipes produced the film himself through his Amen Ra productions. What can we draw from this fact? That Mr. Snipes is no fool, and over the course of his film career he has come to understand what white males want from him: asexual butt-kicking. If he wants their money, he'll keep his pants on. Simple as that.

This is the biggest open secret in Hollywood. If you want a $20 million actor, you have to put him in a $60 million–plus movie. For that film to earn its money back, it has to earn over $100 million. For a film to earn over $100 million, only white males can have sex in it. That's the equation.

Note the different ways they keep black actors from having sex. Sometimes, as I already mentioned, they have the character already married. This seems reasonable, except that white actors routinely, in almost every movie they make, get the boy-meets-girl story arc—the most common and dynamic arc in all storytelling. When you extract this crucial ingredient from the recipe, what you often get is weak soup.

Remember *Bad Boys* with Will Smith and Martin Lawrence? In this one, Smith is supposed to be a great "playa." Let's see how they got away with not giving Mr. Smith his due. The writers pulled a "funny" and "creative" switch where Martin Lawrence is mistaken for his partner Will. Lawrence becomes the one hanging with the sexy witness, while Will is hanging with Lawrence's wife. Isn't that a riot? Isn't that unpredictable?

When Eddie Murphy got a script originally written for Sylvester Stallone (*Beverly Hills Cop*), it was glaringly obvious where the sex scene was cut out: Sylvester was supposed to visit a former girlfriend, and she was supposed to come to his hotel room. Nada for Eddie. It is interesting to note that immediately after *Boomerang,* one of the last major films in which black people were portrayed as human beings in a normal sexual sense, Eddie's career nose-dived, and he was forced to reinvent himself onscreen as a harmless family man (analogous to Bill Cosby) in movies like *The Nutty Professor* and *Dr. Doolittle* (or, if the point needs to be made more clearly, *I Spy*). He had to give up all of the hard, dangerous edge that made him so fascinating during the first years of his career.

That is exactly what black actors have had to do at the same time black actresses are getting laid in droves.

And do we even need to mention *Shaft,* one of the most disappointing remakes ever? Despite some fine moments and performances, the desperate need to emasculate this most iconic of cinematic black hero images gutted the drama of the film, turning it into an artificial exercise in "how can we choreograph this to keep Shaft from ever being alone with a woman? Especially a white woman." Sickening. John Singleton fought for Shaft's sexuality, and lost to producer Scott Rudin, the same guy who approved of the anal sex between Saddam Hussein and Satan in the *South Park* movie.

Look at the statistics. About 70% of interracial couples are black men with white women. But if you formed your opinion based on what you see in cinema, you'd think it was 90% the other way. To whose benefit is this situation? Therefore, the grotesque inversion of reality one sees on the screen certainly isn't about the preference of white females. Or black males. And even if black females wanted to, they could have no control over the kind of box-office numbers I'm talking about. I'm afraid that this constructed reality is simply a white male fantasy, representing the way they wish the world was: all women attracted to them, all potential cock-blockers removed from the game.

So you have this image of the powerful, aggressive, sexual male survivor. White people pump their boys with this cinematic image a thousand times a day. Black people have real problems creating similar images for a multitude of reasons, one of them certainly being the cost of film production and distribution today. In the '70s a "black exploitation film" could make money, because by definition an "exploitation" film is a movie designed to fit a niche market. Hot-rod movies, monster-on-the-campus movies, beach-party movies—these were all "exploitation" films. *Shaft, Slaughter, Coffy, Cotton Comes to Harlem,* etc., were all films about black men and women being powerful in their localized environment. Such films could be made for under $1 million (the original *Shaft* cost $750,000) and generate a tidy profit (in the case of *Shaft,* $15 million). I would say that this period, between about 1970 and 1975, was the only time in American cinematic history that black people were depicted as full-fledged human beings, with a full spectrum of hopes, needs, and desires. This was the only time when movies could make a profit by showing black men as being intelligent and powerful and sexual. This was the only time when black men could win.

There are no niche markets for major Hollywood studios any more.

Studios and theaters have been eaten by conglomerates, the international market looks larger and more important all the time, and stockholders want every movie to yield a home run. No executive wants to be the one who green-lit Sam Jackson's bare behind and lost 80 million studio dollars doing it. This was the process of homogenization.

The question of what to do with this situation is interesting. I wouldn't want anyone to think I despair in regard to this issue. I've been waiting thirty years to see the day when black boys will get the same instruction on how to pass from childhood to adulthood that every white boy gets a thousand times a day. Over the last couple of years there have been a few small signs that things are starting to change. It takes time to turn the *Titanic* around.

Save the Last Dance made money because women were going to movies without their husbands or boyfriends. Women's finances can actually drive the market. Since women are 51% of the population, if you scale your movie financially so that it can make a profit at, say, $70 million, there is a good chance it can make money. There are filmmakers out there who are conscious of this problem. Take a look at *Matrix II*. Noting the number of minorities in that film, it is obvious that the directors were very aware of the artificiality of ethnic distribution in late-twentieth-century film. There are people trying to find a way to work around this problem—we're not alone in this matter.

Now. Let's bring this all back together. What is the answer? What do we do? Well, do you know something? All we really have to do is wait.

The last time I looked at the statistics, Nickleodeon was the top-rated cable network in the country, and Nick is delightfully well integrated. In other words, children are being programmed to look at human beings as human beings—not as bags of colored skin. In other words, the kids will work this all out, given time.

Can we program this racism out? I think so. Black males don't have as much of a "yuck" factor toward white male sexuality at least in part because we have been motivated since childhood to see white men as glorious creatures: every piece of paper money in your pocket has a portrait of a noble white man. Ninety-nine percent of screen, comic-book, or literary heroes have been white—and don't get me started on the image of a blue-eyed blond Christ located in black churches all over the country! Programming works, if you can start the conditioning early enough.

So what will make a difference? Very specifically, since the '60s, lip-service has been given to the idea of equality. If your parents say this aloud, regardless of what they're thinking, it makes a difference. We've all heard of white kids who thought their parents were "liberal" on racial issues until they brought home a black friend. Given a neutral environment in which to make up their own minds, exogamy, the natural tendency to be sexually attracted to members of the "Other" group, will overcome the thickest walls of racial prejudice. We're all one species, folks. All else is just trivial variation. You have to have powerful social prohibitions to keep people from getting together.

So . . . all we have to do to win this game is wait for about 80% of the white males born before 1950 to get old and die. And, frankly, I think it's worth the wait.

SAMUEL R. DELANY &
CARL FREEDMAN

A Conversation with
Samuel R. Delany about Sex, Gender,
Race, Writing—and Science Fiction

The following is a written—and much-revised—text that was composed gradually throughout the calendar year 2003; it is based primarily on e-mails between the two principals. We style it a "conversation" by formal—indeed fictional—artifice; and we hope that, as with so many literary texts from Plato onwards, this artifice will help to give the discussion a liveliness and dialectical nimbleness that no actual conversation could possess. It is perhaps worth adding that we [Delany and Freedman] have, however, had numerous conversations "in real life" and that, though none of them was very similar to what follows, what follows might never have been written without them.

Among the most interesting points in Delany's discourse is the importance he ascribes in his development to his intellectual partnership with the poet Marilyn Hacker, his close friend from high school to whom he was also married for a number of years. His reminder is salutary that, though race and gender are today among the most fashionable topics in literary circles, both (and especially gender) were mostly invisible during the 1950s and early 1960s, when Delany and Hacker were educating themselves and each other. Even more important, perhaps, is Delany's characteristic protest against the vulgar empiricism that would regard race, gender, and sex as merely innocent or pre-given realities "out there." He explains at considerable (but necessary and absorbing) length that our experience and understanding of such realities are always shaped by almost unimaginably complex networks of linguistic, formal, and ideological conventions—a point that is, of course, of considerable importance for grasping the nature and function of science fiction.—CF

CF: Though you've produced important work in a number of different genres, there's no question that you remain most widely known as a writer of science fiction; and I think it's fair to say that nearly all serious SF critics regard you as one of the most interesting and accomplished SF novelists ever. Certainly I've written about you myself in exactly those terms (and we might as well get on the record right now that our personal friendship came about as a result of my long-standing interest in and admiration for your work; things did not happen the other way around, that is, I did not take an interest in your work because you happened to be a personal friend). There are those who prefer your earlier SF and those who prefer your later SF; and of course some critics rank you higher than others do. But there's general agreement that the name of Samuel R. Delany is sol- idly associated with high achievement in science fiction. Yet I can think of several places where you've written that, at the beginning of your career, you never made a conscious decision to write SF and did not, at first, think of yourself as a SF writer. On the face of it, that seems rather unusual, even counterintuitive. Perhaps you could begin by explaining what you meant?

SRD: Yes, I've written any number of places, such as my autobiographical memoir *The Motion of Light in Water* (1988), where I've described the process at length, as well as in the "Toto, We're Back!" interview (*Silent Interviews* 1992) and in any number of others, that when I started writing SF, I never made a decision—any sort of decision, at all—to be a science fiction writer, or to devote my life to writing sci- ence fiction. The words, "I'm going to be a science fiction writer," or "I'm going to write science fiction from now on"—or even "I'm going to write science fiction, now, for the length of this book"—never passed through my head, at least not at any time while I was writing and publishing my first three or four SF novels. When I've said that in the past, perhaps it sounded too glib for people to take it seriously. But it's the truth. Writing science fiction just happened. During my adolescence I'd written nine grittily realistic novels (as I perceived gritty realism, at the time) and a couple of dozen urban short stories about New York adolescents. And I was working on a tenth novel, none of them having anything to do with science fiction or fantasy, when I turned to write still another novel—my science fantasy, *The*

Jewels of Aptor (1962). The three volumes of *The Fall of the Towers* ('63, '64, '65) followed, with *The Ballad of Beta-2* ('65) interrupting the conclusion of the trilogy's difficult second volume. Both were completed at about the same time and sold within a couple of months of each other. Then I started and finished the trilogy's third book. But not until I was finishing *Beta-2* (which would be my fourth published novel) did it strike me, one day, that I was—that I had become—a science fiction writer. I was a bit surprised, but happy at the development. Still, it was the first time I realized I'd strayed and stayed across a genre boundary. Possibly it took so long to register because neither *Jewels* nor the *Towers* included any space travel. Though they were set in "the future," they were about devolved cultures, rather than superscientific advanced societies—not greatly different from the one depicted in *They Fly at Çiron* (a sort of place in the country off from Toron's version of urbanity, not surprising since Çiron's first draft was initially written just before the *Towers* began to topple). Perhaps because all were basically idea driven, I reached for whatever narrative conventions I could to dramatize those ideas, wherever I would find them, without paying much attention to those conventions' writerly provenance. Now, since that time, at several points I've put considerable thought—and I've written about this, too—into how to become a *better* science fiction writer. But I never made any positive decision to become one in the first place.

To clarify:

I don't mean the words "science fiction" never passed through my head, while I completed the manuscripts, read over contracts, and sold them to Ace Books. That would be absurd. I only mean the subject-bound predicate—the Althusserian self-acknowledgment of some social interpellation or hailing ("I am a science fiction writer" / "I am going to write science fiction") never occurred. The originary, inciting, bifurcational moment—"Hey! *Now* I'm going to write science fiction!" at least in any form that *I* can look back and recognize it—never happened.

While I was writing those early novels, I certainly realized what I was writing was science fiction. But this is a fine point about freewill, decisions, intention, and the subject—not about science fiction.

The fact that I'd read enough SF that I knew how to do it—that I'd internalized enough of both the codes it shared with literature and the singular codes of the genre per se—meant I didn't have to give it that isolate entification that such a decision would have demanded of someone else (who, perhaps, had given up on fandom).

But at nineteen I thought of myself as a writer who decided to write a SF novel, rather than the sort I usually wrote, rather than the sort I assumed I would go back to writing.

To go on at such length about a point as small as this—especially a point that you, yourself, are already aware of—might seem a willfully obtuse beginning to a discussion such as this, an unnecessary harping on the smallest of rhetorical fine points, or even a disingenuous side-stepping of your initial question. (If I never made a decision to write science fiction, how *could* SF's treatment of race and gender have played any part in that decision, even for a black gay man like myself?) But it's the "lived-experience" linchpin to a larger and important theoretical point, which perhaps we'll get into in more detail later. For now, suffice it to say that, around every "marginal" enterprise—sexual, social, aesthetic (and science fiction is nothing if not a marginal aesthetic enterprise)—there is a rhetoric already in place, a rhetoric of choice, of decision, of intentionality, generally used to denigrate those marginal topics—in the same way that such rhetoric is used to dignify the topics considered to reside at that center: heterosexuality, white culture, literature. But if the discussion is allowed to go on and develop over any time, this rhetoric invariably turns around and becomes accusatory. In terms of science fiction, this becomes: "Why would someone as intelligent as you, who writes as well as you, choose to write something as trivial/unrealistic/ and finally pernicious as science fiction—only a pull for second-rate minds and talents—when you could have chosen some central enterprise such as literature to commit your talents to?"

Now I don't for a moment expect *you* to take the discussion in that direction. But the point is, there exists a rhetorical scaffolding, a discourse "always-already" in place, to support such a development to our argument, should you, I, or anyone else lean it that way. (Notice: specifically I don't say "decide to take it" in that direction. I don't think *any* of these *are* decisions. They are not explainable by an easy or naïve concept of intention. For the record, I think you can decide *not* to take it in that direction, and if you put out a fair amount of analytical energy, you may be successful. Though even *with* the decision, sometimes you may not be. But if you let the discourse already in place do the speaking for you, that's the direction it will go.) It's the old deconstructive problem—which is to say I'm trying to counter a sedimented discourse with an old-fashioned deconstructive move.

By denying a certain agency, a certain specific order of agency at the beginning/origin/commencement of things, the *last* thing I want to do is say, "Because I didn't 'decide' to be a SF writer, therefore I am not responsible—in the sense of answerable—for what I wrote." I am very much responsible for it. Rather, it's an attempt to make a small, rhetorical intervention at the beginning, which may help shunt us away from the whole system of praise *or* blame that relies on the concept of a genre itself as reasonably judgeable as good or bad, socially helpful or socially dangerous *at* the level of genre.

Because I don't think genres are.

Remember, science fiction is a "genre" that comes with a history: In the '30s and '40s, parents might snatch the science fiction pulp magazines from their children's hands, tear them up, and throw them in the garbage (Theodore Sturgeon reports his stepfather doing just this when Sturgeon was twelve), because they mistily intuited that pulp fiction in general and science fiction in particular was part of the encroaching "Jewish menace" recently infiltrating the United States from Europe. Such a history, even loosed from its specific anti-Semitism, still alerts us to the underlying discursive structure controlling the behavior of, say, the last person who came up to me when I was doing a bookstore signing in a smaller Borders outlet in a city north of Detroit to ask: "You write science fiction, don't you?"

Me, with a friendly smile from behind the table piled with my latest Vintage reprint volume: "That's right."

Him: "You know, I don't *like* science fiction very much." Then he turned around and wandered off among the bookstore shelves. Were this a single occurrence, it wouldn't bear mentioning. But it's happened dozens of times—in my forty years as a published SF writer, it's happened *hundreds* of time—in ways that it never happens to poets or to biographers or to the authors of cookbooks.

("I don't *like* food very much . . . !" Imagine it.)

Most of these people today do not know why they have learned that, when it is written by multiethnic and multigenre writers hiding largely under Protestant and Catholic pen-names and edited by Protestant and Catholic editors hired by European-born, Jewish publishers, what is fantastic and unrealistic, used in the service of relatively politically liberal allegories for one's time, and aimed at the working classes, is considered unrealistic, irresponsible, and dangerous. But the same or similar fantastic and unrealistic strategies are accepted when used by English Protestant writers like Shakespeare, Milton, Stapledon, Orwell, and Tolkien—edited by rigorously restricted Protestant editors who worked for rigorously restricted Protestant publishers in the middle years of the last century, or more recent editors among whom, by 1960, the reigning wisdom was (I quote from memory a conversation I overheard at a table full of such editors while I was a waiter in 1960 at the Bread Loaf Writers' Conference at Middlebury, Vermont):

"There's nothing wrong with Jewish editors' intelligence, you understand. It just the things that they tend to like are so . . . well, *weird!*"

The classic works which these editors had charge of reprinting, along with the new literature of the epoch, purveyed an only slightly more conservative set of allegories than did the pulp ones of that date, as they were generally aimed at the middle classes. But they were considered the glories of literature. The two are rarely brought together in order to consider the history of the contradiction between these two "purely aesthetic" judgments.

That is why, paradoxically, I am so opposed to the contemporary pedagogic move that claims those works—for example, *De Rerum Natura, Orlando Furioso, Il Commedia, Paradise Lost, A Midsummer Night's Dream,* and *The Tempest*—for science fiction, because it muddles the categories on which an understanding of their history depends. As an intervention, I approve of what I take to be such an appropriation's intent. But without a firm hold on their history, with all it entails of politics, immigrations, anti-Semitism, not to mention racism (it was Franz Fanon's philosophy professor from the Antilles who told him, "When you hear anyone abuse the Jews, pay attention, because he is talking about you," an exhortation Fanon found to be "universally" correct), I think it is a premature intervention. But since historical forgetting is the way that (as Paul Goodman wrote) "nature heals"—heals the good things injured by evil, and heals the evil forces briefly smitten down by the good—perhaps the final forces of forgetfulness that battle against history itself can only be opposed so far.

CF: That certainly does answer my first question in a way that opens up some theoretical issues to which I suspect we'll want to return. For now, let's turn to some of the other terms of our interview's title. Like nearly all other science fiction writers, you read a good deal of SF before beginning to write your own. What do you recall about your early reading in the genre with regard to the categories of race and gender? Did the ways that these matters were treated—or not treated—in the SF you read play any particular role in the process by which you became a SF novelist yourself? Most critics, of course, regard you as a pioneer in bringing to SF a more substantial and sophisticated understanding than ever before of race and gender—and of sex. But did you ever have any conscious ambition to be such a pioneer?

SRD: Did I want to do something new, different, creative? Yes. Most certainly. But I'd hesitate to assume a metaphor like "pioneering" for the same reason I distrust all those other initiating or originary mantles—even one so harmless-looking as the "decision/nondecision" we were discussing above. Again, this is not to deny consciousness of the subject itself as a set of questions. It is only to forestall premature, sedimented, answers.

By the same token, we can discuss race and gender, too—in the same interrogative mode. But I feel that a certain vigilance is still needed—perhaps more than ever—in such discussions, especially if such a discussion would aspire to any historical sensitivity.

Today, when every third graduate student paper is entitled "Questions of Race and Gender in—" (fill in the blank with whatever), every bright high school student is aware that an ideology inhabits *every* representation of male and female characters, every representation of Caucasian and non-Caucasian characters, every representation of gay or straight characters. Today, that's what "being bright" means. But this was not always the case—even among highly educated readers. (One might even argue: *especially* among highly educated readers.) It certainly wasn't the case for the general reader during the first half of the '60s, when I started writing science fiction. It was even less true during the '50s when I did most of my formative science fiction reading.

To ask a reader from the '50s or the first years of the '60s what he or she had noticed about the equity or inequity of gender presentations in a piece of fiction of the time would be like asking a reader today, "What did you notice about the equities or inequities of the presentation of domestic and business furniture distribution in the novel you just read last night?" And the facile reductions of the old "New Criticism" then in place in the academy (which held that a text was a wholly self-contained and artificial construct; the text had nothing to do with the world) didn't help.

To such questions about gender, the '50s reader would have almost certainly frowned at you and, as one might answer the question about furniture today, said, "I'm not even sure what you're talking about—and I certainly have no idea why you're asking."

Before the middle '70s the conventions of gender representation (not to mention racial and object-choice representation) that most fiction deployed at the time were generally considered *the* conventions of fiction itself.

I can remember when, in the late '50s, I first intuited that not only were there literary conventions, but that those conventions inhabited a certain economy, a set of relationships which controlled the way in which they could be interpreted. This didn't happen with my SF reading. It happened with the range of popular narratives in presumably "realistic" films and novels. One of my earliest inklings of this came with a Martin Ritt film, *Edge of the City* (1957), starring black actors Sidney Poitier and Ruby Dee and white actor John Cassavetes. When I was fourteen, I saw it for the first time at a preopening release in a midnight showing, sponsored by disk jockey Jean Shepherd. I went with my white high school friend Chuck Abramson. For the time, when you could easily go to fifty films in a row and not see a single black face, male or female, even as an extra walking by on the street, the number of black actors in it made it extraordinary. The three main actors were, of course, superb. The people who made the film certainly believed in it—and so did Jean Shepherd, who, wholly on his own, promoted the film and pretty much single-handedly arranged the midnight showing that Chuck and I and some 300 other people attended. One felt that one was going to a socially significant event—and the little 300-seat Eastside Theater was packed with eager and committed New Yorkers. Chuck and I were the youngest people there, I'm sure, by five or even ten years. In no way was this something for kids. Kids were not Shepherd's audience; he was a proto–Garrison Keillor.

In the movie, Cassavetes played a young white man, Axel North, estranged from his family, who starts to work on the New York docks, where he meets Poitier, who plays a black loader named Tommy. Tommy befriends Axel.

Poitier/Tommy is a good, decent man, with a warm, loving wife, Lucy (played by Dee), and, I believe, a little daughter. The very ordinariness of their names, Tommy and Lucy, are signs of the good, decent American values they represent. And Axel North's slightly unusual name lets us know he's a young man (not from the South, but from the North) enough outside the mainstream so that he might actually let these good people (who are, after all, black) befriend him. Poitier brings Cassavetes home to dinner and makes him part of the family. Meanwhile, at work, political tensions arise that separate the black and white dock workers. Finally there's some kind of mob violence, in which Poitier, fighting for a *rapprochement* between black and white workers, is killed—and Cassavetes is left bereft of his second family, mourning over Poitier's body, on the docks. At the movie's end, everyone is devastated that the good Tommy is dead: Cassavetes, Lucy, the audience—and, of course, Chuck and I.

I saw it revived only once, two or three years later, when I ran to see it again and realized that, despite the acting, it wasn't a very good movie. As a piece of filmic rhetoric it was extremely thin, and the devastating effect it had had on me at age fourteen had been mostly button pushing. Obviously it had gotten financed because it had struck some producer as a kind of *On the Waterfront* (1954) look-alike, and the race relations theme had seemed a daring social gamble—socially desirable, but finally fundamentally justifiable only because of this generic resemblance to this prior film that had been highly successful. But what I realized from my seventeen-year-old viewing that I hadn't realized at fourteen was that the film's message was: "Isn't it tragic that the forces of racial tension are great enough so that the values of good, decent black men like Tommy cannot survive in the contemporary world? Because of that violent racial antipathy, both the black family (represented by Lucy) and liberal whites (represented by Axel) must live in a far more impoverished world."

Another thing the seventeen-year-old realized, which the fourteen-year-old had not, was the basic statement on which the more elaborate question was founded: "The forces of racial antipathy are such that good, decent values of black men like Tommy *cannot* survive." "Cannot" includes "will not"; and since all stories happen in the past, it means that these values are fleeting and rare, and have been largely stamped out already. (It was not a piece of science fiction saying that such values are common today, but *if this goes on*. . . .) When I looked around me, at my family, at my friends, black and white—and after all, I was a black kid who'd grown up in Harlem and gone to school with (and been on detention with) Stokely Carmichael—I'd seen such values working. I had seen the interracial *rapprochements* they facilitated all around me, and I had seen them since I'd been a child. They weren't being stamped out, murdered, destroyed. They were growing, getting larger; and while there certainly were problems, the ones shown in the film were not what those problems were. More and more black and white people were getting on pretty well. Sure, the situation was by no means perfect. I had two uncles—two black men—who were crusading judges in the fight for black rights, the one on my father's side of the family, more liberal and better-known, and a more conservative one on my mother's. But the goals were not some impossible thing to achieve. They were scattered and visible and yielding fruit all over the place. And they still are.

What was wrong with the film was that, first, on the grossest level it wasn't realistic. It wasn't characteristic of what was currently occurring in the world: The same year the film came out, the schools were first integrated in Little Rock, Arkansas—with a good deal of white protest and even violence. But it happened. Second, reality (read: the political world around me) and its discrepancy with what the film purveyed gave me the ideological reading. The film was unrealistic in the same way that a film on the integration of the schools in Little Rock would have been unrealistic if, at the end, Autherine Lucy had been killed and the protesting white segregationists had been successful—and the audience was asked to feel sad and left the theater shaking their heads, saying, "It's too bad they couldn't make that integration stuff work."

Hey! someone would have had to object. *It didn't happen that way!*

Ninety years before, in his criticism of the novel, Mathew Arnold wrote that a novel's overall story has to be believably characteristic of the social group portrayed. Basically he's right. For a certain kind of realistic film, this is true as well. And that's the first place where *Edge of the City* went off.

Fundamentally, the film's message said that something was rare to impossible that was actually common and getting more common. Also, the general grossness of the filmic rhetoric prevented the film from showing the far more subtle problems that real people, black and white, had to face. Only by using a moment of mob violence lifted gratuitously from another film—*Waterfront*—could it make any statement at all. And the filmmakers weren't really concerned with statement. They just wanted to make the audience feel sad.

Here is the hardest point to follow without having seen the actual movie or unless you've had a similar insight with other similarly bad films: to preserve the rhetorical grossness of the filmic rhetoric (the lack of visual analysis scene by scene, the long takes across thin dialogue, the one-dimensionality of the characters, the melodramatic and/or banal microsituations that contributed to the major situations) and make it into something aesthetically interesting, the writer, the producer, or/and the director—to revert to an old-fashioned term, whoever was the *auteur*—would have had to come up with a set of far more carefully and intelligently chosen subsituations leading to a wholly different and more truthful macrosituation to present in that alienated filmic style (alienated in the Brechtian sense, not the Marxian). The ending might, indeed, be tragic or at least dark. Black men *can* get killed on the docks; and prejudice can certainly be a factor. But you must have that death result from something believable. You'd have to work some current of the absurd and blackly comic through it, as well as the social. This would, of course, have cut the film off from a certain audience—certainly the audience who loved it that night in 1957. It would have made the film appear "experimental" and "eccentric," rather than "hard-hitting" and "emotionally" effective. That Brechtian distance is what, a few years later, dealing with matters of sex rather than race, Paul Morrisey would use in his Warhol-produced films *Flesh* (1968), *Trash* (1970), and *Heat* (1972), all of which stand up very well today—experimental and eccentric films all, and which have survived far better than Ritt's *Edge of the City.*

Again and again this is Fassbinder's method.

But that's how you take simplistic filmic rhetoric and make it into art. By changing its relation to truth, you can move it toward the aesthetic.

There is, however, another possibility.

Throw out the distanced rhetoric (which, in the case of *Edge of the City* as it was actually made, was probably laziness, lack of filmic talent, or possibly even a rushed job on a low budget), and put much more analysis and intelligence into the fine points of both the incidents and their filmic presentation: a host of microincidents conceived to dramatize and anchor things to a more complex psychology, showing how *this* situation on the city docks was *idiosyncratic* and *different* from anything that might *generally* be occurring in the world. Time, intelligence, and filmic invention should have been spent making the good guys *and* the bad guys far more individual and believable; and we needed not only to see Tommy's decency but also to explore the source of a certain naïveté in him, and how it got there, because otherwise for a black man in *this* society to walk into the situation Poitier rushes into is just not comprehensible. In short, what the distanced rhetoric would render darkly comic, a more intricate and intimate filmic rhetoric (many more things and far more kinds of things shown in many more artfully interconnected close-ups) would have rendered more human, analyzed, and believable—and it would have further exploited the wonderful actors, and probably required much more talent from a more complex cast of minor actors, not to mention the film technicians. This is Nicholas Roeg, Roman Polanski, and Ridley Scott, the Coen Brothers and Scorsese.

But in either the distanced (Brechtian) or the intimate (call it Hitchcockian) case, it would have been a more demanding film.

Gay British filmmaker Derek Jarman made beautiful, sensuous, politically astute nonnarrative films, like *Sebastiane* (1976), *Caravaggio* (1986), and *Wittgenstein* (1993). In the side comments to his 1991 script for *Queer Edward II,* an impressionistic film based on (or, as he puts it, "improved from") Marlowe's *Edward II,* Jarman remarks that the extended time and the increased number of camera setups required to construct realistic/intimate (Hitchcockian) narrative make them relatively expensive, which mitigates against the financing of ambitious realistic treatments of themes and topics without an (assumed) surefire popular "plot"—a situation which begs for congruences like the one we noted between *On the Waterfront* (Marlon Brando's highly successful film from 1954) and 1957's *Edge of the City.* Wrote Jarman, as far as film was concerned, "essentially narrative is an exercise in censorship because of that"—a pretty good materialist analysis.

Scorsese is a fine enough filmmaker so that one winces at the postproduction butchering of *Gangs of New York.* (Do the producers think that audience can't see where the cuts have been made or can't hear where voice-overs or refilming attempts to splice-over the breaks that were filled with sequences that had once connected things far more smoothly?)

But whether we like it or not, we're still children of Plato. When a change in the rhetorical surface of the art object is perceived as facilitating a move closer either to truth or to beauty, the work is generally counted a success—even if it takes people a little while to become comfortable with that new surface.

Only a few years after *Edge of the City* appeared, in '60 or '61 Nabokov made this statement (which I certainly read before I wrote my first published novel): "The most shocking novel you could write today is about an interracial couple who marry without incident, love each other very much, and have a long and happy life together—with lots of smart, contented children, no one of whom ever got involved with drugs—who lived to a contented old age."

That's when it hit me. With America's history of racial genocide, with blacks, Native Americans, and Mexicans (Billy the Kid purportedly killed over a dozen of all three, who were not even counted among his twenty-one adolescent murders, because, at the time, they were not considered human), the death of someone black, Native American, or Mexican at the end of an "American story" *cannot* be shocking. Surprising? Yes. Surprisingly banal. But shocking? In terms of the larger text with which we have to deal—the greater text that subsumes art *and* life—it's been done.

I've known of several such interracial couples as Nabokov described. My grandmother once told me that when Harlem was a German-Jewish neighborhood, with a scattering of Dutch still living there, she moved into the first house in Harlem open to blacks in

1902, on 133 Street between Seventh and Lenox. Her landlord, living in the same building, was a white woman married to a black man. The woman had owned the building. My black grandmother and grandfather lived there four years, before, in 1906, several blocks closer to Fifth Avenue, history records another house as the first one opened to blacks in Harlem: white landlords who did not live on the property owned it. In one month they moved out all the white tenants and moved in all black tenants, and the results were riots in the neighborhood. People tried to fence the building off. It became a site of contention and started the white flight that left Harlem an overwhelmingly black neighborhood by World War I.

My grandmother's integrated building, with its interracial owners and its black and white tenants—and its relatively peaceful acceptance by the neighborhood (I'm sure there was *some* grumbling)— is *so* shocking, however, that it has dropped out of history. Those shocking situations have been elided from the range of American fiction—and thus have been historically all but forgotten. But I think the story of the *two* buildings makes both take on sociological highlights that the tale of each lacks alone.

I may seem something of a Pollyanna, but history always displays alternatives. That's what justifies our deploring the destructive currents that grow up and sweep away knowledge of more peaceful and better possibilities for change.

In 1959 the *New York Times Book Review* published a version of Leslie Fiedler's 1948 essay, which would shortly form a chapter in his then-new critical work, *Love and Death in the American Novel* (1960), "Come Back to the Raft Ag'in, Huck Honey." In it Fiedler teases out some of the homosexual implications of the Huck Finn and Nigger Jim story and of the American "buddy novel" in general, a subgenre that includes everything from *The Last of the Mohicans* (1826) to *On the Road* (1957). In the course of it, he gave a generation of general readers the methodological tools for looking at a certain kind of plot significance. In the full critical book, which I read a year-and-a-half later, just after I was married, Fiedler actually tried to do the same thing with the American novel's handling of women. But because he was committed to the rather idiotic Leavis notion (which Leavis had put together almost solely to redeem the novels of D. H. Lawrence for the Great Tradition) that the only right and proper topic for the authentically great novel (at a time when "mature" meant accepting what the world dealt you, no matter how unfair) was "mature heterosexual relations"—in which case Lawrence's *Rainbow* (1915) and *Women in Love* (1916), and perhaps *To the Lighthouse* (1927) and *The*

Years (1937), are among the only mature novels around, dismissing all the writers, male and female, who wrote about courtship. They are only leading up to the real thing.

The result is that Fiedler could not quite come out and condemn either the world or the fiction. But a lot of his readers could.

I can remember even giving that one—the mature heterosexual relation—some serious consideration. In the same section of his book, Fiedler also claimed that serious fiction about the insane must finally be, by definition, boring or banal. I remember sitting in the wingchair in the corner of our 4th Street bedroom/living room, with the Dell Paperback in my hand, and saying to myself, in about the same tone of voice Huck Finn decides, "All right, then. I'll *go* to hell." All right, then. I won't *write* a proper and authentic great novel. I'd write some *other* kind. And when, two years later, through overwork and a host of other tension, I ended up in a mental hospital, and locked in obsessive repetitious behavior patterns that frightened me, I was pretty sure some of that "boring" material would have to make its way into anything I did, banal or not.

Have I said? I still think Fiedler is *the* great mid-century American critic. Without his efforts, one, we never would have had the intellectual scaffolding on which to wrestle with these problems. And, two, there has been no one more generous to me personally, as a writer. Fourteen years later, on the strength of a handful of argumentative letters, he offered me my first visiting professorship at Buffalo, in 1975.

The first of those letters survives in part as the basis of my essay "Letter to a Critic." The others were lost in the Fiedlers' catastrophic fire in the middle '90s, in which many far more valuable texts than mine were incinerated, including a first edition of *Ulysses,* an early correspondence with Saul Bellow, and exchanges with numerous other writers.

Is anyone today *not* aware of the statistic that something over 10 percent of all black males spend time in jail? Half of those incarcerations are for drugs, so that ten or twenty years from now, if those drugs are made legal, half of those incarcerations will be reread as a form of civil disobedience—such changes are brought about by material pressures, and, as Marxists know, the morality is then adjusted to reflect or challenge it only as much as is materially required. The half of those incarcerations that are a matter of actual crime is *still* an appalling statistic. But it also means that almost nine out of ten of us have not spent time in jail.

If you're going to talk about the "black male" experience, you've got to talk about those nine-out-of-ten, as well as the one-out-of-ten, remembering that the nine-out-of-ten are still the overwhelming majority. You also have to consider the relationships between them. When 10 percent of 50 percent of your population have experienced jail, it means that the other 95 percent of the total male-and-female population are much more likely to know someone now in jail or who has been in jail, or to know people who are on the verge of some illegality, or to have been tempted themselves and overcome that temptation. That's part of the black experience, too. As a community, black people have a much greater first- and second-hand knowledge of the police system and its many warts, which only secondarily has anything to do with whether you personally have or haven't been arrested—whether you are or are not one of the one-in-ten. This strikes me as the true and cultural significance of that statistic.

The ideological reduction of any given narrative is a factor of the statistical availability of specific occurrences in the world in tension with the statistical prevalence of certain experiences in other narratives—both the similar experiences and different ones.

Another Hollywood convention: in a film, you rarely see anyone read a book. Even more rarely does anyone say anything about one. The pivotal scene in *The Great Gatsby* (1925), in which Nick, Daisy, and Jordan Baker listen to Tom bluster on about Goddard's *Rise of the Colored Empire,* never makes it to the screen in any of the film versions. But I can't imagine a couple like Tommy and Lucy at that time who would not have been devouring the essays of James Baldwin and discussing them from soup to nuts over dinner, especially with a young man such as Axel—just as a few years later Lucy would have devoured Betty Friedan's *The Feminine Mystique* (1962). These were bestsellers during their times, and middle-class people, black and white, discussed and argued over them incessantly. I wonder if Hollywood's refusal to show folks reading and talking about what they read, as real people still do all the time, has anything to do with helping TV knock reading even further out of the center of our cultural experience than it has naturally fallen out over the last fifty years? More accurately, I suspect it's a factor of individual and group *perception* of the statistical awareness of these occurrences: thus the ideological "meaning" of a text is a dialogue between *this* text, *all* texts, and the *world.* In a historical field, this is a fundamentally unstable relationship, which accounts for why the ideology of a given narrative constantly changes through time, even as the world changes and as the statistical deployment of other narratives change.

What I am describing here is the complex of intertextuality, in which the world itself (or rather our perception of it) can finally be seen to operate identically to the perception of a text—a play of differences, of presences and absences, a mental construct that is only put together through the textual process Freud described as *Nachträglichkeit*. The only thing we have access to is that mental construct; for the construct to cohere, we also have to have a number of metaphysical concepts—those "facts"/beliefs about the universe that we can have no direct access to, but, whether we believe the universe to be matter and energy or whether we believe it to be an idea in the mind of a deity greater than we are, or even if we believe solipsistically it is only an idea in our own minds, it would not hold together.

The complexity and the malleability of this web (which also explains its great stability and ability to recover from rips, tears, and momentary violences committed by the irruptions of other texts/occurrences upon it) are hard or impossible to keep in one's mind for any length of time; the reduction we all always make of it—or have "always already" made—is to some notion of a "content"—fixed, stable, unchanging—in terms of written or visual texts, and to an "objective reality," in terms of the text of the perceived world. But as far as what we actually have access to, those notions are at best provisionally useful illusions. (Essays such as "Critical Methods/Speculative Fiction" [1969] and "Russ" [1979] were among my tentative and clumsy attempts to convey my perception of the interconnected webs which constitute language and the world.) You can find hints of an awareness of this textual complexity of life and language in writers back through Nietzsche, Pater, Hegel, Kant, and even Augustine and Plato. But what they all say is that such complexity is too complicated to hold onto and finally unnecessary; and each eventually turns to a simpler model—but that's largely because each saw himself as writing not for readers in a multiplicity of cultural positions but for a single culture, and even for the members of a single class within that culture. Given many day-to-day situations, critical judgments, and what-have-you, the reductive illusions of "content" and "reality" suffice. But finally they are—like the story told in *Edge of the City*—unrealistic. In a situation where we have to consider a given text—a given narrative—in a larger context, one where it must pass from one culture to another, say, or from one time to another, or be discussed or even argued over by members of two different cultures or culture groups, the illusion only fosters confusion, and often hostility and anger. This is one reason why literary theory, which tries to promote a more realistic view of how the judgment of texts, the interpretation of texts, and even the very reading of texts occur, has become such a necessary part of university studies, despite all its difficulties and complexities of rhetoric and all its counterintuitive ideas.

Well, when we were adolescents, the only person I had to discuss all these new ideas with was my friend and later wife, Marilyn Hacker. (What is it Ogden Nash asked: "What makes adolescents adolesce?") Discuss them we did. From the moment we were married in late August of 1961—she was eighteen, I was nineteen—immediately Marilyn began to make me aware of her similar thinking on these problems in terms of the situation of women in life and as represented in art as I was making her aware of about race. I've written in my autobiography how, on a rainy afternoon, when Marilyn came in wet from shopping at the grocery store, and I gave her a pair of my jeans to change into, she was astonished to learn that men's pants (and men's clothing in general) possessed real pockets. I was equally astonished to learn that the pockets in most women's clothing up to that time were practically artificial and basically only for show—tiny little things, three inches deep, in which clearly no one was meant to put or carry anything. From this, over the next few weeks of conversation, we elaborated an entire sociology/anthropology of men's and women's culture as lived in the United States since World War II. This led to a critique of the range and lack of complexity in women characters in recent American fiction and also in older English and French novels. The results of all of this litter were my first seven science fiction novels—*The Jewels of Aptor* through the three books of *The Fall of the Towers,* to *The Ballad of Beta-2, Babel-17, Empire Star,* and *The Einstein Intersection.*

While you can find the most passing references to women having abortions in fiction written during the '30s (the largely international Djuna Barnes and the English Jean Rhys), between the end of World War II and the passage of *Row vs. Wade,* there is not a single piece of fiction written in America that I'm aware of (and I've looked) in which a woman has an abortion and does not die in the process. In America the phrase "died-during-an-abortion" was practically a single word, as the phrase "drunken-Irish-laborer" was a single word in England during the '60s and '70s. Well, during the '50s, '60s, and '70s I knew no women personally who had died from an abortion, though I'd known several who'd had them and lived on happily enough, even though the operations were then illegal—and I'd known one twenty-year-old woman who committed suicide because abortions *were* illegal, and, though she'd wanted and needed one, there was no way she could get it. The discrepancy between the texts displaying that fictive convention (all abortions lead to death) and the text of the world is what made the fictive convention into an ideological strategy for political intimidation *across* the world's text.

A series of popular '70s films with Clint Eastwood about a police detective named "Dirty Harry" finally drove that particular *Edge of the City* narrative trope out of general usage. The villains of the *Dirty Harry* films were usually from some marginal cultural group (black, Latino, gay)—in one, the villain was a white serial killer, but in tracking him down, white Harry (Eastwood) got to kill half a dozen other unsavory folk from the margins. In the largely liberal cinema, the films offered the white audience the pleasure of seeing a white man beat up and/or slaughter half a dozen folk from the social margins. The gimmick was, however, that in each film Harry was assigned a partner, always from a "marginal" group: a young, idealistic policeman—now black, now Hispanic, now a woman—would be full of liberal ideas and outrage, which Harry has no time for. But the Cop Code would prevail—and invariably they would save each other's lives, proving that Harry wasn't *just* a hopeless bigot and psychopath. Then, at the end of the film, the young, liberal partner would be killed. There would be a moment of pathos, in which hardhearted Harry would . . . well, we didn't know what was going on inside him, because he was too stony-faced for us really to tell. But the audience felt sad.

This was so obviously a way of furthering the slaughter machine which was the film itself that it provoked a flood of protesting articles. A fair amount of the audience, white and black, began to realize how, ideologically, the films functioned. From the fusillade of articles in papers from the *Village Voice* to the *New York Times* that responded to the *Dirty Harry* films, a notable percentage of the audience began to be able to do the kind of ideological reduction of the gross plot of the films and separate it from the transparent emotional manipulation that was used to overlay it and make it acceptable.

Not too long after the *Dirty Harry* films had been jeered off the screens, Michael Cimino made *Thunderbolt and Lightfoot* (1974), again a film with Clint Eastwood and this time Jeff Bridges. In this case the mayhem revolved around a pair of criminals, the older Eastwood and the younger Bridges.

Now, another filmic convention that, as a gay man, I had noted was that whenever a male character put on a piece of female attire in a noncomedic film, invariably that character died sometime in the next half-hour. Again, in pre-WWII films—and narratives—this is not the case. Various forms of cross-dressing are a regular staple of '30s and '40s comedy, romantic and otherwise, from the Marx Brothers to Abbott and Costello, from Gable and Colbert to Grant and whoever. And in '20s and '30s pulp novels, particularly masculine heroes flaunt their masculinity through appropriating the feminine. They are *so* butch that they can act effeminate without "polluting" themselves by the deadly feminine itself. For example, in Hammett's novel *The Thin Man* (1933), when Nick and Nora Charles are in bed together in their room in the Plaza, a hoodlum bursts in with a gun. To show his bravery, Nick responds (I quote—inaccurately, I'm sure—from memory): "Will you put that thing away. It doesn't bother my wife. But I'm pregnant, and I might just have it right here." Clearly there's a sexist element in this, because the appropriation of the cross-gender rhetoric doesn't usually go in both directions to the same end. (That is to say, it is the discrepancy between *this* text and *another*-text-that-is-too-rare, too-slight, too-ephemeral, too-statistically-uncommon, which gives this one its iniquitous ideological weight. But what *looks* like sexist content is *all* intertextual. If society encouraged women to joke in the same way that men do, then the *social content* of Nick's line would be entirely Other. The sexism we perceive "in" the line is the dimly perceived constraint on women's making the same sort of joke in the same hail-fellow-well-met mode in a parallel situation. The social forces that lead to the fact that women might not even *want* to make that sort of joke is, however, *part* of the constraint.) After the war, however, when the House Un-American Activities Committee began to hound homosexuals as "security risks," this kind of joking became *verboten*—and banned from the movies. Masculinity had become too precious (an aspect of male power rather than an aspect of female pleasure, a power too fragile, too authoritarian, too beleaguered) to be seen joking about itself in this way. The necessity of killing anyone who even jests with the possibility of cross-gendering in popular films probably grew out of the same anxiety.

At any rate, in 1974 I went to see *Thunderbolt and Lightfoot* with a sophisticated, heterosexual English friend, John Witton-Dorris. About a third of the way through the movie, in order to commit a robbery, Bridges dresses up as a not-very-attractive woman. I laughed and said, "Well, *he'll* be killed soon."

Frowning, John glanced over at me, "Of course he won't. He's the sexy young star. You can't kill the sexy young star."

Well, about thirty minutes later—in movie-time *long* after Bridges has discarded his female attire and clearly been (re-)marked as straight through his lusting after one young lady or another—the bad guys set on him and literally kick him to death in one of the most brutal murder sequences either one of us had yet seen in a commercial film.

Much of the kicking focused on his genital area and kidneys— *one* of the things that makes the sequence so excruciating.

"How did you know that was going to happen?" John asked me, astonished.

"It's a convention," I told him.

And a month later he phoned me up and said, "You're right. I've seen three more or them, since then—just on late-night telly. I've been watching films all my life, and I never noticed that before."

I told him, "Probably the people who make the films aren't even aware of it, as such. They stick in the bit of cross-dressing, then suddenly they feel like they *have* to put in the other—the deadly payoff, or it doesn't feel like real fiction to them. That's how 'real' fiction works."

The first film that I'm aware of to violate this convention was, incidentally, Ron Howard's spectacularly unsuccessful *Willow* (1988; produced by George Lucas)—a film whose general approach to the human body was far more radical than, say, Jackson's in *The Lord of the Rings* (2001), which, for all the different sizes and types of Caucasian bodies it shows (Dwarf, Elf, Hobbit, human . . .), basically homogenizes them all, so that even the hairy feet of the hobbits and Elijah Wood's cunningly bitten nails tend to escape all margins of signification.

Well, only a few years ago, with a working-class friend, a relatively *un*sophisticated man (who by his own admission has only read a single novel in his life), I went to see *Boys Don't Cry* (1999), the film about the young female-to-male transsexual, Brandon Teena, who was raped and murdered in Nebraska a few years back. When we came out of the theater, the first thing my friend said was: "Well, I guess the point of *that* movie was that it's all right to kill lesbians if you're sorry about it afterwards."

Today this particular kind of ideological reduction is easy to make and almost everyone can do it. If anything, we begin to see that, as a method, it can be almost too glib. But this has been a social process that has grown up over the years.

In the '50s and the first half of the '60s, if you pointed out that the deaths of Maggie Tulliver, Emma Bovary, and Anna Karenina created an ideological pattern to which the death-in-life of Natasha Rostov at the end of *War and Peace* and the death of the heroine at the end of Chopin's *The Awakening* only contribute, most '50s intellectuals, at least in this country, would have simply frowned at you and said something about your lack of understanding of tragedy, though neither Flaubert nor Tolstoy thought of the suicides of his leading lady as tragic, but rather as the deserved comeuppance for feminine stupidity and immorality.

It's hard to convey how very much, in the dozen years between 1962 and 1973 (to pick an arbitrary date), Marilyn and I were on our own in all this—or at least how much we felt as if we were.

Well, Marilyn and I shared an intellectual language, which we had learned in the same high school and from the same texts: we had even helped teach it to each other. But we were from two very different cultures. I don't think it's an accident (as Adorno might put it) that Marilyn's subsequent history as a writer and as an editor is such a stellar one in helping new black and Latino writers—especially during her extraordinary tenure as editor at the *Kenyon Review*—such as Reginald Shepherd, Cyrus Cassels, John Keene, Jr., and Raphael Campo, just as she helped me; or that she has chosen to translate someone like the Lebanese novelist and poet Vénus Khoury-Ghata, who writes in French (*Here There Was Once a Country* 2002).

But, again, in the '50s and '60s, there were no bookstore shelves filled with volumes containing "race" and "gender" in the titles and dozens of introductory books to acquaint you with the thinkers and the particular passages in their works where they interrogated such intertexual complexities, such textual realities.

Written between my nineteenth birthday and the spring of my twenty-fifth year, those first eight science fiction novels struggle with all this in a halting, clumsy way, as you might imagine from someone who wasn't terribly sure if anyone was going to understand the presuppositions on which they were based, anyway, however incomplete and rickety they were.

Now, the way in which all this history redounds on your question is to say that, at the time, I had no way to perceive what I was writing—nor do I believe very many other people would have perceived it that way—as part of a general cultural project which I had the choice of joining or not joining, or of joining or not joining to a greater or lesser extent. And that, finally, is what I suspect, when asked today, your question has to imply.

Having run all around Robin Hood's barn like this, I can return to the last part of your question. When I was writing my first nine science fiction novels, did I see myself as some sort of pioneer? Not only did I *not* see myself in such a way, I *couldn't* have seen myself in such a way. The best I could say is that I was trying not to make the kinds of mistakes I saw being made all around me, mostly in contemporary fiction and narrative film. I succeeded in not making a few of them—and failed wildly, laughably, ludicrously in avoiding many, many others.

None of those early novels has any more than provisional interest. I don't mean that I abnegate the responsibility for having written them. But if you asked me, "Who are you as a writer?" and wanted me to respond by presenting you with a text to read, I wouldn't pick any of them. But if you asked me, "Who *were* you as a writer before, say, arbitrarily, 1975?" I might give you *Nova,* possibly the stories in *Aye, and Gomorrah,* and perhaps *The Einstein Intersection*—though I would have to assume that your reasons for wanting to know were all but unfathomable.

That is to say, even for such a provisional task, I'd choose books blatantly not among those most likely to be labeled "pioneering" in the way that I take you to mean. That doesn't mean these areas aren't still terribly important from a political point of view.

But that's why answering your very rich question in some simple way, without all this historical elaboration, would be, by implication, to miswrite or rewrite history. While, in those years, clearly a project was going on in the text of the world, making great strides, changing laws, changing lives (in 1961 our landlord owned a dozen Lower East Side buildings, in one of which he put *all* the interracial couples who came to him looking for apartments—without telling them, of course. But the fact that he had such a building, and that Marilyn and I ended up living there for four years, is an emblem of the change), there was as yet no concomitant project in the text of literary fiction or film—and certainly not in SF; though, because of those '30s currents which were far more alive in SF than they were in mainstream literature, SF was certainly the logical place to mount (or, more accurately, to continue) such a project. For such a project is never begun; it can only continue—even if the people involved think they are starting it.

During the years I wrote my first eight novels, I often said that one reason I liked science fiction was that it was a *little* less bound by these incredibly conservative genre and racial conventions that strait-jacketed film and literary fiction. (Perhaps you can see now why I need the literary/paraliterary distinction. The paraliterary provides a place to stand, as it were, from which the literary can be positively critiqued. It really does have a different history, however much interchange there has been with the mainstream.) The women characters were more varied in type than you found in mainstream fiction (Luise White discusses this very well in the 1975 *Women in Science Fiction Symposium: Jisbella MacQueen, Olivia Presteign, Kathy Niven*), not richer in the sense that Forster suggests with his notion of flat and round characters, but in fundamental type. And there was a general liberalism and sense of relatively forward political thought in the genre.

What you can possibly see in those early SF novels of mine that might, indeed, look like the beginnings of such a project are probably better seen as a struggling attempt to speak intelligently to a good friend, who would give me a sympathetic hearing and to whom I happened to be married, but who hailed from a culture very different from mine, as I hailed from one very different from hers, and about which differences we were learning more and more, day by day, both to appreciate and to question.

Back then, yes, I thought the genre itself was ahead of its times. Today, I'm aware that these "forward-looking" currents were actually holdovers from the '30s, even unto the variety of female characters (a response to the women's movement of the teens and '20s), which had been stabilized by the marginal position of pulp fiction outside that of the literary mainstream, whose culturally backsliding people such as Maxwell Geismar (*Henry James and the Jacobites* 1960) had made much of, though few people paid (or pay) heed to it then (or today). But as far back as 1961, Marilyn had pointed out to me that the scientist's plucky daughter, whose dad had taught her to fix anything with vacuum tubes, resistors, and capacitors in it, had actually evolved from the rancher's plucky daughter from the traditional Western, whose dad had made sure she knew how to "ride and shoot like a man"—but I didn't think of the Western genre as a specifically *historical* forerunner of SF until later.

During the '50s I read science fiction and read it passionately—but I also read it relatively uncritically: the way you would expect someone between the ages of eight and eighteen to read it. And when, at fifteen, sixteen, seventeen, I began to analyze what was going on in fiction, my analytic gaze was focused on literature and films, as you might expect that of a bright adolescent at the time to be. The very small innovations that I made in my early science fiction novels, written in the first half of the '60s, came almost entirely from considerations of changes I'd seen in the world and through my rather extreme reactions against what I took to be flaws in literary fiction—and relatively little from what I'd seen in science fiction itself.

However ludicrous and hopelessly inadequate the results, the conscientious models for *The Fall of the Towers* (as I've written in *The*

Motion of Light in Water 1988) were Balzac, Tolstoy (and my own critique of Fiedler), and Wilde, as much as, or more than, they were Heinlein, Sturgeon, McLean, or Bester. This is only to confirm what I've indicated here and in the sections of my autobiography in which I discuss more the sources of, and influences on, those early books. Most of my thinking was about narratives and films outside the science fiction genre. Written science fiction, with its slightly wider array of female character types, was there to receive the benefits of that analytical thought. And receive it, it did.

The enterprise of the *Tower*'s three books grew out of my frustration with American involvement in the Vietnam War: since so many Americans were simply *not* going to accept the self-evident moral objection to war (we were murdering other people and being murdered), I would try to show what the whole process was doing to *us,* to the soldiers, yes, but even more to those of us not actually fighting—what we were losing of our own selfhood. If they couldn't hear the blatantly moral argument, perhaps a few might be able to hear a blatantly self-serving one.

I did this by using some science fiction precepts to de-realize the war *qua* war in my story, in order to throw the spotlight back on the society.

Years later, when I read Conrad's *Heart of Darkness* for the first time, carefully and all the way through (I had been reading *at* it since I was a teenager), I found the same theme there—with Imperialism substituted for War.[1] Many critics do not agree—certainly Chinua Achebe did not, in his well-known 1974 Chancellor's Distinguished Faculty Lecture, given at the University of Massachusetts, later my home university (a lecture I was honored with an invitation to give two dozen years later). One of the things you learn from contemplating the web-like qualities of life and language is that a theme, by the time it is recognizable as a theme, is an always-already ordained pattern that one imposes on the text in which one thinks one is discovering it. As such, it functions identically to a political prejudice. But from having written science fiction, that is how I was prejudiced to read Conrad's 1898 story that grew out of his 1890 visit to the Congo. As prejudices go, I think it's a fairly good one, and one I find supported by Conrad's text in myriad ways; thus, that is how I continue to read it, to reread it, and to teach it—even as that same web experience has shown me—convinced me—that other readings are perfectly possible; and I try to urge others toward their own, equally rich, readings.

But that's the lived experience behind my regularly repeated contention that the boundary between genres is quite as important for what it allows to pass back and forth across it—from literature to science fiction and from science fiction to literature—as for what it keeps out and impedes from traveling back and forth. But I also believe that the results of the crossing and the impedance are interdependent.

CF: I wasn't expecting quite such a lengthy answer, but I think you're absolutely right to insist that these issues can't be intelligently discussed without a good deal of historical contextualization; and I think that the history lesson you've given us is especially valuable because so much of what you've said will come as news to many readers today, especially, perhaps, readers younger than either you or I. On the more personal side, I was especially interested in the extent to which you recall your earlier SF novels as being written for a single individual, namely, your wife, Marilyn Hacker. Of course, many works that now have a wide audience were originally composed with just one person, or one small group, in mind: *Alice in Wonderland* (1865) really was written for one young girl, Alice Liddell; and most of Kafka's fictions were designed only to be read aloud to a small circle of his personal friends. An interesting twist, though, is that Kafka's friends are now remembered just for being Kafka's friends, and Alice Liddell just for inspiring Lewis Carroll; whereas Marilyn, as you've already indicated, is herself a writer and editor of major achievement. So maybe the early friendship of Wordsworth and Coleridge would be a closer analogy.

Perhaps we could now move from the genesis of your early SF to its reception, especially with regard to the reception of your representations of race and gender. My own understanding is that this is a very mixed story—that early Delany received much praise and honor but also a significant amount of hostility and incomprehension. I suggest, too, that we broaden the conversation to include your representations not only of nonwhite and female characters but also of minority sexualities. Here, surely, there is a significant change as we move from early to middle Delany. *The Einstein Intersection* (1967), for instance, radically probes issues of race and biology, and also of masculinity and femininity. But the plot is structured on a pretty conventional heterosexual quest—even if, as some readers have felt, Friza, the ardently desired female love-object, seems female only in the notional sense that applies, say, to all those lasses and maidens in A. E. Housman's *A Shropshire Lad* (1896). (As you know, Housman sent a copy of that volume to Oscar Wilde in prison, and Wilde, of course, understood exactly what was going on.) There's a big change, clearly, by the time we get to *Dhalgren* (1974), with the open bisexuality of the Kid.

SRD: I'm going to shy away from directly responding to your statement to provide a bit more context. Bear with me, and I'll come back to take up both your notion about individual address and the treatment of minority sexualities, in *The Einstein Intersection* (1967) and, three to eight years later, in *Dhalgren* (1975). Perhaps I can show why this context is so important.

Those first eight SF novels—really the first nine, because the ninth, *Nova,* appeared in the late spring of '68 and arrived in paperback in April of '69—all came before an extremely important year. More than a year, actually: the period overlapped both 1968 and 1969.

You recall Virginia Woolf's famous remark, "Around 1910, everything changed"? Well, in the same way, around 1968, everything changed.

I'm talking about a period that began on April 4, 1968, with Nobel Peace Prize winner Dr. Martin Luther King's assassination. The shooting at the Loraine Motel in Memphis was followed, weeks later, by the assassination of Robert F. Kennedy in Los Angeles, after five out of six successful primary elections had suggested a pretty good chance for a win from a relatively liberal presidential candidate (if not as liberal as his opponent Eugene McCarthy, who'd beaten him in Oregon)—an assassination which, incidentally, wiped an attempt on the life of artist Andy Warhol by radical feminist Valerie Solanis off the front pages of the nation's papers: it had happened only the day before.

A week or so after King's death, the police fomented a major nightlong riot with the students sitting in at Columbia University. Millions of people in the greater New York area followed, horrified, as it was broadcast live till five o'clock in the morning over WBAI-FM. April 1968 in America was, I have always contended, pivotal on the occurrences of May 1968 in France; the French incidents started as a sympathy strike for Algerian students protesting Vice President Humphrey's visit to Tunis and for the students in New York.

I wonder if, incidentally, this isn't typical. F. Scott Fitzgerald says in the opening essay of *The Crack-Up* (the assemblage of pieces Edmund Wilson put together four years after his friend's death, which chronicle Fitzgerald's decline), that the Jazz Age actually began with the 1919 May Day riots in New York City, when the police attacked and brutalized the hundreds of young men who had gathered to listen to the leftist speakers at Madison Square—as it was brought to an end a decade later with the stock market crash of October 29. But new cultural periods are often marked at their beginnings and ends with political and/or economic violence.

In postpartum depression, exacerbated by the nation's violence, the wife of a writer friend, Michael Perkins, herself a talented painter, Rennie Perkins, died after three days in the hospital from a suicide attempt. Two months later, the writer himself was in the hospital with a stab wound in the stomach, received in a neighborhood riot in the Lower East Side. And I have written about going to dinner at comic-book writer Denny O'Neal's in those same weeks and having to cross Avenue C with an ashcan cover held over my head because people were throwing bricks from the roof at people in the street. In July 1969 this period more or less finished with the three days of Stonewall riots throughout New York City's Greenwich Village area. People who lived through it—at least in the cities of America—tended to experience that period as one continuing eruption of change. Certainly I did.

In that sixteen-month period—a year and a season—laws about what could and could not be published in the country were radically amended: it became legal to publish, unexpurgated, writers like D. H. Lawrence and Henry Miller. With this new freedom, yes, outright pornography with no particular redeeming social value also became legal—as a far more aware public now realized there was simply no hard-and-fast way to ascertain an absolute difference. In New York the death penalty was repealed.

That period saw the formation of NOW, the National Organization for Women—an organization whose doings were regularly reported in the popular press, bringing the idea of Women's Liberation to the general public. Before, while people such as Marilyn and I and a few of our friends had debated these questions from sun-up till sundown for some six or seven years, these same questions had received relatively little public discussion. Nor had the discussion been supported with a growing shelf of literature, including Kate Millet, Shulamith Firestone, Sheila Rowbotham, Andrea Dworkin, and Jill Johnston, all of whom first began to emerge about now, with their books—or with the articles that would make up their books a few years later. That's when Gloria Steinem became a household name as someone passionate over the concerns of women. The honorific "Ms." was first seriously proposed. The magazine of that name, under Steinem's editorship, followed soon after. Already known among a circle of intellectuals as an eccentric novelist and an astute critic with a penchant for films and a sympathy for popular culture, Susan

Sontag (1933–2004) became even more widely known for her article "Notes on Camp."

The Hopkins seminars, which had started in 1966 and which were so influential in bringing literary theory to this country, climaxed in 1969—that is to say, by the end of that period, people indeed knew about the existence of literary theory, at least in various sectors of the academy, in a way they simply hadn't before those years. In 1970 piles of the Pantheon hardcover translation of Foucault's 1966 volume, *The Order of Things,* sat on the front desk of the Eighth Street Bookshop, and the book become a neighborhood bestseller.

Before that time, while there had been a small homophile movement, centered on the Mattachine Society (the lesbian contributor to their newsletter, Carol Lee Haine, who wrote a monthly column entitled "Move Over, Boys," was a friend of Marilyn and mine and crashed with us for a few days at our 4th Street apartment), there *was* no Gay Liberation Movement. By the end of that time, there *was*—a movement whose doings were regularly reported in the *Village Voice.* Indeed, by the end of this period, there were the beginnings of something you could call a Gay Press.

Though there had been an alternative press, now the regular press began to take cognizance of the *East Village Other* and the *Berkeley Barb* as alternative sources and sites of ideas and debate—both of which, for the next few years, in issue after issue, ran a poignant personal ad in their back pages, complete with photograph, entreating a young man who had vanished from his home at the age of ten back in the early 1950s, Roger Calkins, to get in touch with his family. ["Roger Calkins" is the name of a character in Delany's *Dhalgren.*—CF]

In the same period, the nation's urban centers mounted a massive educational and medical campaign to end the venereal diseases gonorrhea and syphilis—a campaign that dwarfs anything done fifteen to twenty years later in the age of AIDS. Though, along with syphilis, gonorrhea had been curable since 1948, the disease had been rampant in the armed forces, as well as in the general population, since World War II. The 1968 campaign was largely successful. Along with the educational push, public health facilities changed their policies; and those changes worked. Up until then, from '62 through '68, regularly I'd gotten gonorrhea two and three times a year. Though I certainly made no major change in my sexual practices, since '69 I haven't had it once—which gives you some idea of how successful this campaign was. One of Marilyn's poetic japes from about 1964 was a bit of doggerel including this quatrain:

Gonorrhea, gonorrhea!
Oh, the shame! I'll not outlive it!
But before I have it treated,
Let me think to whom I'll give it!

Clearly this bit of verse speaks from *before* the urban venereal disease cleanup, when, among the sexually active, this particular sexually transmitted disease was as prevalent as the common cold.

The civil rights movement was the only one of the liberation movements that had achieved any social presence at all. But even then, it had been perceived as a social cause, focused on ending racial "discrimination/segregation," whether in the South or in the North. Discrimination and segregation were seen as specific social institutions and policies—in hotels, restaurants, schools. Over this period, the focus shifted from discrimination to "racism"—and with that change it now became a *social* project, whose focus was the elimination of a set of stances, attitudes, and actions among people. That is to say, at the end of this period it *was* a social project which anyone and everyone could take part in, even if you didn't get on a freedom bus and troop down into the South to help register black voters.

In that same spring, black students broke into libraries and tore down the signs on the shelves saying "Negro Literature" and replaced them with signs saying "Black Literature." Some of the guys who were slated to carry out this raid on the Tompkins Square and St. Marks branches of the library—Lamar, Noel, Tony (all three gay, incidentally)—met in my living room. My mother was a library clerk at the 135th Street branch of the New York Public Library, and I had to come up a few days later and defend their action to her and her (white) superior—an extremely intelligent and politically astute woman. My mother was initially and quietly outraged, but calmed down a bit after I came up to talk to them. During my spiel I reminded them how the term "black" had been Dr. DuBois' preferred term. (My parents had been acquaintances of DuBois—my father had known him since he was child, when DuBois was a guest of my grandfather's at St. Augustine's, where he stayed with my father's oldest brother, Dr. Lemuel Delany—some eighteen or nineteen years older than my father.) At the end of my speech, I remember my mother's boss finally saying, "Well, if it brings them in here to read it, I don't care what they call it. I'm for letting it stay." And the library system knuckled under—as did the *New York Times* a year later, followed by the rest of the literate world.

The shift from the specific fight for "civil rights" to the generalized battle against "racism" as the focus of concern was, or would soon be, mirrored in the other liberation movements—the specific fight for "women's rights" to the generalized battle against "sexism," from the fight for "gay rights" to the battle against "homophobia." It's arguable that, in all three cases, something had been lost in the transformation, and that '68/'69 were pivotal years in that transformation for all three. A number of people believe that, on all three fronts, the shift was premature—an argument I can understand and concur with. Still, under that shift, tremendous social strides were made—precisely in terms of the public awareness of the existence and situation of the groups *as* groups.

Before that time, there were no film-studies programs in any university; no black-studies programs, no women's studies. Afterwards, there were.

I've already assembled a book called *1984,* as a sort of nod in the direction of Orwell's year. Someday I would really like to write one about *this* particular period.

If I had to characterize it succinctly, I'd say that before that time there was no perception of precisely the cultural project that you began by asking me about. After it, however minuscule, there was. At least there was among SF readers. And more than that, now a number of different conceptual tools were in place with which to think about implementing that project. I will always believe that it was carried over the generic border *from* science fiction *into* the literary precinct. By no means did it start there. (As I said, it doesn't start. It continues.) But I believe it was reflected there first.

In the first late-night conversations I had with him in London in April of 1966, I told John Brunner how Marilyn, who had edited a number of John's novels at Ace Books, had already noted that he must have done some thinking about this question because he invariably *had* women characters in his novels. He confirmed this, and explained that as the husband of a wife who was a decade his senior, and who remembered the women's suffrage movement from her childhood, they'd had a number of discussions similar to Marilyn's and mine. John had made a point of having *at least* three women characters with notably different personalities in *every* novel. It doesn't sound like much today. But given that most SF novels at the time had none, and a few had a single woman who provided a love interest alone, even this much social thought was visible on the other side of an ocean by an eighteen-year-old editor/reader (Marilyn). The greater point is that this was another personal discussion, in John's case, with his wife, Marjorie, which Marilyn and I had overheard, as it were, a continent away—as John, indeed, had overheard Marilyn's and mine.

I say it started/continued in the SF precincts and moved into the literary. But that's because too many of the writers who helped bring this project into the literary, from Marge Percy to Bertha Harris to Jewel Gomez, I know were avid SF readers—and they read Joanna Russ and Ursula Le Guin, and, yes, before them, John Brunner and myself. But the change was brought about on pretty much every level of society, in a period of violence and legal and educational reform.

I drafted my novel *Hogg* in the opening days of 1969. Basically, it was written out in longhand, filling most of four notebooks through March, April, May, and June of that year, when I was in San Francisco. The retyping, the polishing, the general pumicing took place, desultorily, over the next four years. But I feel secure in saying that very little of that reworking was substantive in terms of plot or occurrences dealt with in the story. And the conception and the initial execution are pre-Stonewall. Often I tell people—and I stand by it—that really *Hogg* is the *last* pre-Stonewall gay novel written in America. And certainly from the time, that June, people phoned me in San Francisco to tell me about the three days of the Stonewall riots occurring in New York and I read the various newspaper accounts, this one sympathetic, that one appallingly wrong-headed, I would not have been able to conceive a novel in a similar vein. *Hogg* is a hugely angry novel, by a gay man who is ready to see the whole of bourgeois society destroyed, top to bottom, by a creature like my main character, Hogg.

As I've said, the Stonewall riots in New York City from June 27 through 29 were the climax of some currents in that period. At the end of those days, a change was . . . complete? No. But it was visible, markable, known about and knowable *as* a change, and in place. As soon as I learned that there was now an active and organized Gay Liberation Front, which was the all-but-immediate fallout of Stonewall, now there was another mode into which to channel that anger, those feelings—a mode that I do not hesitate to call constructive. And over a month's time the blatant nihilism of *Hogg* was suddenly consigned—at least for me as an active and creative force—to the past.

But now we can drop back five or six years to your question as it concerns science fiction.

My first four SF novels went all but unnoticed. I had no social contacts within the SF world—and later I learned that the SF field's general wisdom of the time was that "Samuel R. Delany" was an Ace Books "house name"—a pseudonym maintained by the publisher as a catchall for poor-quality novels that had stacked up in inventory or that the writers didn't want to see appear under their own names.

The otherwise relatively socially isolated *Analog* reviewer, P. Schyler-Miller, was a personal friend of Don Wolheim's and so, apparently, knew I was a real person—and was extremely generous to me in his early reviews. (I never met him, alas—or, if I did, it was only years later, a little before his death. If it happened, it must have been a brief "hello" at a social event that I just don't remember. I hope, though, if I did meet him, I said, "Thank you.") But his were the *only* reviews I received for my first four books. The rest of the field ignored me.

My second novel, the first in a trilogy, elicited a wonderfully nutty fan letter, explaining that the secret identity of "Samuel R. Delany" was now revealed. The writer carefully rewrote my name out:

"S-amuel R. De-*lan*-y."

Because my name contained all the letters of *Slan,* Van Vogt's best-known SF novel, obviously Delany was a pseudonym for A. E. Van Vogt! No unknown newcomer, the letter went on, could possibly have begun with such a well-written and well-crafted book. I had to be an old pro playing a trick on people.

And a year or so later, for the trilogy's concluding volume, there was that letter from John Brunner.

Another thing I had carried across the literary-paraliterary boundary with me into my science fiction writing was something I took to be a specifically literary ethic. Anything you wrote at all *had* to be written and rewritten until it was as good as you could possibly make it. The notion of writing quickly and facilely for money was one I never adopted. Possibly because I was so acutely dyslexic (which you would realize had you seen the illiterate jumble that some of the early drafts of these responses began as), the idea of writing quickly in any way was, for me, a contradiction in terms. And the $1,000 (sometimes $750) I was getting for each novel, though it went a bit more than ten times as far as it does today (my rent was, after all, about $750 a *year*!), was still not a living wage.

Things like that first letter are not a lot for a young writer to live on. But that and the Miller reviews and John's good words and generous support were about all, as a writer, I had as far as public support, until I returned from my first six-month trip to Europe in mid-April of 1966.

Another thing that changed over this '68/'69 period was the SF community itself.

For one thing it doubled in size over the three- or four-year period in which those sixteen months are at the center. A pre-1968 statistic that remains in my head: the number of original SF novels that were published around '66 or '67 was approximately 314 per year. By 1975, that number was up to approximately 600 novels per year.

By the same token, the SFWA's membership also doubled, from just under 200 to over 400. This growth was accompanied by a politicization of the sort that all these other incidents suggest as well. That year the *Magazine of Fantasy and Science Fiction* ran two facing-page ads, one censuring the American involvement in the Vietnam War and one saying that in trying political times, we should support the government. The wording of the two ads was such that, really, there was nothing that stopped one from signing both ads—though nobody did. And the facing-page presentation made it look very much as if one group (almost entirely East Coast writers) opposed the war and the other (almost entirely West Coast writers) supported it. That same year in Chicago, the 1968 Democratic Convention produced another round of rioting. (Science fiction writer Judith Merril [1923–97] and her daughter, Ann, on their way to Canada, were there and observed and took part in some of it.) About that time, a relatively mindless adaptation of William Faulkner's novel *The Sound and the Fury* (1929) hit the country's movie screens. The producers had been wholly unsure whether the association with the literary, through the Nobel Prize–winning novelist, or the novelist's association with the South, would be a selling point or would alienate audiences, and so they finally decided to change the film's title to *The Long, Hot Summer,* which is how it appeared. The media (perhaps responding to the euphony of the new title) picked up the phrase as a euphemism for summer protests and political riots and unrest, and for the next handful of years "long, hot summer" became a media figure of speech to indicate a summer of political riots—either anticipated or regretted.

At any rate, the Nebula Awards presented in 1969 in Berkeley—to Harlan [Ellison], Ursula [Le Guin], and me—were presented by an organization notably different from the one that had presented them to me in '68 and '67, where I had taken my first three. My sense is that there was far more publicity connected with the 1969 Nebula Awards than with any of the previous ones. Previously, there was coverage in only one paper—I recall that in 1967 the Saturday *New York Post* ran a single article, and only about the winner for the novel. In 1968, the year I won two, I seem to remember only two inches of text on the back page of one paper or another—even less than the previous year. But a year later, half a dozen papers carried mentions of 1969's awards, and pretty much every one of the winners received some attention. That Harlan, Ursula, and I had all won before perhaps added a certain momentum to that attention, but there was certainly more of it there to give.

Well, these are some of the things that made those of us who lived through this period feel that some major change was occurring and, when it was over, that some change had, indeed, occurred. All my "unproblematically" SF works were written before this period. *Hogg* was first drafted in the midst of it, just before its end. *Dhalgren* was conceived and written at the very end of it—or just afterward—and executed over the following four years.

Before that time, while there *was* individual protest—or relatively small group protests—there was no broadly social project. Now, however, there was a social project that you *could* choose to join or not join. Radicals wanted to implement these changes. Conservatives were majorly opposed to them.

Today, while there is still a conservative streak in the country that is violently against these changes, I don't think either of the two major parties can be called opposed to this social project. Rather, you have some people who are interested in furthering it or furthering some part of it, and other people who simply do not find it of interest. (Reagan, the politician most closely associated with a lack of interest in this project, was first elected governor of California during this same transitional period.)

Those who actively oppose it are somewhat in the same position as the radicals of the '50s and '60s—though the success we radicals have had in sedimenting this *as* a social project is a warning of just how possible it might be for the radical right and the religious right to make their own desires into such a national social project. (That's basically what happened in Germany in the '30s and '40s.) But I can't stress enough how that year—1969 and four months—instituted a change.

If you read his imposing preface to his 1904 play *Heartbreak House* (the preface was written after World War I), Shaw talks about the same changes that Woolf noted in 1910—and relates them brilliantly to what his Edwardian play was actually about. Anyone who lived through '68/'69 as an adult, who reads that essay, will recognize the emotional effect of living through such a change that Shaw describes—the growth in uncertainty about society at the same time as society itself grows more homogenized and, in many ways, for many people improves.

Before that period, there was no community project—because

these groups did not conceive of themselves as communities. They had not been encouraged to conceive of themselves as such. By "a community," I mean a community within a greater community. In terms of matters gay, for example, this was not just the fact that much gay activity was clandestine—although that certainly contributed. Gay men and women have always been social. And gay men often had larger or smaller circles of gay friends. But before this time one could not conceive of a political candidate who might be sensitive to the needs of gay men and women. One could not conceive of a section in a bookstore, much less a whole bookstore—or even a shelf in a bookstore set aside—for books of interest to gay men and women. If you were a writer, and you wanted to say something to gay men or women, you wrote a book or story for the heterosexual community (because, though it was not the only social group, it was the only *community* there was); and here and there, in highly coded form, you dropped in little asides that were for the gay readers. Sometimes these asides were local. Sometimes they were aspects that moved through the entire plot. But the *communal* thrust, if one can speak of such, was for the heterosexual (*not* a gay) community.

Although at a slightly different saturation, this is also how one had to put things in texts that were for women—as it were. This even went for women writers. Male or female, you could write novels for male editors and male publishers about women's fantasies that were sold by men largely to women. But there were few if any ways to write a story that in any manner related to real women and real women's reality— unless, in the same way, you dropped it in on the side. This is how the portrait of the "little priestess" functions in *The Jewels of Aptor.* This is how making Rydra Wong a poet *and* space-ship captain functions in *Babel-17.* In *The Fall of the Towers,* the prisoners exchanged a couple of coded remarks about homosexuality in the prison mines. The highly politically active Duchess of Petra (the first character I based on Stendhal's Duchess San-severina from *The Charterhouse of Parma*), the mentoring relationship between the Mathematician Clea and the young circus acrobat Alter (find me *any* other American novel written between World War II and 1969 which shows a positive friendship between two women; believe me, you'll have quite a hard time)—these were things dropped into the overall plot in the same way for women. Years later, when Joanna Russ finally read the books in the '70s, she paid me what I've always felt was a wonderful compliment. "My God, Chip!" she wrote me. "You were trying to write radical stuff back in '63 and '64!" And the fact is, however badly, however inadequately, however clumsily, I was.

All these were a way of saying, "Hey, look. I know there's a problem!" But part of the reason you could do little more was that there was no sense of a gay community, no sense of a women's community, and no sense of an antiracist social project to address or join. In *The Einstein Intersection* this is how Le Dove and the three sexes function—or the reference to the drag actor Mario Montez (which, in the first edition, a printer blithely changed to Maria Montez, under the impression that it must be a slip of the typewriter—which was about par for the course with the subtler of these coded references). Now, the problem with the homosexual codes was that they were "contagious." The assumption—and it was a fairly safe one at the time—was that the only people who would possibly want to use the codes must, themselves, be gay. But at the same time, the contagion went so far that if, as a straight person, you acknowledged that you understood the codes, that was tantamount to declaring yourself homosexual—and so you didn't. Indeed, the only way—as a straight person—you could address these coded statements was from the position of medical or legal discourse. And even that was highly risky, so one thought twice about doing even that.

Let me conclude my discussion of this period of change with one more anecdote. In 1911, André Gide wrote his defense of homosexuality, *Corydon*. Now and again, in various articles that would slip by, various people would refer to this book. I had no idea what a "defense of homosexuality" could even be. How did you defend a disease that was presumably and only possibly treatable by psychoanalysis? (If today someone published a book entitled *A Defense of Diabetes,* it would sound equally odd.) But because there was so little published about the topic of homosexuality, the notion of a nonfiction book entirely devoted to the topic was fascinating. Well, sometime in 1966 the book was translated and republished.

As soon as I could, I got hold of it.

Now you have to understand, no one—or certainly no one in any of the circles I moved in—knew that an extensive homophile movement had existed in Germany in the 1880s. We did not know that people had been trying to change the laws about homosexuality since before the turn of the century. We had not read Freud's "Letter to an American Mother." We did not know about the work of Klaus Ulrich or Magnus Hirschfield, or what John Addington Symmonds had done trying to enlighten both Richard von Kraft-Ebbing and Havelock Ellis. We did not know that Gide's own novel *The Immoralist* from 1904, nor Robert Musil's *Young Törless* from the same year, fell at the end of this movement and that Gide's 1911 book had been an attempt to reawaken interest in the movement in France. In short, we had no way to know that *Corydon* was, indeed, part of a social project.

Besides myself, another black gay man read the book in the year of the American reprint—James Baldwin. Baldwin went so far as to review it. I read his review eagerly. And what I found is that he had been almost as baffled by the text as I had been. In that first, hungry reading, I found almost exactly what Baldwin found. It began with some rather odd-sounding considerations of biology, relating to farm animals, which Gide claimed practiced homosexuality. (Could anything be more absurd? Animals were "natural." They simply couldn't be "sick" in that way—because homosexuality was "unnatural"—thus the book started off with a complete contradiction in terms. I simply could neither read nor comprehend that Gide was actually arguing that homosexuality *was* "natural.") Then, for the bulk of the text, there was a tortuous argument that neither Baldwin nor I could make heads or tails of. Gide kept going on as if he were writing about some sort of *social* oppression and completely sidestepped all discussion of the self-evident aspect of illness clearly at the center of the topic. This is how both Baldwin and I read Gide's book in 1966—even after I had been in Mt. Sinai Mental Hospital and had had the personal revelations about how inadequate the public language I had been given was for discussing the "disease" that I describe in my autobiography.

Baldwin's uncomprehending review has been collected in *The Price of the Ticket* (1985). It's easily accessible and there to be read today.

Like my own confused reading, clearly it's a product of the world before the '68/'69 transition I'm writing about.

Twenty-three years later, in 1992, I taught *Corydon* in an upper-level graduate/undergraduate seminar at the University of Massachusetts on "Representations of Male Sexuality," which looked at several of Gide's novels as well as *Corydon,* along with novels by D. H. Lawrence and Robert Musil. On the near side of that transition period, when I reread *Corydon,* I had no trouble at all following Gide's argument. More to the point, neither did any of my graduates or even undergraduates. *Corydon*'s "impenetrable argument" is a clear exposition of an oppressive technique today known as "blaming the victim." It is a strategy that almost every liberation movement—including the early black abolition movement—has had to work its way through. "Blaming the victim" is, of course, shorthand for the strategy the oppressor mounts against an oppressed group by saying, "Look, if you didn't struggle so hard and just accepted your condition, you wouldn't be so unhappy. All your problems really come from you—from your trying to fight against a situation that isn't really all that bad." This argument had been used against slaves; it had been used against women; and in 1911, it had already been used against the existing homophile movement. Gide had taken it on himself, as part of a social project, to show it up for what it was. But the one position from which you cannot follow the argument is the one in which you have been sincerely hoodwinked into believing the problem *is* your fault—if, indeed, you are the victim. Gide (and presumably any number of his readers) could understand this in 1911. Any bright undergraduate could understand it in 1993. But some rather considerable intellects were baffled by it in 1966—which is simply another sign of the extraordinary practical change in the reigning structure of discourse the years 1968 through 1969 represented, when essays and analyses of "blaming the victim" became commonplace, not only in academic discourse but in the daily press, so that relatively ordinary readers were already familiar with the general idea.

An incident from this period that might be characterized as the transition from a homosexual (or a set of homosexual) subsociety(ies) to that of a gay community is one that occurred about this time. Truman Capote was widely known to be gay, but he had never announced himself as such in any public way (in much the same way that, in the entertainment field, the pianist Liberace was out, or, on another level entirely, any number of female impersonators were known, such as Mr. Charles Pierce, who from time to time, performed in drag on *The Ed Sullivan Show* in the '50s); and because there were neither legal nor medical reasons to do so, he was, so to speak, protected.

On one evening, after he'd given a talk at the 92nd Street Y, during the question-and-answer period one man raised his hand and, when called on, stood up and asked loudly and belligerently, "Mr. Capote, are you homosexual?"

Without missing a beat, Capote put his hand against his chest, fingers spread, and returned, with all disingenuousness: "Is that a proposition?"

The audience laughed.

The questioner was silenced.

The discussion moved on. But what Capote was saying, in the coded manner of the times—a code clearly accessible to everyone who laughed—was: "You don't want to go there. You know as well I do, I can make this turn around and bite you in the ass. So shut up and sit down." The laughter was confirmation of his rightness. And the message was heard.

Because we *have* a gay community today rather than a set of strictly guarded social codes, such an answer would have a very different effect—and probably not be anywhere nearly as powerful. But the famous repartee of the drag queen begins as the rapier-like wielding of such social codes.

In your question, you say that Friza is the problem in *The Einstein Intersection*. Believe it or not, you're the first person who's ever suggested that to me. You may very well be right. If I ever go back and reread it, I'll certainly pay attention to that. But, again, you may be just balking at the conventions of what represented the feminine in 1967.

Neal Gaiman in his introduction to *The Einstein Intersection* has commented that the hero, Lo Lobey, is an "unconvincing heterosexual." But I never read that as a critique of the *female* character per se. All sorts—indeed, the overwhelming majority—of heterosexual male writers (and a good number of female writers as well) have problems presenting convincing women characters—had and have both before and after the transition period I've been speaking of. (Would that it *had* solved most of those problems!) That may very well be how Lo Lobey strikes a reader today. But I think what is more to the point is that Lobey is an unconvincing bisexual. And the way Le Dorick (the member of the third biological sex of this species) accepts his exclusion or the way Le Dove (the other member of the third sex we see) has appropriated the feminine for his self-presentation is an unconvincing representation of homosexuality. And certainly, five years after the novel was written, it was particularly unconvincing, though at the time there was all too much justification for it.

If you want to get a sense of the difference of the before and after to those years, read the Pearl and Le Dove from *The Einstein Intersection* against Teddy and Bunny in *Dhalgren*—and bisexual Kid against bisexual Lobey. My description of the Pearl was inspired by my first visit to the Mineshaft [a New York City gay male sex club], just as directly as, thirty years later, in *The Mad Man,* my direct portrait of the place would be from another visit fifteen years later. The grope room in the back would be transformed in *The Einstein Intersection* and become the downstairs chamber, visible through the polarized flooring which rotates to reveal the couples below. But the point is not that the room had to be rerendered in believably heterosexual form but, rather, that it had to be rendered into something recognizably heterosexual. Its unbelievability becomes the sign that it is probably code for something other, which is there specifically in that form so that homosexuality can be read *out* of the text in any public interrogation—that is to say, any interrogation that is not medical (psychoanalytic, say) or legal—if a legal tribunal wanted to chance the contagion.

Unlike *The Einstein Intersection*, *Dhalgren* is a book written for the heterosexual *and* the gay communities. (*The Einstein Intersection* wasn't written for the gay community, because, as I said, none existed.) As important as they are, novels such as Vidal's *The City and the Pillar*, Baldwin's *Giovanni's Room*, and even Proust's explorations in *Sodome et Gamorre* and Hall's *Well of Loneliness* and *Finisterre*, are fundamentally exposés for the straight community. (Proust's *Sodome* is, in particular, exposé. You recall his advice to Gide: "You can say anything as long as you don't say 'I'"—which Gide rather heroically rejected. The prohibition on that "I," direct or implied, is one of the things that prevents you from addressing a community, once it's there; and with the "I" but without a community, you can only confess/expose.) But when that's all there is, gay readers must crowd around and look over the shoulders of provisional straight readers and look just as hard for coded bits of gay reality as they would in any other text.

In that, *Dhalgren* may be one of the first novels—at least of such size and ambition—to be written aware that such a gay community had now formed. (In Bellona we know who *owns* the gay bar; we know the *same man* publishes the newspaper; etc.; etc.) And Kid is someone who moves back and forth between the two communities, as pretty much most gay men have always moved back and forth, since we are almost all born and raised in the heterosexual community.

I remember, during my first read through Proust, how astonished I was to realize that the fundamental model for this monumental verbal edifice was the soft-core lesbian novels endemic at the turn of the century in France. Indeed, it's as if he started to write one of these things and then just let it run wildly out of control until it turned into something else entirely. By the conclusion of the first volume, all the women are going to bed with each other, Odette with Madame Verdurin, little Cecile with someone or other, and, by the end, Odette with the Duchesse de Guermantes, till, finally, she replaces the *Duchesse* by marrying the *Duc*. But it is all so off-handed—and so clear that Proust is completely uninterested in the sensual reality of these affairs. Only the most conscientious plot synopsis even mentions them. While it propels the machinery of the plot, it concerns the narrator-and-analyst of what is going on not at all—so that a critic could write endlessly on the book and not even mention it, as many do.

This is the genre which that other great *fin-de-siècle* writer, Colette (for a number of years Proust's intimate and confidante), turned into something memorable in her *Claudine* novels, written at the demand of her first husband, the pornographer Willy. Only a couple of years ago, a feminist scholar wrote a little book—and it *was* little—called something like *Proust's Lesbians,* as though nobody had even noticed this till now. No, it's the enabling genre that allows the book to be. But it has to be ignored to acknowledge what is new in this obsessively analytic Matterhorn.

When I say that those early novels—my paltry first SF novels—were written for Marilyn, I don't mean that I was speaking a private language that only she could understand. Oh, there was an occasional private joke—as when a cell number in a jail was the same as the one on our apartment door, or when the number on a government report was recognizably our street address. But we are talking about the public speech available at the time. The public speech available to talk about homosexuality was a highly coded one—and that's the one which these books are written, so awkwardly, in.

CF: You've said a good deal already about the importance of race, sex, and gender in your life; perhaps we should talk a bit more about writing itself, since that's obviously been another hugely important thing for you. Do you consider yourself a graphomaniac, that is, someone for whom nothing is entirely real or valid until and unless you've somehow gotten it down on paper? I've wondered about this from time to time, but was especially struck by this sentence I found in a recent private communication from you: "When I'm not writing, suddenly I'll have the conviction that I'm dangerously close to death." Not marble nor the gilded monuments, as Shakespeare said!

SRD: I guess I am. Napoleon used to write himself messages and then tear them up. What he once wrote down, he could remember. What I write, I'm far more likely to recall. That particular comment you quote reflects an observation I found in Harold Bloom, which just sounded right. Artists create, said Bloom, from a fear of not creating. Perhaps it's a particular kind of repetition compulsion. The painter likes that repeated, back-and-forth brush movement of the hand, of the brush, which happens hundreds of thousands of times to produce the twelve-foot luminous oilscape. The writer likes the feel of the fingers falling again and again on the typewriter keys—six- or seven-hundred-thousand times in a four- or five-hundred-page novel.

My childhood was blighted by intense anxiety attacks in which I'd be struck with sudden, acute apprehension of the amount of time

I would have to remain dead. It was like being struck with a bat. They only lasted a few seconds, but they prostrated me for a couple of hours afterward, before I could get it back together. By the time I was fourteen or fifteen I'd learned that, while nothing could ward off these attacks entirely, when I was writing a lot, they went down from three and four times a day to once every day or even day-and-a-half.

Soon writing had become a habit—the easiest way to keep it together, to ward off a certain kind of fear. The attacks grew less and less and went away when I was thirty-five or thirty-six. But, by then, the habit was fixed and the journey had become too interesting to give up.

CF: But surely it's not habit alone that keeps you writing as prolifically as you do; and, *pace* Dr. Johnson—since you are certainly not a block-head!—I don't think it's mainly the money. Not only do you write furiously, but you write all sorts of different things. Surveying your whole career so far, one might say that whenever you've really mastered a particular kind of writing, you pretty soon seem to lose interest in it and move on to something else.

SRD: I write furiously, yes—and slowly. Probably I take more time at it than most people. Twenty hours may produce perhaps ten first-draft pages—fifteen if I'm on a roll. That will have to be redrafted five or six times, possibly even ten or twelve, with perhaps two or three hours per draft. You can read ten pages aloud in under half an hour—fifteen in just over that. But writing is how I do my thinking. Talking out loud proceeds at about three times the speed of thought—so in ten pages there's about ten minutes of actual thought—and about two 24-hour days of rethinking.

To put forty or fifty hours into refining ten minutes of thought feels very good. I think slowly. I write slowly. I like how that feels—at a sensual, bodily level. That's why I keep doing it.

It looks prolific. But it isn't really—which is to say, it only looks so because I've been doing it for fifty years.

CF: I'm reminded of something Anthony Burgess once said in an interview. He was evidently a bit fed up with the widespread assumption that, because he produced so much, he must write pretty fast; and he said that, no, he actually wrote quite slowly, but managed to put in more hours per day on the job than most writers seemed to. You appear to be saying something of the same thing (minus Burgess's characteristic asperity). But I'd like to press you a bit further on the variety as well as the bulk of your output. When you followed *Nova* (1968) with *Dhalgren* (1974), you began producing a radically different kind of SF—and upset a good many of your early fans. Then you published *Triton* (1976) and *Stars in My Pocket Like Grains of Sand* (1984), and, after that, stopped publishing SF altogether. But, by that time, you'd begun the radically original sword-and-sorcery stories, novellas, and novels of the *Nevèrÿon* sequence (1979–87). Since then, you've mostly published fiction that might be described as more "realistic," though I think we need the quotation marks to cover such things as *The Mad Man* (1994) and *Atlantis: Model 1924* (1995). And I haven't even mentioned the large, important, and internally various body of your nonfiction. Could you talk a little about what drives you to do so many different things?

SRD: Burgess's point is my point exactly, though he puts it not only with asperity, but with more wit than I do. I think what you're kind enough to call a drive is there because somewhere in my teens I picked up the modernist notion that writing—and writing fiction—was not just the creation of a product, which, for the great producers of those wonderfully bulky and baggy nineteenth-century novels, from Balzac and Stendhal, Sand and Dumas, Hugo and Flaubert, the Goncourts and Zola, to Austen and Thackeray, the Brontës and Dickens, Eliot and Hardy, Meredith and Trollope, not to mention the Russians, is largely what it was. (It had aspects of the obsessive and the selfish, which are inescapable, even then.) But—possibly from the introduction to some Bantam Paperback of François Mauriac or Roger Martin-DuGard (it *had* to be French)—or possibly it was something from Gide's old two-volume Vintage Paperback Edition of the journals, which as a teenager I devoured—I picked up the idea that writing was an intellectual, even a spiritual, adventure.

Now the question is: What kind of spiritual adventure can someone have who doesn't particularly believe in spirits? But that's a real postmodern question, and one worth wrestling with. The adventure has nothing to do with self-actualization, by the by—although I think it does result in one's developing (a process that goes along with age itself) a colder eye to cast on life, on death.

And we hear the horseman.

It means you *don't* do the same thing twice, though. Now add to that the modernist fetishization of originality. . . .

CF: Well, that postmodern question certainly is worth wrestling with; so let's wrestle with it a little. I'm naturally sympathetic, since I believe in the human spirit or soul in the sense of the psyche—the sense Freud meant by the German term *Seele*—but certainly not in spirits in the sense of gods, demons, pixies, fairies, angels, higher powers, and the like. Could you pick one or two of your books and discuss them as adventures in what we might agree to call materialist spirituality—a term, by the way, that I once saw used to describe that wonderful SF masterpiece, Olaf Stapledon's *Star Maker* (1937)?

SRD: You tempt to me start speaking about what my books mean—and that's a question I'm still enough of a modernist to feel that, however diplomatically or even brutally, I have to avoid. It isn't mete for the author to take that one on, especially in a public forum. The larger adventure I'm speaking of, the one that keeps you from doing the same thing again and again, lies primarily between the books. I will go so far, though, as to say that most of my adventures—the ones between the covers of any given book—tend to be textual ones. Where has this text been hidden? What is this text really about? What will that text's effects be once it gets to where it's supposed to be delivered? How should a text be written? I'm sure you can see how all these might be used as allegories of the writer's relation to his material, his audience, his tradition. And I do. But that's as far as I'm willing to take it.

Note

1. Conrad had been to the Congo. He'd seen the mountainous piles of black human heads and black hands piled beside the roads. The Belgians had instituted the insidious system of requiring a black right hand in exchange for bullets that the black mercenary soldiers needed to keep the more peaceful black native peoples from rising up and slaughtering both them and the Belgians. These hundreds of thousands of humans hands were in huge, rotting piles along the highways: Conrad knew Imperialism was monstrously barbaric. While he had been there, a black African woman had saved his life, taking him into her hut and nursing him back from a fever, when whites had abandoned him to die, sick, in a ditch beside one of those same highways. This was the material for the self-evident argument that other whites were simply not prepared to listen to. So while he made much of these incidents in his personal tales among his friends and acquaintances, he did not use them in his story. If such evidence would have swayed anyone, it was too common and already would have done so. So in the story, for the benefit of his powerful friends lounging together on the yawl *Nelly,* Marlow carefully tells the tale of his own corruption, and what has made him the interesting ne'er-do-well—a good raconteur, but a mediocrity nevertheless—that he is. Marlow, who "hates

a lie more than anything," is forced by his encounter with the other *whites* in the Congo, paramount among them the totally monomaniac Mr. Kurtz (who would have been a mediocrity had he remained at home, but whom the other white mediocrities have ele-vated to the position of demi-god *because* of his ruthless monomania with the natives), to become a liar when he returns to civilization. That is how Imperialism corrupts.

KEVIN WILLMOTT &
MARLEEN S. BARR

Black "Science Faction"

An Interview with Kevin Willmott, Director and Writer of
CSA, The Confederate States of America

MSB: *CSA* [2004] relates to science fiction in that it is very definitely an example of alternative history. How did the fact that your film is rooted in science fiction alternative history influence your thinking?

KW: I wanted to use the genre in a new way. By telling an alternative history, I actually tell you our real history. A living history. It is the history that we feel. That is why people sometimes feel uncomfortable watching the film. We are touching areas where we never go in society. I didn't want it to be distant. I wanted it to confront. I didn't want a safe parlor game of "what if." I wanted the film to use the genre to reveal a deeper truth. For me, that is the science fiction I enjoy. The kind that reveals something about our present, that responds to a reality that we have difficulty expressing. I jokingly call it science faction.

MSB: The cliché scenario of science fiction alternative history of course involves speculation about Hitler winning World War II. Questions relating to this scenario are very easy for Americans to pose because Hitler was unquestionably evil—and not American at that. In contrast, your question about what would ensue if the South won the Civil War very definitely positions some Americans as villains. Nobody wants to be called a villain. How do you respond to the point that your alternative history science fiction scenario is very difficult for some Americans to see and discuss? How are you coping with the consequences of breaking the taboo in America about directly confronting the fact that slave owners were our founding fathers?

KW: That's the big one. America as "slaveocracy," but that is exactly what it was. A democracy with slavery central to its core. The film illustrates how the country was actually founded as the CSA. And then Lincoln comes along and wants to create a new nation without slavery.

But he is assassinated and we get 100 years of slavery-lite (Jim Crow segregation, chain gangs, peonage, lynching)—finally, the civil rights movement changes things and we get the USA. We have been struggling ever since as to what country we really want to be—the CSA or the USA. I think when authors make that less dramatic choice of not saying that America was based in white supremacy, just like Nazi Germany, they are trying to downplay the reality of slavery. That is what our film doesn't do. It places slavery center stage in relation to the cause of the Civil War. The idea that slavery wouldn't have continued is part of that "Big Lie." You fight the bloodiest war in American history for an institution (slavery) that is dying. For those few slave owners that directed the Confederate secession, slavery was very much alive and well. We had to tell the "Big Lie" to reunite North and South, as our film points out. And hence the change from slavery to states' rights ensues.

MSB: Black science fiction writers such as the late Octavia E. Butler and Samuel R. Delany have depicted blacks confronting apocalyptic situations. Hurricane Katrina made their science fiction visions real. If Katrina hit the CSA instead of our USA, how would the response of the CSA federal government differ from the real Bush administration response?

KW: In the CSA, the response would have been different because those African-Americans would have been slaves and worth a lot of money. So property would have been rescued. Just like if Katrina hit Palm Springs, do you think we would have watched rich folks up to their necks in sewer water on CNN? But in the metaphorical sense, the Bush administration's response to Katrina is another example of how the CSA won.

MSB: How would the CSA slaves respond to present-day technology? Would they have Internet access? Would the CSA conduct high-tech lynchings? Would the slaves write science fiction slave narratives?

KW: Slaves would use the technology the way they used the means available in the 1800s to free themselves. In the film we use the example of an escaped slave, Henry "Box" Brown, who sealed himself in a box and shipped himself up North. We change it to Confederate Express—"slaves are 'overnighting' themselves to freedom." Slaves would not be lynched; they would be punished. Lynching came out of freedom, not slavery. Slaves' price as slaves prevents destroying chattel property. The Internet would be used to send messages to slaves about escapes and rebellions. Slave narratives would be published on the Internet in the hope that slaves would find access. However, the CSA would restrict Internet content, like today in China and other countries, so it would be difficult to assist captive slaves through technology. Just like in South Africa in the 1980s, the black majority was controlled by IBM technology through an elaborate government passbook system of monitoring all movement and activity. So those choices again come from the "what is" not the "what if."

MSB: Both you and Henry Louis Gates, Jr. are black academics who are boldly going beyond the confines of the academy. I think that Gates's *African American Lives,* a PBS television program about black families, relates to science fiction in that it discusses the search for black identity via the use of new DNA technologies which until very recently were science fictional. Why is it that black male academics are the ones who are most visibly combining science fiction and popular media to break out of academic structures?

KW: I don't know for sure. Maybe African-Americans know that the media have always been a major resource for change and effect. Black men really are aware of this because it is a very visible example of success and effectiveness. It gives many people hope for the future. I wanted to make the film in the hope we could get people thinking about slavery and the real CSA. Science fiction for blacks has always been a way to tell that part of our story some people don't want to hear. The genre is big and very flexible, so it can be used in various ways. Like the best of the *Twilight Zone* and Rod Serling.

MSB: In *Kindred,* Octavia E. Butler used a time travel scenario to transport her protagonist back in time to meet an enslaved ancestor. Butler turned to science fiction to connect the present with the real historical past. Why did you concern yourself with a science-fictional historical past instead of the real historical past? The science fiction writer Greg Bear says that a sense of freedom is at the heart of both his and Butler's involvement with science fiction. Does "freedom" figure in your intermingling of history with science fiction?

KW: Freedom is also central for me. It is the thing the CSA is against. The CSA doesn't even understand what the concept means. It is anti-freedom. By defining the CSA, we start to understand what freedom means in the USA. It is a reminder of how we attained rights in this country through struggling and fighting against smaller minds and a lack of vision. The CSA becomes a much bigger issue than just American slavery; it connects us to world domination, torture, violence, and a complete institutional intolerance of others. It is the other America—America's evil twin.

MSB: What would a CSA version of *Star Trek* look like? Would the Starship *Enterprise* have slave quarters?

KW: Wow. *Star Trek* wouldn't exist in the CSA. It is too multiracial and the vision is too big. The show examines a world where democracy and justice are central and slavery and injustice have been removed from the universe. *Star Trek* came out of the 1960s when we thought we could create a better world. It is closer to a reflection of Dr. King's "Beloved Community"—the struggle for a just society. The CSA would actually be an alternate *Star Trek* world where slavery sells someone like Lt. Uhura (now a house slave) to the highest bidder.

MSB: Let me turn to your portrayal of women. A reality-based black woman living in Canada is the authority figure who unifies the narrative flow of *CSA*. Why did you position a black woman as the voice of media-centered authority? I find your choice extraordinary in that in American reality, before Katie Couric, no woman had ever been a solo network news anchor. Why ensconce a real-world black woman within the mass media space which so far only white people have inhabited?

KW: The choice originated with Barbara Fields and Shelby Foote in the Ken Burns documentary *The Civil War*. But it takes on an added dimension in our film. It is an expression of the equality former slaves are experiencing in Canada—both as people of color and as women. It again reveals the distance we still have to go in the USA and how the CSA did win in various ways.

MSB: To my mind, the most hysterically funny *CSA* scene involves the analogue between the Home Shopping Network and the Slave Shopping Network. Shopping is such a quintessentially female activity. Why did you think of shopping? Why did you not portray a woman being sold on the Slave Shopping Network?

KW: We do show a family, Jupiter's family. We wanted to get across how an actual slave auction worked, that the auctions were normal. Families were often split apart, and children and spouses sold away never to meet again. I simply took how we shop today and placed it in the world of the slave-based CSA. The television show's two hostesses are women, and shopping reflects that deeply entrenched shopping culture you refer to that is sold to women. The hostesses simply talk about the slave family analogously to how the real home shopping shows sell jewelry or exercise equipment.

MSB: As opposed to the cliché of the white woman as damsel in distress, *CSA* depicts white women as rescuers. Why?

KW: We show a few damsels in the play "A Northern Wind" which includes a Scarlett O'Hara–type character. But the white-women-as-rescuers notion comes from Susan B. Anthony, Elizabeth Cady Stanton, and Lucretta Mott and their involvement in the abolitionist movement. They would lead the women's movement, but they first learned about equality from the fight against slavery. Of course, most women, like most men, didn't understand the idea of racial equality. But I wanted to acknowledge these women and their prophetic vision. In that sense, these women did rescue us.

MSB: *CSA* concludes in the early twenty-first century. If you make a sequel, will you consider doing a science fiction future vision *CSA*? What if the slaves revolt and win and send whites off to different planets in starships/slave ships? Would you make the ship captain a black woman?

KW: I have a different idea that involves other planets and the issue of race and class. Again, for me, I always look to the reality first. I ponder what is at the core of how we are actually living. You can then determine how to use science fiction to explore that reality. I think the future of the CSA is right here on Earth, and that will determine what our future will be.

Octavia's Healing Power

A Tribute to the Late Great Octavia E. Butler

I named my daughter, Anya, after Anyanwu, a character from Octavia E. Butler's book, *Wild Seed*. Anyanwu means "Eye of the Sun" in the Igbo language, which is the ethnic group that my daughter's father and I come from, though we were both born in the United States.

Octavia's character was the first African, Nigerian, Igbo fantastical being that I ever came across in fiction.

Anyanwu was a shape shifter who could become any animal whose flesh she'd tasted. I've always been fond of birds and their ability to fly, and when Anyanwu changed into a bird, my imagination soared.

Anyanwu could make herself a man or a woman, young or old. She had superhuman physical strength and, in my opinion, a superhuman capacity to care for and nurture other people. She could heal herself of any disease, once she'd figured out how it worked. She was practically immortal, having already lived for 300 years when we first meet her in *Wild Seed*. And she was a leader but could follow when she had to.

To sum it up, she was the strongest, most amazing black woman I'd ever read about. There are several reasons why the name is perfect for my daughter.

Wild Seed is Octavia's greatest influence on me as a writer. She documented ideas and characters that I had only dreamed about. And by putting them in writing, she made them real—she made them possible.

I uncovered my first Octavia E. Butler novel, *Wild Seed,* at the Clarion Science Fiction & Fantasy Writers' Workshop at Michigan State University in 2001. I noticed the book at a bookstore because on the cover was a picture of a mysterious-looking, dark-skinned black woman with wild hair, and this book was in the science fiction and fantasy section. A very rare combination indeed.

At the time in the workshop, I was writing a story about an Efik woman in Nigeria who learned to fly. The story was set in the 1920s. This character was mean, selfish, promiscuous, and strong-willed, and quite frankly, she disturbed me. When I read *Wild Seed,* I practically cried. There, in the book's pages, living in a remote Nigerian village long ago was Anyanwu, complex, Nigerian, and mythical. It was after reading that book that I went through my own "transition" and started to call myself a writer of science fiction and fantasy.

Octavia's fiction contained a lot of firsts for me: black people and other people of color featured at the forefront of stories set in well-imagined strange worlds and situations; stories where race and gender were thoughtfully factored and woven into the type of fiction that I've loved since I could read; and the most memorable characters I've ever read.

And all of this was written in and rendered by sparse, bold prose that grabbed me by the neck and didn't let go even after the story ended.

On the other hand, Octavia also deeply disturbed me. In the *Xenogenesis* series, I was forced to seriously question my ideas about gender when she introduced me to the Oankali, aliens who have three sexes: male, female, and ooloi.

The ooloi enabled the others to reproduce by blending elements of their genetic makeup. And they did the same with human beings, shifting the entire dynamics of human male-female relationships.

Needless to say, Octavia's ideas stretched my mind so much that it never recovered to its previous shape. I was changed.

Butler was only fifty-eight when she passed in February 2006. Among her many awards were the MacArthur Foundation "genius grant" and multiple Nebula and Hugo awards. She had many more books in her. I met her for the first time a few months before her death, at the Gwendolyn Brooks Writers' Conference. She was such a charming lady, and she had a real sense of humor. When I interviewed her for *Black Issues Book Review,* she told me why it had been six years since her last novel appeared.

"It's taken me this long because of all sorts of unpleasant things," she said. "Health problems, writer's block, the kind of medicines that makes you more interested in dozing off."

She'd wanted to write but could not. Her last novel, *Fledgling,* came out in September 2005. Octavia said that she was able to focus and write it because it was a chase story that was "avalanching toward an end."

A friend of mine who is an African-American fantasy writer summed it up best when she said: "What do I love about Octavia Butler? She dared.

She dared to create characters who had the audacity to be black and female and exist in the future, with aliens at that! She dared to be powerful, to create nations, and birth religions. She is an unapologetic writer. And she succeeded."

Octavia E. Butler
June 22, 1947–February 25, 2006

MARLEEN S. BARR

AFTERWORD

The Big Bang

Or, The Inception of Scholarship about
Black Women Science Fiction Writers

My preface focuses upon bringing Italo Calvino's "All At One Point" to bear upon black science fiction. I explain how Calvino's vision of Mrs. Ph(i)NKo unleashing the expansion of the universe when she says "I'd like to make some noodles for you boys!" (Calvino 46) applies to black science fiction's present burgeoning. I also point out that it is rather unusual to situate black science fiction in terms of an Italian imaginative vision. (Ditto for the juxtaposition between Japanese and black science fiction I discussed.) Unusual, but not unheard of. As I said, according to Calvino's story, an Italian mother's words serve as a catalyst for the universe's inception; I know that the beginnings of scholarship about black women science fiction writers emanated in part from the words of a woman of Italian ancestry.

I know because I witnessed it—and I was responsible for it. I offer an anecdote of historical importance in relationship to the development of black science fiction criticism: the story of how Ruth Salvaggio—who hails from New Orleans and now teaches at the University of North Carolina—witnessed a big bang, agreed to write about Octavia E. Butler, said that she'd like to cook some gumbo, and participated in the start of scholarly writing about black women who author science fiction.

Time: 1984
Place: Blackhole State University
Dramatis Personae: Young Marleen and Dr. Ph(d)SalvagGlo (aka Ruth)

Once upon a time, Young Marleen and Dr. Ph(d)SalvagGIo "were packed in there like sardines" in the patriarchal academy when hardly anyone "knew then there could be [feminist] space" (Calvino 43). In their attempt to create new feminist literary criticism spaces, Dr. Ph(d)SalvagGIo was turning from Dryden to women writers, and Young Marleen defiantly focused upon feminist science fiction. She decided to enlist her friend in her cause.

"I'm editing a Starmont House Press *Readers' Guide* on three women science fiction writers. All the other books in the series are about one male author. No one realizes that women science fiction writers are important enough to warrant their own individual studies. So three women authors have to be packed in like sardines in one volume. I'm writing on Suzy McKee Charnas and I've lined up someone to do a Joan Vinge chapter. Will you contribute something on a woman science fiction author?" Marleen asked Ruth.

"Science fiction? I don't know anything about science fiction."

"Ruth, science fiction is *literature.* You're a literature scholar. You can write about literature."

"I'm not sure about this."

"*Please* do it. Tell ya what. I have a whole shelf filled with science fiction written by women. To make you more comfortable with the thought of writing about science fiction, why don't I take all my women's science fiction books and throw them in the air. You can write about the text that falls closest to you."

"Okay. It's 1984 and Big University Patriarch is watching us. We young feminists have to stick together. Yes, Marleen, as always, I will stand with you in solidarity—even if it does mean that I have to write about [gasp] science fiction."

Marleen took her books in hand and hurled them upward. They crashed with a resounding big bang. One book, after nearly decapitating Ruth, landed on Ruth's foot.

"Fate has decreed that I write about this book—about *Kindred* by Octavia E. Butler. Who is Octavia E. Butler? Is *Kindred* good?" said Ruth.

"Ruth, Butler is awesome. Even though *Kindred* has a white woman on its cover, Butler is a black writer who writes about black women. You must realize that feminist science fiction scholars exist. Two years ago, Frances S. Foster and Beverly Friend published *Extrapolation* articles about Butler."

Breathing a sigh of relief after hearing that there was life in alien feminist science fiction criticism, but still reluctant to touch an actual science fiction novel, Ruth gingerly took *Kindred* in hand.

"Time travel? Plantations? Slavery? *Kindred* is an American epic, and Butler is a descendant of Mark Twain. I can bring my experience as a Southerner and a daughter of Italian immigrants to bear upon Butler. I'd like to make some gumbo for tonight's department feminist reading group. As soon as I finish cooking, I'll start reading *Kindred* immediately."

And so it came to pass that at the same time Dr. Ph(d)SalvagGIo uttered the word "gumbo"—and consummate New Yorker Young Marleen wondered if gumbo contained sardines—"the point that contained her and all of us was expanding in a halo of distance in light-years and light-centuries and billions of light-millennia . . . and, properly speaking, space itself, and time" (Calvino 47). Two young women friends who were together facing the slings and arrows of outrageous sexism which the patriarchal academy directed against women in 1984, united in Big Sisterhood, participated in the birth of the feminist criticism that would elucidate the new space called science fiction created by black women—whose time and expanding space had come. They wanted to make one point: the literary universe is certainly big enough to preclude women writers and women scholars from being treated like fruitless sardines confined within the good ol' boys fishing pond.

This is a true story. Salvaggio really did agree to write about Butler after I threw my science fiction books in the air and *Kindred* landed at her feet. She went on to publish "Octavia Butler and the Black Science Fiction Heroine" in *Black American Literature Forum*, the initial essay about a black woman science fiction writer that ever appeared in a journal devoted to black literature. And Salvaggio contributed the chapter on Butler to the first Starmont House *Readers' Guide* devoted to female science fiction writers. That volume marked the first time that Butler's work was discussed between hard book covers.

The part I played in generating the big bang which brought Salvaggio to Butler is pertinent to *Afro-Future Females*. When I asked Butler if I could include one of her stories, she said that she fondly remembered the chapter about her work in the Starmont House *Readers' Guide*. With that memory in mind, she graciously granted me permission to include "The Book of Martha" sans monetary remuneration. "Just send me a copy of your anthology and that will be payment enough," she said.

I can never fulfill her request. So, instead, I want to share the story about how feminist solidarity and gumbo cooking led to generating scholarship that played a role in the history of literary criticism about black women science fiction writers—and (most importantly) made Octavia E. Butler happy.

Works Cited

Barr, Marleen S., Ruth Salvaggio, and Richard Law. *The Readers' Guide to Suzy McKee Charnas, Octavia Butler, and Joan Vinge.* Mercer Island, WA: Starmont House, 1986.

Calvino, Italo. 1965. "All At One Point." *Cosmicomics.* Trans. William Weaver. New York: Harcourt Brace & World, 1968. 43–47.

Foster, Frances S. "Octavia Butler's Black Female Future Vision." *Extrapolation* 23 (1982): 37–49.

Friend, Beverly. "Time Travel as a Feminist Didactic in Works by Phyllis Eisenstein, Marlys Millhiser and Octavia Butler." *Extrapolation* 23 (1982): 50–55.

RESPONSE TO THE AFTERWORD

Connecting Metamorphoses

Italo Calvino's Mrs. Ph(i)NKo and I, Dr. Ph(d)SalvagGlo

It seems unimaginable that back in the 1980s Octavia E. Butler was just beginning to be recognized for her remarkable stories of transformation, and almost unbelievable that she is now gone, way too soon. Yet I'm not surprised that Barr should invoke Italo Calvino to praise Butler. He would be especially appreciative of the wonderful crossroads she inhabited—in her time travels, in her planetary journeys, through her strange mutations of bodies and species. He had praised Ovid for her same reason—the ability to see how everything is connected in worlds constantly undergoing metamorphoses.

I'm so grateful that Marleen introduced me to Octavia E. Butler two decades ago, because over the years I've come to find in Butler what literature is ultimately all about: the connections that bind us. Calvino's description of what he calls the "manifold text," recently invoked by Charles Martin to describe Ovid's *Metamorphoses* (11), seems a perfect way to understand Butler's sometimes tragic but always magic transformations. Such a work, Calvino says, "would let us enter into selves like our own but give speech to that which has no language, to the bird perching on the edge of the gutter, to the tree in spring and the tree in fall, to cement, to plastic" (117, 124). What a haunting way to understand the slaves who would jump ship and swim as wild fish in the ocean, and then return again to their human form to take up their place in Butler's novels. What a tribute her work is to the imagination in all its metamorphoses. Even after death, continuity is all.

⟩ Works Cited

Calvino, Italo. *Six Memos for the Next Millennium.* Cambridge, MA: Harvard University Press, 1988.
Ovid. *Metamorphoses.* Trans. Charles Martin. New York: Norton, 2004.

NOTES ON CONTRIBUTORS

The Editor

Marleen S. Barr, who is known for her pioneering work in feminist science fiction theory, teaches in the Department of Communication and Media Studies at Fordham University. She has won the Science Fiction Research Association Pilgrim Award for lifetime achievement in science fiction criticism. Barr is the author of *Alien to Femininity: Speculative Fiction and Feminist Theory; Lost In Space: Probing Feminist Science Fiction and Beyond; Feminist Fabulation: Space/Postmodern Fiction; Genre Fission: A New Discourse Practice for Cultural Studies;* and *Oy Pioneer!: A Novel.* She has edited many anthologies and coedited the special science fiction issue of *PMLA.*

The Contributors

Steven Barnes has taught writing at UCLA and the Clarion Writers' Workshop, written for television, hosted radio shows, and created life-writing workshops. He is the author of fifteen novels (including the 2003 Endeavour Award winner, *Lion's Blood,* which imagines a pre–Civil War United States where whites are slaves and blacks are the masters). He says, "After publishing about two million words of science fiction [including the *New York Times* bestsellers *The Legacy of Heorot* and *The Cestus Deception*] and having about twenty hours of produced television shows [including *The Twilight Zone, Outer Limits, Andromeda,* and *Stargate,* as well as four episodes of the immortal *Baywatch*], I've got opinions on the writing life. After earning black belts in judo and karate, and practicing the Indonesian art of Pentjak Silat Serak for the last ten, well, I have some opinions there, as well."

Octavia E. Butler—whose love, talent, and generosity are beyond words—wrote these words to Marleen S. Barr about her participation in this volume: "I hope your readers enjoy 'The Book of Martha'" (January 11, 2004).

Samuel R. Delany is Professor of English and Creative Writing at Temple University. Walter Mosley says this about him: "Mr. Delany is it. He is the *center*. He is one of our most amazing writers and thinkers. You're sitting in a room with one of the greatest men in American literature. Period."

Mark Dery, who teaches in the Journalism Department of New York University, is a prominent commentator on new media, unpopular culture, and the digital age. He edited *Flame Wars: The Discourse of Cyberculture*, a seminal anthology of cybercrit. He is the author of the critically acclaimed *Escape Velocity: Cyberculture at the End of the Century*, and an essay on guerrilla media, "Culture Jamming: Hacking, Slashing, and Sniping in the Empire of the Signs." Dery has written a column on fringe literature, "Invisible Lit," for *Bookforum* and has done cultural commentaries for *Radio Nation*. His most recent book is the essay collection *The Pyrotechnic Insanitarium: American Culture on the Brink*.

Madhu Dubey is Professor of English and African American Studies at the University of Illinois, Chicago, where she teaches courses in African-American literature and culture. Her research interests include African-American literature, cultural studies, and postmodern theory. She has published two books: *Black Women Novelists and the Nationalist Aesthetic* and *Signs and Cities: Black Literary Postmodernism*. *Signs and Cities* is the first book to consider what it means to speak of a postmodern movement in African-American literature. She is also the author of various articles on twentieth-century African-American literature, nationalism, and postmodernism. Dubey asserts that for African-American studies, post-modernity best names a period, beginning in the early 1970s, marked by acute disenchantment with the promises of urban modernity and of print literacy.

Tananarive Due has written seven books ranging from supernatural thrillers to science fiction to a civil rights memoir. *The Living Blood* received a 2002 American Book Award. *Publishers Weekly* named both *The Living Blood* and *My Soul to Keep* as being among the best novels of the year. *The Good*

House was nominated as Best Novel by the International Horror Guild. *The Black Rose,* based on the life of entrepreneur Madam C. J. Walker, was nominated for an NAACP Image Award. *My Soul to Keep* will be a major motion picture at Fox Searchlight Pictures. Due's newest novel, *Joplin's Ghost,* juxtaposes the supernatural, history, and the present-day music scene. *Freedom in the Family: A Mother-Daughter Memoir of the Fight for Civil Rights*—which Due coauthored with her mother, civil rights activist Patricia Stephens Due—was named Best Civil Rights Memoir by *Black Issues Book Review.*

Carl Freedman, Professor of English at Louisiana State University, is the author of many articles and of *George Orwell: A Study in Ideology and Literary Form.* Freedman is the recipient of the Science Fiction Research Association's 1999 Pioneer Award. His *Critical Theory and Science Fiction* was selected by *Choice* as an Outstanding Academic Book of the Year. In *Critical Theory and Science Fiction,* Freedman traces the fundamental and largely unexamined relationships between the discourses of science fiction and critical theory, arguing that science fiction is (or ought to be) a privileged genre for critical theory. He asserts that it is no accident that the upsurge of academic interest in science fiction since the 1970s coincides with the heyday of literary theory, and that likewise science fiction is one of the most theoretically informed areas of the literary profession.

Andrea Hairston is Professor of Theatre at Smith College where she directs and teaches playwriting and black theatre literature. She is the Artistic Director of Chrysalis Theatre and has produced original theatre with music, dance, and masks for over twenty-five years. Her plays have been produced at the Yale Rep, Rites and Reason, the Kennedy Center, and Stage West, and on Public Radio and Public Television. Hairston has received many playwriting and -directing awards, including a National Endowment for the Arts Grant to Playwrights, a Rockefeller/NEA Grant for New Works, an NEA grant to work as dramaturge/director with playwright Pearl Cleage, a Ford Foundation Grant to collaborate with Senegalese Master Drummer Massamba Diop, and a Shubert Fellowship for Playwriting. Since 1997, her plays produced by Chrysalis Theatre—*Soul Repairs, Lonely Stardust,* and *Hummingbird Flying Backward*—have been science fiction plays. She garnered a 2003 Massachusetts Cultural Council Fellowship for her *Archangels of Funk,* a science fiction theatre jam. She is the author of *Mindscape,* a speculative novel.

Jennifer E. Henton is Assistant Professor of English at Hofstra University where she teaches African, Caribbean, and African-American literature as well as women's studies and film. She is currently working on a manuscript that considers black literature's connection to Lacanian psychoanalysis.

Nalo Hopkinson is the author of three novels and a short story collection: *Brown Girl in the Ring, Midnight Robber, The Salt Roads,* and *Skin Folk.* She has edited the fiction anthologies *Whispers from the Cotton Tree Root: Caribbean Fabulist Fiction; Mojo: Conjure Stories; So Long Been Dreaming: Postcolonial Science Fiction* (with Uppinder Mehan); and *Tesseracts Nine* (with Geoff Ryman). Hopkinson's work has received honorable mention in regard to Cuba's Casa de las Américas Literary Prize. She is a recipient of the Warner Aspect First Novel Prize, the Ontario Arts Council Foundation Award for emerging writers, the John W. Campbell Award for best new writer, the World Fantasy Award, and the Gaylactic Spectrum Award. *The New Moon's Arms* is her latest novel.

De Witt Douglas Kilgore is Associate Professor of English and American Studies at Indiana University. He is the author of *Astrofuturism: Science, Race, and Visions of Utopia in Space,* an incisive engagement with the science writing and science fiction produced by the modern spaceflight movement. As a history, the book takes seriously the (sometimes progressive) hopes of those scientists and engineers who wrote the Space Age into being as a great cultural project. He says, "My general field is twentieth-century American literature and culture. I am particularly concerned with exploring the political (utopian) hopes expressed by our society through its projects in science and technology. Race, as both a social and an analytic category, stands for what is most often at stake in the histories I engage and the readings. My general research agenda is to recoup the liberatory potential of sciences and narratives ordinarily prescribed as closed to nonwhite, nonmale, non-middle-class people."

Nnedi Okorafor-Mbachu has had her first novel, *Zarah the Windseeker,* described by Nalo Hopkinson in this way: "[Okorafor-Mbachu's novel is a] fantastical travelogue into the unknown of a young girl's fears, and the magical world that surrounds her town. Written in the spirit of Clive Barker's *Abarat,* with a contemporary African sensibility, Okorafor-Mbachu's imagination is delightful!" *The Shadow Speaker* is her second novel. Okorafor-Mbachu says, "I named my daughter, Anya, after Anyanwu, a character from Octavia E. Butler's book, *Wild Seed.* Anyanwu means 'Eye of the Sun' in the Igbo language, which is the ethnic group that my daughter's father and I come from, though we were both born in the United States. Octavia's character is the first African, Nigerian, Igbo fantastical being that I ever came across in fiction."

Ellen Peel is Professor of English and Comparative Literature at San Francisco State University. She is the author of *Politics, Persuasion, and Pragmatism: A Rhetoric of Feminist Utopian Fiction*, which focuses upon developing original theories of feminism and narrative persuasion. The book examines how people come to believe what they do—in particular, how they are influenced by reading feminist novels, especially those that represent pragmatic feminism. Peel is currently completing *The Text of the Body / The Body of the Text*, a study that examines texts about the physical and mental construction of human bodies. In this work, she pays particular attention to self-referential literature in which construction of the human body parallels construction of the textual one.

Alcena Madeline Davis Rogan is Assistant Professor of English at Gordon College. Her articles and book reviews focus on science fiction studies, with an emphasis upon feminist science fiction. Rogan is currently working on a book called *The Future in Feminism: Reading Strategies for Feminist Theory and Science Fiction*. She describes her book in this way: "I examine feminist science fiction that either implicitly or explicitly engages feminist theory's presuppositions and positions. My object is to use these texts to illuminate the pitfalls and potentialities presented by various works of feminist theory. Each of the works of feminist science fiction that I analyze presents a portrait of how some feminist theoretical tenet might be enacted, and the problems that such an enactment might encounter." Rogan coedited a special issue of *Socialism and Democracy* called "Socialism and Social Critique in Science Fiction."

Ruth Salvaggio is Professor of English at the University of North Carolina. She works in the areas of feminist and critical theory, eighteenth-century studies, and poetics. Her authored books include *The Sounds of Feminist Theory; Enlightened Absence: Neoclassical Configurations of the Feminine; Dryden's Dualities;* and a monograph on Octavia E. Butler. She coedited, with the Folger Collective on Early Women Writers, the anthology *Women Critics, 1660–1820*. She served as Director of Graduate Studies in the interdisciplinary American Studies Department at the University of New Mexico, and as Director of the Women's Studies Program at Purdue University. She has also served as President of the Women's Caucus of the Modern Language Association. Her current book project concerns questions of ecology and poetics.

Nisi Shawl is the coauthor of *Writing the Other: A Practical Approach*. Her short stories have been published in *Asimov's SF, Strange Horizons,* and *Infinite Matrix*. Her reviews and essays appear regularly in the *Seattle Times,* and she has contributed to *The Encyclopedia of Themes in Science Fiction and Fantasy* and to *The Internet Review of Science Fiction*. She has edited *Beyond* magazine, an online magazine of Afrocentric speculative fiction by teens. Shawl is a founding member of the Carl Brandon Society and is currently a board member for the Clarion West Writers' Workshop. She has been a guest lecturer at Stanford University and at the Science Fiction Museum and Hall of Fame.

Hortense J. Spillers is the Frederick J. Whiton Professor of English at Cornell University. She has, over the past twenty years, enormously enriched African diasporic literary and cultural criticism. Spillers' present work is at the intersection of psychoanalysis and black feminist criticism. She says, "In some ways, I don't believe in the collective unconscious, or racial unconscious, because if that's true then that means that we will all never be anything but haunted, each generation. If that's true, then there is an original sin, it has not been ransomed or somebody has paid the price for that, and if that's so, then we're talking about human and social fatalism and historical fatalism that I don't think I can afford to believe; that I don't want to believe. . . . But if that's so, then human agency is not going to make any difference. In some ways, politically speaking and aesthetically speaking, I can't believe it because that would then make a lot of what else I believe untrue or questionable."

Jarla Tangh, a writer at the inception of her career, is described this way by Nisi Shawl: "Jarla Tangh is well worth watching out for. Though 'The Skinned,' her tale of a guilty African immigrant facing down undead canine vigilantes, is her only published work to date, it's a strong debut that leaves its readers wanting more." De Witt Douglas Kilgore says this about "The Skinned": "Tangh's narrative combines the familiar with the new. Africa is familiarly depicted as a place of danger, a catastrophic land in which easy faith in human goodness or sanity is challenged. But Tangh's Africa is not Joseph Conrad's unknown and unknowable Africa. . . . In accordance with fantasy and horror traditions, the evil that Tangh depicts also seems to be familiar. . . . Tangh uses the convention of horrific racial invasion and violation to designate Europe as the source of primal danger."

Sheree R. Thomas is a writer, editor, small press publisher, educator, and visual artist. She is the copublisher of the literary journal *Anansi: Fiction of the African Diaspora* and founder of Wanganegresse Press. Her fiction and poetry are anthologized in *Role Call: A Generational Anthology of Social and Political Black Literature and Art; 2001: A Science Fiction Poetry Anthology; Bum Rush the Page: A Def Poetry Jam;* and *Mojo: Conjure Stories*. In 2003, she was awarded the Ledig House/LEF Foundation Prize for Fiction for her novel *Bonecarver*. As a journalist and occasional book critic, her reviews have appeared in *AALBC.com, Upscale, Washington Post Book World, Black Issues Book Review, QBR, American Visions,* and *Emerge* magazine.

Kevin Willmott is Associate Professor in the University of Kansas Theatre and Film Department. He is the author of *Colored Men*, a study of the 1917 Houston riot. For television, he cowrote *House of Getty* and *The 70s*, both miniseries for NBC. Willmott wrote and codirected *Ninth Street*, an independent feature film starring Martin Sheen, Isaac Hayes, and Queen Bey; he plays the role of "Huddie," one of the film's main characters. *Ninth Street* is a comedy/drama based on Willmott's experiences growing up in the small town of Junction City, Kansas. Set in 1968, the film deals with the last days of one of the most notorious streets in the nation. He also adapted *The Watsons Go to Birmingham* for CBS, Columbia Tri-Star, and executive producer Whoopi Goldberg. His most recent film, *CSA: The Confederate States of America,* is about an America in which the South won the Civil War.

CPSIA information can be obtained
at www.ICGtesting.com
Printed in the USA
BVHW070639151118
533157BV00001B/31/P

9 780814 255056